U·X·L
Encyclopedia
of Science

U·X·L
Encyclopedia
of Science

Second Edition
Volume 10: Su-Z

Rob Nagel, Editor

U·X·L®

GALE GROUP

*
TM

THOMSON LEARNING

Detroit • New York • San Diego • San Francisco
Boston • New Haven, Conn. • Waterville, Maine
London • Munich

U·X·L
Encyclopedia of Science
Second Edition

Rob Nagel, *Editor*

Staff

Elizabeth Shaw Grunow, *U•X•L Editor*

Julie Carnagie, *Contributing Editor*

Carol DeKane Nagel, *U•X•L Managing Editor*

Thomas L. Romig, *U•X•L Publisher*

Shalice Shah-Caldwell, *Permissions Associate (Pictures)*

Robyn Young, *Imaging and Multimedia Content Editor*

Rita Wimberley, *Senior Buyer*

Pamela A. E. Galbreath, *Senior Art Designer*

Michelle Cadorée, *Indexing*

GGS Information Services, *Typesetting*

On the front cover: Nikola Tesla with one of his generators, reproduced by permission of the Granger Collection.

On the back cover: The flow of red blood cells through blood vessels, reproduced by permission of Phototake.

Library of Congress Cataloging-in-Publication Data

U-X-L encyclopedia of science.—2nd ed. / Rob Nagel, editor
    p.cm.
    Includes bibliographical references and indexes.
    Contents: v.1. A-As — v.2. At-Car — v.3. Cat-Cy — v.4. D-Em — v.5. En-G — v.6.
H-Mar — v.7. Mas-O — v.8. P-Ra — v.9. Re-St — v.10. Su-Z.
    Summary: Includes 600 topics in the life, earth, and physical sciences as well as in engineering, technology, math, environmental science, and psychology.
    ISBN 0-7876-5432-9 (set : acid-free paper) — ISBN 0-7876-5433-7 (v.1 : acid-free paper) — ISBN 0-7876-5434-5 (v.2 : acid-free paper) — ISBN 0-7876-5435-3 (v.3 : acid-free paper) — ISBN 0-7876-5436-1 (v.4 : acid-free paper) — ISBN 0-7876-5437-X (v.5 : acid-free paper) — ISBN 0-7876-5438-8 (v.6 : acid-free paper) — ISBN 0-7876-5439-6 (v.7 : acid-free paper) — ISBN 0-7876-5440-X (v.8 : acid-free paper) — ISBN 0-7876-5441-8 (v.9 : acid-free paper) — ISBN 0-7876-5775-1 (v.10 : acid-free paper)

    1. Science-Encyclopedias, Juvenile. 2. Technology-Encyclopedias, Juvenile. [1. Science-Encyclopedias. 2. Technology-Encyclopedias.] I. Title: UXL encyclopedia of science. II. Nagel, Rob.
    Q121.U18 2001
    503-dc21

                                                                    2001035562

Printed in the United States of America

10 9 8 7 6 5 4 3 2 1

Table of Contents

Contents

Reader's Guide

Demystify scientific theories, controversies, discoveries, and phenomena with the *U•X•L Encyclopedia of Science,* Second Edition.

This alphabetically organized ten-volume set opens up the entire world of science in clear, nontechnical language. More than 600 entries—an increase of more than 10 percent from the first edition—provide fascinating facts covering the entire spectrum of science. This second edition features more than 50 new entries and more than 100 updated entries. These informative essays range from 250 to 2,500 words, many of which include helpful sidebar boxes that highlight fascinating facts and phenomena. Topics profiled are related to the physical, life, and earth sciences, as well as to math, psychology, engineering, technology, and the environment.

In addition to solid information, the *Encyclopedia* also provides these features:

- "Words to Know" boxes that define commonly used terms
- Extensive cross references that lead directly to related entries
- A table of contents by scientific field that organizes the entries
- More than 600 color and black-and-white photos and technical drawings
- Sources for further study, including books, magazines, and Web sites

Each volume concludes with a cumulative subject index, making it easy to locate quickly the theories, people, objects, and inventions discussed throughout the *U•X•L Encyclopedia of Science,* Second Edition.

Suggestions

We welcome any comments on this work and suggestions for entries to feature in future editions of *U•X•L Encyclopedia of Science.* Please write: Editors, *U•X•L Encyclopedia of Science,* U•X•L, Gale Group, 27500 Drake Road, Farmington Hills, Michigan, 48331-3535; call toll-free: 800-877-4253; fax to: 248-699-8097; or send an e-mail via www.galegroup.com.

Entries by Scientific Field

Boldface indicates volume numbers.

Acoustics

Aerodynamics

Aeronautical engineering

Aerospace engineering

Agriculture

Anatomy and physiology

Astrophysics

Biology

Entries by
Scientific Field

Primatology

Psychiatry/Psychology

Radiology

Robotics

Seismology

Sociology

Subatomic particles

Subatomic particles are particles that are smaller than an atom. In 1940, the number of subatomic particles known to science could be counted on the fingers of one hand: protons, neutrons, electrons, neutrinos, and positrons. The first three particles were known to be the building blocks from which atoms are made: protons and neutrons in atomic nuclei and electrons in orbit around those nuclei. Neutrinos and positrons were somewhat peculiar particles discovered outside Earth's atmosphere and of uncertain origin or significance.

That view of matter changed dramatically over the next two decades. With the invention of particle accelerators (atom-smashers) and the discovery of nuclear fission and fusion, the number of known subatomic particles increased. Scientists discovered a number of particles that exist at energies higher than those normally observed in our everyday lives: sigma particles, lambda particles, delta particles, epsilon particles, and other particles in positive, negative, and neutral forms. By the end of the 1950s, so many subatomic particles had been discovered that some physicists referred to their list as a "particle zoo."

The quark model

In 1964, American physicist Murray Gell-Mann (1929–) and Swiss physicist George Zweig (1937–) independently suggested a way out of the particle zoo. They suggested that the nearly 100 subatomic particles that had been discovered so far were not really elementary (fundamental) particles. Instead, they suggested that only a relatively few elementary particles existed, and the other subatomic particles that had been

▼ Words to Know

Antiparticles: Subatomic particles similar to the proton, neutron, electron, and other subatomic particles, but having one property (such as electric charge) opposite them.

Atomic mass unit (amu): A unit of mass measurement for small particles.

Atomic number: The number of protons in the nucleus of an atom.

Elementary particle: A subatomic particle that cannot be broken down into any simpler particle.

Energy levels: The regions in an atom in which electrons are most likely to be found.

Gluon: The elementary particle thought to be responsible for carrying the strong force (which binds together neutrons and protons in the atomic nucleus).

Graviton: The elementary particle thought to be responsible for carrying the gravitational force.

Isotopes: Forms of an element in which atoms have the same number of protons but different numbers of neutrons.

Lepton: A type of elementary particle.

Photon: An elementary particle that carries electromagnetic force.

Quark: A type of elementary particle.

Spin: A fundamental property of all subatomic particles corresponding to their rotation on their axes.

discovered were composed of various combinations of these truly elementary particles.

The truly elementary particles were given the names quarks and leptons. Each group of particles, in turn, consists of six different types of particles. The six quarks, for example, were given the rather fanciful names of up, down, charm, strange, top (or truth), and bottom (or beauty). These six quarks could be combined, according to Gell-Mann and Zweig, to produce particles such as the proton (two up quarks and one down quark) and the neutron (one up quark and two down quarks).

In addition to quarks and leptons, scientists hypothesized the existence of certain particles that "carry" various kinds of forces. One of those particles was already well known, the photon. The photon is a strange type of particle with no mass that apparently is responsible for the transmission of electromagnetic energy from one place to another.

In the 1980s, three other force-carrying particles were also discovered: the W^+, W^-, and Z^0 bosons. These particles carry certain forces that can be observed during the radioactive decay of matter. (Radioactive elements spontaneously emit energy in the form of particles or waves by disintegration of their atomic nuclei.) Scientists have hypothesized the existence of two other force-carrying particles, one that carries the strong force, the gluon (which binds together protons and neutrons in the nucleus), and one that carries gravitational force, the graviton.

Five important subatomic particles

For most beginning science students, the five most important subatomic particles are the proton, neutron, electron, neutrino, and positron. Each of these particles can be described completely by its mass, electric charge, and spin. Because the mass of subatomic particles is so small, it is usually not measured in ounces or grams but in atomic mass units (label: amu) or electron volts (label: eV). An atomic mass unit is approximately equal to the mass of a proton or neutron. An electron volt is actually a unit of energy but can be used to measure mass because of the relationship between mass and energy ($E = mc^2$).

All subatomic particles (indeed, all particles) can have one of three electric charges: positive, negative, or none (neutral). All subatomic particles also have a property known as spin, meaning that they rotate on their axes in much the same way that planets such as Earth do. In general, the spin of a subatomic particle can be clockwise or counterclockwise, although the details of particle spin can become quite complex.

Proton. The proton is a positively charged subatomic particle with an atomic mass of about 1 amu. Protons are one of the fundamental constituents of all atoms. Along with neutrons, they are found in a very concentrated region of space within atoms referred to as the nucleus.

The number of protons determines the chemical identity of an atom. This property is so important that it is given a special name: the atomic number. Each element in the periodic table has a unique number of protons in its nucleus and, hence, a unique atomic number.

Neutron. A neutron has a mass of about 1 amu and no electric charge. It is found in the nuclei of atoms along with protons. The neutron is normally a stable particle in that it can remain unchanged within the nucleus for an infinite period of time. Under some circumstances, however, a neutron can undergo spontaneous decay, breaking apart into a proton and an electron. When not contained with an atomic nucleus, the half-life for this change—the time required for half of any sample of neutrons to undergo decay—is about 11 minutes.

The nuclei of all atoms with the exception of the hydrogen-1 isotope contain neutrons. The nuclei of atoms of any one element may contain different numbers of neutrons. For example, the element carbon is made of at least three different kinds of atoms. The nuclei of all three kinds of atoms contain six protons. But some nuclei contain six neutrons, others contain seven neutrons, and still others contain eight neutrons. These forms of an element that contain the same number of protons but different numbers of neutrons are known as isotopes of the element.

Electron.   Electrons are particles carrying a single unit of negative electricity with a mass of about 1/1800 amu, or 0.0055 amu. All atoms contain one or more electrons located in the space outside the atomic nucleus. Electrons are arranged in specific regions of the atom known as energy levels. Each energy level in an atom may contain some maximum number of electrons, ranging from a minimum of two to a maximum of eight.

Electrons are leptons. Unlike protons and neutrons, they are not thought to consist of any smaller particles but are regarded themselves as elementary particles that cannot be broken down into anything simpler.

All electrical phenomena are caused by the existence or absence of electrons or by their movement through a material.

Neutrino.   Neutrinos are elusive subatomic particles that are created by some of the most basic physical processes of the universe, like decay of radioactive elements and fusion reactions that power the Sun. They were originally hypothesized in 1930 by Swiss physicist Wolfgang Pauli (1900–1958). Pauli was trying to find a way to explain the apparent loss of energy that occurs during certain nuclear reactions.

Neutrinos ("little neutrons") proved very difficult to actually find in nature, however. They have no electrical charge and possibly no mass. They rarely interact with other matter. They can penetrate nearly any form of matter by sliding through the spaces between atoms. Because of these properties, neutrinos escaped detection for 25 years after Pauli's prediction.

Then, in 1956, American physicists Frederick Reines and Clyde Cowan succeeded in detecting neutrinos produced by the nuclear reactors at the Savannah River Reactor. By 1962, the particle accelerator at

Brookhaven National Laboratory was generating enough neutrinos to conduct an experiment on their properties. Later, physicists discovered a second type of neutrino, the muon neutrino.

Traditionally, scientists have thought that neutrinos have zero mass because no experiment has ever detected mass. If neutrinos do have a mass, it must be less than about one hundred-millionth the mass of the proton, the sensitivity limit of the experiments. Experiments conducted during late 1994 at Los Alamos National Laboratory hinted at the possibility that neutrinos do have a very small, but nonzero, mass. Then in 1998, Japanese researchers found evidence that neutrinos have at least a small mass, but their experiments did not allow them to determine the exact value for the mass.

In 2000, at the Fermi National Accelerator Laboratory near Chicago, a team of 54 physicists from the United States, Japan, South Korea, and

Electronic display of energies from subatomic particles. *(Reproduced by permission of Photo Researchers, Inc.)*

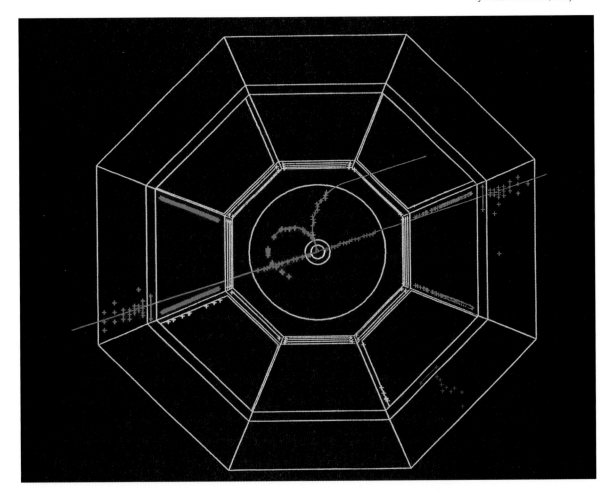

Greece detected a third type of neutrino, the tau neutrino, considered to be the most elusive member of the neutrino family.

Positron. A positron is a subatomic particle identical in every way to an electron except for its electric charge. It carries a single unit of positive electricity rather than a single unit of negative electricity.

The positron was hypothesized in the late 1900s by English physicist Paul Dirac (1902–1984) and was first observed by American physicist Carl Anderson (1905–1991) in a cosmic ray shower. The positron was the first antiparticle discovered—the first particle that has properties similar to protons, neutrons, and electrons, but with one property exactly the opposite of them.

[*See also* **Antiparticle; Atom; Electron**]

Submarine

A submarine is a ship capable of operating underwater. Because its great advantage is its ability to stay hidden, the submarine has developed as a tool of warfare.

In 1578, in his book *Inventions or Devices,* William Bourne described a ship with two hulls (bodies), one made of wood, the other of leather. According to Bourne, the ship could be submerged or raised by taking in or expelling water from between the double hulls.

The first known submarine to be built was by Dutch inventor Cornelius Drebbel. It consisted of greased leather over a wooden framework. It was propelled either on or beneath the surface by eight oars sealed through the sides with leather flaps. During a demonstration for English king James I in 1620, Drebbel's vessel was successfully piloted just under the surface of the Thames River in London. However, it did not make deep descents.

During the American Revolution (1776–81), American inventor David Bushnell built a one-man submarine called the *Turtle*. It was 6 feet (2 meters) tall and resembled a slightly squashed egg. It had two hand-cranked screw propellers, a hand-operated control lever connected to the rudder, foot-operated pumps to let water in or send it out (to submerge or surface), and a control panel. The *Turtle* also had a large explosive attached to it in the hopes the operator could maneuver under an enemy ship, screw the explosive into the ship's hull, and depart before the explosive's timing device discharged it. On its only test mission, the *Turtle* failed to sink its target.

Robert Fulton

Perhaps the most successful early submarine was designed by American inventor Robert Fulton. He lived in an age of naval battles, but hated war. Fulton hoped that a device that could make warships ineffective would end war altogether. In 1801, he built a 21-foot (6-meter) vessel with a two-bladed propeller, which he called *Nautilus.* After he was unable to interest both the French and English governments in his idea, Fulton abandoned the submarine project, returned home, and went on to produce his famous steamboats in the United States.

After the American Civil War (1861–65), designers sought alternatives to human-powered propulsion for submarines. Several systems proved unsuitable; for instance, steam engines made the craft unbearably hot and an electric battery could not be recharged at sea.

In the late 1890s, Irish-born American John Holland solved these problems by adding a second power source, the gasoline engine, to the batteries then in use. Because it needed oxygen, the gasoline engine could not be used while a submarine was underwater. When the ship was above water, its engine could provide propulsion and charge the batteries used while the ship had been submerged. Holland's vessels incorporated many of the features found in modern submarines: a powerful engine, advanced control and balancing systems, and a circular-shaped hull to withstand pressure. The United States Navy accepted his submarine, the U.S.S. *Holland,* in 1900.

Periscopes and diesel engines

Around this time, two other improvements were introduced. Inventor Simon Lake created the first periscope specifically for submarines. A periscope is a vertical telescope that provides a magnified view and a wide angle of vision. In the 1890s, Rudolf Diesel invented an engine that was fired by compression rather than an electric spark. The diesel engine was more economical than the gasoline engine and its fumes were much less toxic (poisonous) and volatile (explosive). This new engine became essential to all submarines until nuclear power was introduced as a means of propulsion in the 1950s.

In World War II (1939–45), submarines played a large role in Germany's repeated attacks on Allied (English, American, and French) ships.

Meanwhile, American submarines crippled the Japanese by sinking nearly 1,400 merchant and naval ships. During this time, the snorkel was developed. It was a set of two fixed air pipes that projected from the sub's topside. One tube brought fresh air into the vessel, and the other vented engine exhaust fumes. Now a sub could stay hidden below the surface when running on its diesel engine and recharging its batteries.

Nuclear power

The greatest modern advance in submarine technology was the introduction of nuclear power. With the encouragement of U.S. Navy captain Hyman Rickover, American inventors designed the U.S.S. *Nautilus,* the first nuclear-powered submarine. Launched in 1955, the U.S.S. *Nautilus* carried a reactor in which controlled nuclear fission provided the heat that converted water into steam for turbines. With this new power source, the submarine could remain underwater indefinitely and cruise at top speed for any length of time required.

However, the traditional needlelike shape proved inefficient for such a submarine. A new teardrop design was introduced in the United States. Vessels with this improved shape easily drove through the water at speeds of 35 to 40 knots (about 40 to 46 miles or 64 to 74 kilometers) per hour. The U.S. Navy later adopted this shape for its submarines.

[*See also* **Diesel engine; Nuclear power**]

A trident submarine under construction in Groton, Connecticut. *(Reproduced by permission of Phototake.)*

Succession

Succession is a process of ecological change in which a series of natural communities are established and then replaced over time. Ecologists (scientists who study the relationships of organisms with their living and nonliving environment) generally recognize two kinds of succession, primary succession and secondary succession. Primary succession takes place on an area that is originally completely empty of life. As an example, an area that has been covered by a flow of lava has, for a time, no life at all on it. Over a period of time, however, various kinds of organisms begin to grow in the area. Over time, the variety of life-forms changes as succession continues.

Secondary succession is far more common. It occurs in an area where life once existed but has then been destroyed. For example, imagine a forest that has been destroyed by a wildfire. Again, for a period of time, no living organisms may exist in the area. Before long, however, certain types of plants begin to reappear. And, as with primary succession, the nature of the plant communities gradually change over time.

The stages in ecological succession

The changes that take place during any form of succession depend on a variety of environmental factors, such as the amount of moisture, temperature, and wind. One possible scenario for primary succession might begin with the appearance of simple plants, such as lichens and mosses. Such plants are able to spring up in tiny cracks in the rocks in which water and dissolved minerals collect.

When these pioneer plants die, they decompose and begin to form soil in which other, more complex plants can begin to grow. The second stage of plants might consists of grasses, herbs, and small shrubs. A characteristic of these plants is that they devote a great deal of energy producing huge numbers of seeds. They may live only one year, and spend the greatest part of their energy to ensuring that offspring will arise the following year. Species of this kind are known as opportunist species. Grasses are a common example of opportunist species.

Plants that make up the early stages of succession also die, decompose, and contribute to the growing layer of soil. This process takes place over hundreds or thousands of years, however. Eventually, the soil is able to support more complex plants, such as larger shrubs and small trees including aspen, black spruce, and jack pine. These plants gradually take over from earlier communities since they are taller, have more leaves, and can capture more sunlight that was originally captured by simpler plants.

Words to Know

Climax community: A relatively stable ecosystem characterized by large, old trees that marks the last stage of ecological succession.

Ecosystem: An ecological community, including plants, animals, and microorganisms, considered together with their environment.

Opportunist species: Plant species with short life-spans that devote most of their energy to producing seeds.

Pioneer plants/communities: Plants or communities that are the first to be established in an area previously empty of life.

Primary succession: Succession that takes place on an area that was originally completely empty of life.

Secondary succession: Succession that occurs in an area where life once existed but has then been destroyed.

In the final stages of succession, taller trees begin to grow. They, in turn, block out the sunlight needed by smaller trees and replace them. The final stage of ecological succession is known as a climax community. A climax community in the scenario outlined here might consist of birch, white spruce, and balsam fir.

Secondary succession

The general trends that take place during secondary succession are similar to those for primary succession. Imagine that a forest has been cleared for agriculture and then abandoned at a later date. In this case, a pioneer community consisting of lichens and mosses is not needed. Soil, rich or not, is already available.

In such a case, the first plants to reappear might be annual (living one year) weeds, such as crabgrass. At a somewhat later date, the weedy community might be replaced by perennial (those that live year after year) weeds, and then by shrubs, a pine forest, and finally a mature forest consisting of oaks, maples, elms, and other large, long-living trees.

As succession goes forward, the nature of plant communities changes significantly. Instead of sending out many seeds each year, as in a pioneer community, trees in more mature communities devote their energies to sending out roots, branches, leaves, and other structures. Indeed, as

they grow larger and create more shade, they actually prevent the germi-
nation (first life stages) and growth of their own seeds and seedlings.

Climax community

Ecologists refer to the final, highest stage of ecological development in an area as the area's climax community. That terms refers to a
relatively stable community that is environmentally balanced. Climax
communities are more a theoretical than a real concept. Certainly it is
possible to recognize in old-growth communities areas that change relatively slowly compared to the earlier, more dynamic stages of succession.

Climax forest

1.

— Ash layer
— Buried
seeds
— Deposition
of minerals

2.

Species
from other
sites invading

3. Buried seeds   Roots
sprouting   regenerating

Recovered forest

4.

Illustration of (1) a climax
forest (2) destroyed by wildfire and (3 and 4) its even-
tual recovery. Secondary
succession occurs in an area
where life once existed but
has then been destroyed.
*(Reproduced by permission of
The Gale Group.)*

However, change in ecological communities is a universal phenomenon. Thus, even the climax state cannot be regarded as static.

For example, even in old-growth communities succession on a small scale is always occurring. That succession may involve the death of individual trees and the growth of new ones. As environmental conditions change, even climax communities themselves continue to evolve.

Sudden infant death syndrome (SIDS)

Sudden infant death syndrome (SIDS) is the term used to describe the sudden and unexplained death of an apparently healthy infant. This unpredictable and unpreventable phenomenon is the leading cause of death in babies less than one year old and strikes infants of all ethnic or economic backgrounds. Several theories exist but none can fully explain it or stop it from happening.

SIDS in history

The sudden death of a baby while sleeping, although tragic, is nothing new. It has a history of at least 2,000 years and is even mentioned in the Bible. In First Kings, the story is told of how King Solomon judged who was the real mother of a surviving child. The child's dead sibling was thought to have "died in the night because she overlaid it." "Overlaying" or the accidental suffocation of an infant by an adult who rolled on the baby while sleeping was for centuries thought to be the only reasonable explanation for an apparently healthy infant going peacefully to sleep and never waking up. In ancient Egypt, a mother who was judged to be responsible for doing this was sentenced to hold the dead infant for three days and nights. The first known medical textbook written during the second century A.D. by Greek physician Soranus of Ephesus instructs mothers and wet-nurses (female servants who were nursing or breast feeding their own child and who also would nurse the baby of their mistress or employer) never to sleep with infants in case they should accidentally fall asleep on the baby and somehow suffocate it.

References to "overlaying" are known to exist throughout the centuries, and it appears again and again in church records and doctors' records. It is even found in records from the Plymouth colony in New England where it was called "stifling." The question of whether a baby

¥ Words to Know

Apnea: Cessation of breathing.

Hypoxia: A deficiency of oxygen reaching the tissues of the body.

had been killed deliberately by an adult was always in the background, and often authorities would have to judge the fate of parents whose healthy infant died suddenly and therefore suspiciously.

Nineteenth-century doctors naturally tried to explain scientifically these sudden deaths of babies, and one of the first such explanations was that the infant suffered from some sort of respiratory ailment. By the beginning of the twentieth century, sleep apnea (pronounced AP-nee-uh), in which a baby stops breathing for some reason but does not start up again, was considered a cause. By the 1930s, the role of infection was being considered, and by the 1940s, most American mothers were no longer taking their children to bed with them for fear of accidentally smothering them.

International attention

The first modern study of any and all of the factors that might be involved in a case of sudden infant death was done in 1956. By the late 1950s, many thought that such death was caused by some sort of abnormal function of the baby's breathing reflex. During the 1960s, many new theories were offered, such as a hypersensitivity to milk, an abnormal heartbeat, or some form of hypoxia (pronounced hi-POCKS-ee-uh), which is a lack of oxygen. In 1963, the first international conference on sudden infant death was held in Seattle, Washington, which produced not only more theories but also increased awareness on the part of the public. It was at the second international conference that a definition was agreed upon and the condition came to be named SIDS. The definition also stressed that all possible known causes must have been ruled out by an autopsy, a death scene investigation, and a careful review

(Reproduced by permission of Stanley Publishing.)

TEN LEADING CAUSES OF INFANT DEATH (U.S.)

Congenital anomalies
Pre-term/Low birthweight
Sudden Infant Death Syndrome (SIDS)
Respiratory Distress Syndrome
Problems related to complications of pregnancy
Complications of placenta, cord, and membrane
Accidents
Perinatal infections
Pneumonia/Influenza
Intrauterine hypoxia and birth asphyxia

Source: *Monthly Vital Statistical Report*, 46, no. 1 Supplement, 1996.

of the medical history. These guidelines are still followed today. During 1972, the issue of SIDS received even more attention as the United States Congress held hearings on the subject and increased funding for research.

SIDS victims

Despite this history and attention, it is nonetheless still true that in the U.S., more children die of SIDS in one year than die of cancer, leukemia, heart disease, cystic fibrosis, and child abuse combined. SIDS is, therefore, the leading killer of children between one week and one year of age. What physicians know about SIDS is more of a description than a real understanding. They know that it occurs to infants up to one year old, but most often between the ages of two and four months. It occurs during sleep and strikes without warning. It may occur a few minutes after a baby is put down for the night or after sleeping all night. It has even happened to a sleeping baby in a parent's arms. It affects all types of children in all types of families, and has no relation to ethnicity or income level. However, for some reason, African-American infants die of it twice as often as white infants. Males babies are 50 percent more likely to die of SIDS than females, but neither parents nor doctors can tell which babies will die.

Risk factors

Although no specific cause is yet known, researchers have put together a typical case of what does happen when SIDS strikes. They now believe that certain babies are more at risk than others, and that babies born with one or more conditions can make them especially vulnerable to the normal stresses that all babies experience. Some of these risk factors are stress caused by infection, a birth defect, or a failure to develop. Other factors that are believed to increase vulnerability are premature birth, low birth weight, a sibling who died of SIDS, or babies who have a twin. Other external factors that seem to matter include cigarette smoking or drug use by the mother during pregnancy as well as other medical complications she may have experienced while pregnant. Finally, statistics show that babies who are breast-fed are less likely to die suddenly than those who were bottle fed. The very number of these factors points out how little modern science knows about this syndrome.

Search for a cause

As to what causes SIDS, two major theories best exemplify the hundreds of theories already proposed. One of these says that SIDS happens to normal, healthy babies who have something go wrong with them because of the fact that they are developing so rapidly. This notion of SIDS as a developmental phenomenon argues that because a baby's brain is growing so quickly during its first six months, there is the possibility that it may send an abnormal or wrong message to a critical organ system. For example, it might tell the throat to "close off" instead of "open up" after a breath. The other major theory says that babies who die from SIDS were basically not healthy infants, and that some condition predisposed them to it. This idea says that the baby's developmental experience in the womb before it was born may have made it more at risk. Like the other theory, this theory also focuses on the brain, but argues that it is significant that many SIDS victims have subtle or minor brain abnormalities in the part of the brain that affects sleep.

Over a long period of time, the number of SIDS deaths has tended to remain roughly the same (about 4,000 a year), although starting in 1993 the rate of SIDS decreased some 30 percent. This is thought to be the result of a 1992 effort to educate parents to the fact that infants who sleep

Scientific studies are still inconclusive as to whether it's better to have young babies sleep on their back or on their side. *(Reproduced by permission of Photo Researchers, Inc.)*

on the stomachs are more at risk than those who sleep on their backs. It is now standard practice for doctors to tell new parents that normal babies should sleep face up during the first six months of life.

The death of any child is a terrible thing, but when it occurs with such suddenness and with no forewarning, it can be devastating to the survivors. Often, parents cannot rid themselves of guilt feelings that somehow they were to blame or that they could have done something to prevent it. Fortunately, there are many support groups available for both parents and siblings of a SIDS victim, many of whom feel so bad they become psychological victims themselves. With all the attention and research that SIDS is attracting, the rate of the syndrome may be falling. However, because SIDS is still so unpredictable, researchers must continue their work to seek a cause. Many believe that when SIDS is finally understood, it will have more than one simple explanation.

Sun

The Sun, the star at the center of our solar system, is an average-sized, middle-aged star. It is a gas ball made mostly of hydrogen and helium, with a small amount of carbon, nitrogen, oxygen, and trace amounts of heavy metals. The Sun is roughly 865,000 miles (1,392,000 kilometers) in diameter, about 109 times the diameter of Earth. The Sun, so large that more than 1.3 million Earths could fit inside of it, accounts for about 99.8 percent of the mass of the solar system.

Because the Sun is a gas ball, the rate of its rotation about its axis varies—it spins faster around its equator than around its poles. At its equator, it completes one rotation in about 25 Earth days. At its poles, one rotation takes place about every 35 Earth days. The Sun's surface gravity is almost 28 times that of Earth. Its gravitational attraction holds all the planets, comets, and other solar system bodies in their orbits.

The solar core

The Sun's core is located about 312,000 miles (502,000 kilometers) below the surface. With a diameter of 240,000 miles (386,160 kilometers), the core accounts for only about 3 percent of the Sun's volume. Yet it is so dense that it contains about 60 percent of the Sun's mass.

The temperature in this dense area is an incredible 27,000,000°F (15,000,000°C). It is here that nuclear fusion, the Sun's heat-producing

Words to Know

Chromosphere: Glowing layer of gas that makes up the middle atmospheric layer of the Sun.

Convection zone: Outermost one-third of the solar interior where heat is transferred from the core toward the surface via slow-moving gas currents.

Core: Central region of the Sun where thermonuclear fusion reactions take place.

Corona: Outermost and hottest layer of the solar atmosphere.

Flare: Temporary bright spot that explodes on the Sun's surface.

Granules: Earth-sized cells covering the Sun's surface that transfer hot gas from the Sun's interior to its outer atmospheric layers.

Nuclear fusion: Nuclear reactions that fuse two or more smaller atoms into a larger one, releasing huge amounts of energy in the process.

Photosphere: Innermost layer of solar atmosphere that constitutes the Sun's surface and where most of the visible light is emitted.

Plages: Bright hydrogen clouds on the surface of the Sun that are hotter than their surrounding area.

Prominence: High-density cloud of gas projecting outward from the Sun's surface.

Radiative zone: Central two-thirds of the solar interior.

Solar wind: Electrically charged subatomic particles that flow out from the Sun.

Sunspot: Cool area of magnetic disturbance that forms a dark blemish on the surface of the Sun.

process, takes place. Under tremendous pressure and heat, two hydrogen nuclei are combined to form one helium nucleus, releasing a tremendous amount of energy in the process. The amount of helium found in the Sun indicates that the fusion of hydrogen to helium must have been going on for about 4.5 billion years. Scientists estimate that the Sun has enough hydrogen to continue producing energy for about 5 billion more years.

Enveloping the core is a region called the radiative zone, in which heat is dispersed into the surrounding hot plasma (a substance made of ions [electrically charged particles] and electrons). Above the radiative zone is the convection zone, where heat is carried toward the surface by slow-moving gas currents. The temperature at the surface of the Sun is about 6,000°F (3,315°C).

The Sun's atmosphere

The atmosphere of the Sun consists of three general layers: the photosphere, the chromosphere, and the corona. Since these layers are composed of gases, no sharp boundaries mark the beginning of one layer and the end of another.

Photosphere. The photosphere, the innermost layer of the Sun's atmosphere, is a few hundred miles thick and has a temperature of about 10,800°F (6,000°C). When gas currents in the convection zone reach the photosphere, they release the heat they carry, then cycle back toward the center of the Sun to be reheated. The photosphere is covered with cells in which this heat transfer occurs. These cells, called granules, are Earth-sized chunks that constantly change size and shape.

Another feature of the photosphere is the presence of sunspots, dark areas that may exceed Earth in size. A sunspot has two components: a small, dark featureless core (the umbra) and a larger, lighter surrounding region (the penumbra). Sunspots vary in size and tend to be clustered in groups. They are magnetic storms caused by the transfer of heat stirring up the weak magnetic field lying beneath them. They are dark because they are 2,700°F (1,500°C) cooler than the surrounding area.

Chromosphere. Beyond the photosphere lies the chromosphere, another region through which heat and light pass from the inner layers to space. It is around 1,200 to 1,900 miles (1,930 to 3,060 kilometers) thick. At its greatest distance from the Sun's surface, the chromosphere has a temperature of about 180,000°F (100,000°C). This atmospheric layer is punctuated with plages and flares. Plages are bright patches that are hotter than their surroundings. Solar flares are sudden, temporary outbursts of light that extend from the outer edge of the chromosphere into the corona, the next layer. They produce an incredible amount of energy in only five to ten minutes. A flare can accelerate solar particles to nearly the speed of light. The largest flares generate enough energy to supply the United States's needs for 100,000 years.

Corona. The chromosphere merges into the outermost part of the Sun's atmosphere, the corona. The weak light emitted by the corona (about one-half the light of a full moon) is usually overpowered by the light of the photosphere and therefore is not detectable. During a solar eclipse, however, the Moon blocks the light of the photosphere and the corona can be seen shining around it.

The corona is the thinnest part of the atmosphere. It consists of low-density gas and is peppered with prominences. Prominences are high-density clouds of gas projecting outward from the Sun's surface into the inner corona. They can be more than 100,000 miles (161,000 kilometers) long and maintain their shape for several months before breaking down. The corona extends out into space for millions of miles. As its distance from the Sun increases, so does its temperature, to an incredible 3,600,000°F (2,000,000°C). Astronomers believe that the corona's energy may emanate from spectacular pillars of fiery gas near the Sun's surface, at the bottoms of looping arches of magnetic fields (like those produced by a bar magnet) that stretch for hundreds of thousands of miles above the surface. Hot gases seem to explode upward along the magnetic fields and heat the rest of the corona.

A photograph of the Sun taken with a coronagraph, a telescope that creates an artificial eclipse so that the solar corona is visible. The shape of the corona varies with time and in some areas is nearly absent. *(Reproduced by permission of National Aeronautics and Space Administration.)*

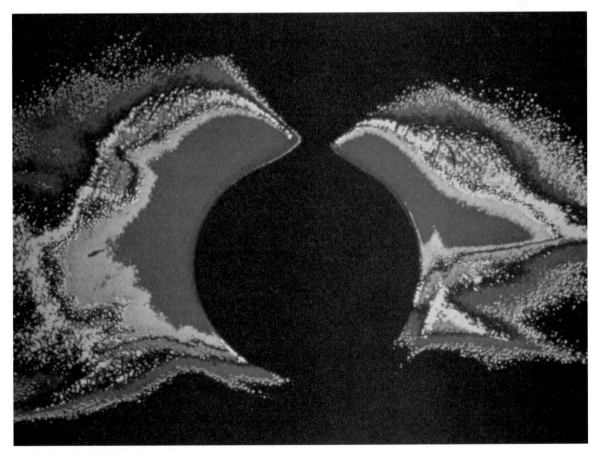

At its farthest reaches, the corona becomes the solar wind, a stream of charged particles (mainly free protons and electrons) that flows throughout the solar system and beyond. When the solar wind reaches Earth, the protons and electrons are flowing along at speeds up to 620 miles (1,000 kilometers) per second. Little of the solar wind reaches Earth's atmosphere because the charged particles are deflected by the planet's magnetic field. The particles that do get through spiral down toward the north and south magnetic poles where they collide with oxygen and nitrogen molecules present in the upper atmosphere. As a result of this collision, the molecules become ionized (electrically charged) and emit the shimmering, green or red curtains of light known as auroras (aurora borealis in the Northern Hemisphere and aurora australis in the Southern Hemisphere).

Solar activity cycle

The solar activity cycle is the periodic variation in active features such as sunspots, prominences, and flares in the Sun's atmosphere and

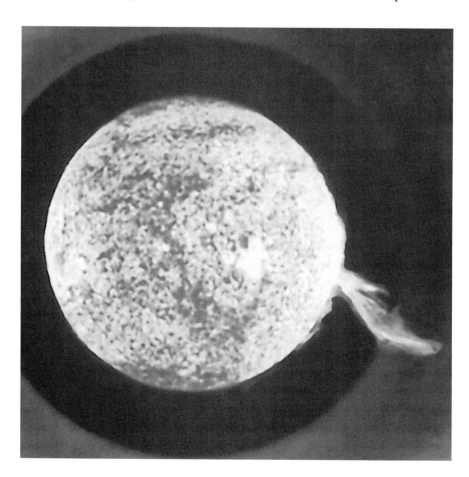

A solar flare, which began erupting about 90 minutes before this photograph was taken. Shading indicates the level of extreme ultraviolet radiation being emitted. *(Reproduced by permission of National Aeronautics and Space Administration.)*

on its visible surface. Sunspot activity generally follows an 11-year cycle from the time when the number of sunspots is at a maximum to the next. During Solar Max or solar maximum, the Sun's magnetic north and south poles flip or reverse. Also accompanying the variations in sunspot number are corresponding changes in prominences and flares. An increase in all of these solar activities increases the solar wind and other matter ejected by the Sun. This, in turn, increases the appearances of auroras in Earth's atmosphere and also causes radio communication interference.

In April 2001, at the peak of the Sun's solar activity cycle, a solar flare erupted from the surface of the Sun near a giant sunspot that was 14 times as large as Earth. According to scientists, the flare was more powerful than any detected in the previous 25 years. Most of the blast was directed away from Earth. Still, two days after the flare erupted, luminous arcs, streamers, veils, rays, and curtains of light were seen in the night sky above Earth. Fortunately, sensitive electrical and communications systems were spared.

The Sun's end

About 5 billion years from now, the Sun will have used up all of its hydrogen fuel and will swell into a red giant, taking on a reddish color as its temperature begins to drop. Because the Sun will shed a great deal of its mass, Earth may be lucky enough to escape being swallowed up in its outer atmosphere, a 3,000°F (1,650°C) plasma. Even though Earth's orbit will be pushed slowly out into the solar system, the oceans will boil off, the atmosphere will evaporate, and the crust may melt. Earth will be a burnt ember. Eventually, the Sun's atmosphere will float away, leaving only a glowing core called a white dwarf that will cool for eternity.

[*See also* **Nuclear fusion; Solar system; Star; Stellar magnetic fields**]

Superconductor

A superconductor is a material that exhibits no resistance to the flow of an electric current. Once a flow of electrons is started in such a material, that flow continues essentially forever.

Superconductivity is an unheard-of property in materials at or near room temperatures. All substances that conduct an electric current—copper, silver, and aluminum are among the best conductors—exhibit at least some resistance to the flow of electrons. This resistance is somewhat

Words to Know

Absolute zero: The temperature at which all atomic and molecular motion ceases. Absolute zero is about 0 K (Kelvin), −273°C, or −459°F.

Cryogenics: The production of very low temperatures and the study of the properties of materials at those temperatures.

Electric current: A flow of electrons.

Electrical resistance: The property of a material that opposes the flow of an electric current.

Electromagnetism: A form of magnetic energy produced by the flow of an electric current through a metal core.

Particle accelerator: A device for accelerating subatomic particles to very high speeds for the purpose of studying the properties of matter

similar to the friction that one observes in sliding a smooth wooden block across a smooth wooden floor.

Resistance is, in most cases, an undesirable property for conductors. When an electric current is passed through a wire, for example, some of the energy represented by that current is wasted in overcoming the resistance of the wire. Only a fraction, even if it is a large fraction, of the energy can actually be put to useful work.

Superconducting materials have the potential for revolutionizing electrical devices. Since they do not resist the flow of an electric current, all the energy represented by that flow can be used for practical purposes.

History

The story of the development of superconducting materials is an especially interesting one. Superconductivity was first discovered by Dutch physicist Heike Kamerlingh Onnes (1853–1926) in 1911. While studying the properties of materials near absolute zero (0 K, −273°C, or −459°F), Kamerlingh Onnes found that some materials lose all resistance to the flow of electric current at these temperatures.

Kamerlingh Onnes's discovery was, for more than 70 years, a subject of purely theoretical interest. As useful as superconducting materials would be in the everyday world, no one was able to find a way to produce that effect at temperatures much above absolute zero.

Then, in 1986, a remarkable breakthrough was reported. Karl Alex Müller (1927–) and Georg Bednorz (1950–), two physicists working at the IBM Research Division in Zurich, Switzerland, found a material that becomes superconducting at a temperature of 35 K (−238°C). Within an amazingly short period of time, news of other high-temperature superconducting materials had been announced. In 1987, for example, a team led by Chinese-American physicist Paul Ching-Wu Chu announced the discovery of a material that becomes superconducting at a temperature of 92 K (−181°C). Shortly thereafter, materials with superconducting temperatures as high as 150 K (−123°C) also were announced.

It may seem strange to call a temperature of 92 K a high temperature. The reason for that choice of terms is that the liquid most commonly used for cryogenic (low temperature) research is liquid nitrogen, with a boiling point of 77 K. The technology for making and storing liquid nitrogen is now well advanced. Many industrial operations can be conducted quite easily at temperatures this low.

Thus, finding a material that becomes superconducting at temperatures greater than 77 K means that such materials can be produced and used very easily. Chu's breakthrough converted the subject of

A small cube magnet hovering over a nitrogen-cooled specimen of a superconducting ceramic demonstrates the Meissner effect. Because the test is so distinctive it is used as a test for identifying superconducting materials. *(Reproduced by permission of Phototake.)*

superconductivity from one of theoretical interest to one that could be applied to practical electrical problems.

Applications

The applications for superconducting materials fall into two general categories: electronics and magnets. All electronic devices will operate more efficiently if they are made from superconducting materials rather than from ordinary conducting materials. However, given the fact that those materials have to be kept at the temperature of liquid nitrogen, those applications have only a limited commercial application so far.

The situation is very different with magnets. The most powerful magnets are electromagnets—magnets that owe their magnetic properties to the flow of electric current through a metal core. The traditional way to make a more powerful magnet is to make the metal core larger and larger. The problem with this approach, however, is that the core needed to make very powerful magnets is larger than can be used on a practical basis. Using superconducting materials, however, the flow of electric current is more efficient, and a more powerful magnet can be made with a smaller metal core.

Perhaps the most famous application of superconducting magnets was the Superconducting Super Collider (SSC). The SSC was a machine designed to be used as a particle accelerator, or atom-smasher, an instrument to be used for the study of subatomic particles (particles smaller than an atom). The U.S. Congress approved the construction of the SSC in 1987 and funded the early stages of its construction. Seven years later, Congress canceled the project because of its escalating costs. The only reason the SSC was practical at all, however, was that the enormous magnets it needed for its operation could be made from superconducting materials.

[*See also* **Cryogenics; Electrical conductivity; Electric current; Electromagnetism**]

Supernova

Ancient astronomers assigned the word *nova,* Latin for "new," to any bright star that suddenly appeared in the sky. They called an extremely bright new star a supernova.

Modern astronomers now know that a supernova, one of the most violent events in the universe, is the massive explosion of a star. Only relatively large stars (those having 1.5 times the mass of our Sun or more)

Words to Know

Black hole: Remains of a massive star that has burned out its nuclear fuel and collapsed under tremendous gravitational force into a single point of infinite mass and gravity.

Chandrasekhar's limit: Theory that determines whether an exploding supernova will become either a neutron star or a black hole depending on its original mass.

Neutrino: High-energy subatomic particle with no electrical charge and no mass, or such a small mass as to be undetectable.

Neutron star: Extremely dense, neutron-filled remains of a star following a supernova.

Nuclear fusion: Merging of two hydrogen nuclei into one helium nucleus, with a tremendous amount of energy released in the process.

Pulsar: Rapidly spinning, blinking neutron star.

Radio waves: Electromagnetic radiation, or energy emitted in the form of waves or particles.

explode in supernovae at the end of their lives. Once a star has used up all its nuclear fuel, it begins to collapse in on itself. During this process, energy is released and the outer layers of the star are pushed out. These layers are large and cool, and the star at this point is considered a red giant. The star continues to expand, however, and soon explodes outward with great force. As a result of the explosion, the star sheds its outer atmospheric layers and shines more brightly than the rest of the stars in the galaxy put together.

What happens next depends on the original mass of the star. Stars up to three times the mass of the Sun end up as densely packed neutron stars or pulsars (rapidly rotating stars that emit varying radio waves at precise intervals). Stars more than three times the mass of the Sun collapse, in theory, to form a black hole (an infinite abyss from which nothing can escape).

The formation of a supernova

Astronomers did not know what causes a star to explode in a super nova until the 1939, when Indian-born American astrophysicist

Subrahmanyan Chandrasekhar (1910–1995) pieced together the sequence of events leading up to a supernova. He also calculated a figure for the mass of a star (known as Chandrasekhar's limit) that would determine if it would end up as a neutron star or a black hole.

Various theories have been proposed to explain the reasons a star explodes outward while collapsing inward. One theory is that the explosion is caused by a final burst of uncontrolled nuclear fusion. A more recent theory is that the explosion is due to the ejection of a wave of high-energy subatomic particles called neutrinos (electrically neutral particles in the lepton family). The neutrino theory gained greater acceptance following the 1987 supernova in the Large Magellanic Cloud, our galaxy's closest companion. Just before the supernova came into view, a surge of neutrinos was detected in laboratories around the world. This supernova, called Supernova 1987A, was the first visible to the naked eye since 1604.

[*See also* **Star; White dwarf**]

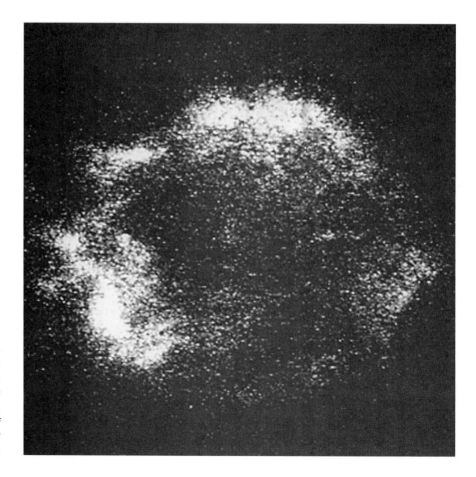

X-ray photo of the supernova remnant Cassiopeia A. The supernova exploded in the late seventeenth century and is still expanding. *(Reproduced by permission of National Aeronautics and Space Administration.)*

Surgery

Surgery is the treatment of disease or injury by cutting into the body to repair or remove the injured or diseased body part. Surgery is usually performed by surgeons in the operating room of a hospital or clinic.

Ancient surgeons

Surgery has been performed since ancient times. The earliest surgical operations were circumcision (removal of the foreskin of the penis) and trepanation (cutting a hole in the skull for the release of pressure or "demons"). Stone Age skulls bearing holes from trepanning have been found around the world. The ancient Egyptians practiced surgery as early as 2500 B.C. using sharp instruments made of copper. The ancient Hindus of India excelled at surgery, performing tonsillectomies, plastic surgery, and removal of bladder stones and cataracts (a clouding of the lens of the eye). The Greeks and Romans used a variety of instruments, including forceps, knives, probes, and scalpels, to operate on wounds and amputate limbs.

During the Middle Ages (400–1450), medical knowledge slowed, and those performing operations, called barber-surgeons, often possessed little education or skill. Without knowledge of antisepsis (techniques to prevent infection), surgery was extremely risky and often resulted in complications or death of the patient.

After the Middle Ages, efforts were made to elevate the status of surgery to a level of some prestige and professionalism. Instrumental in this effort was the great French surgeon Ambroise Paré (1517–1590). Paré introduced the use of ligature (material such as thread or wire) for the tying of blood vessels to prevent excessive bleeding during amputations. His medical writings, which include information on anatomy and discussion of new surgical techniques, greatly influenced his fellow barber-surgeons and advanced the surgical profession.

Era of modern surgery

The era of modern surgery began in the nineteenth century with the introduction of anesthesia (techniques to lessen pain), antiseptic methods, and sterilization of instruments. The discovery of the X ray in 1895 gave surgeons an invaluable diagnostic tool. X rays are a form of radiation that can penetrate solids and are used to generate images of bones and other tissues. Diagnoses using X rays were followed by diagnoses

Words to Know

Anesthesia: Method of decreasing sensitivity to pain in a patient so that a medical procedure may be performed.

Barber-surgeon: Name given to often unskilled and uneducated persons who practiced surgery during the Middle Ages.

Computerized axial tomography (CAT scan): An X-ray technique in which a three-dimensional image of a body part is put together by computer using a series of X-ray pictures taken from different angles along a straight line.

Endoscope: Instrument for examining internal body cavities or organs.

Laser: A device that sends out a high-intensity beam of light.

Ligature: Material such as thread used to tie a blood vessel or bind a body part.

Magnetic resonance imaging (MRI): A technique for producing computerized three-dimensional images of tissues inside the body using radio waves.

Trepanation: The removal of a circular piece of bone, usually from the skull.

Ultrasound: A diagnostic technique that uses sound waves to produce an image.

X ray: A form of electromagnetic radiation that can penetrate solids that are used to generate images of bones and other tissues.

using ultrasound, computerized axial tomography (CAT) scanning, and magnetic resonance imaging (MRI).

Surgery advances in the twentieth century include techniques for performing blood transfusions, brain and heart operations (such as bypass surgery and valve replacement), organ transplantation, microsurgery, and laser surgery. Microsurgery allows surgeons to perform precise, delicate operations on various body structures while viewing the surgical area through a microscope. Lasers, high-intensity beams of light focused at targeted tissues, are used to treat eye disorders, break up kidney stones and tumors, and remove birthmarks, wrinkles, and spider veins.

Some types of surgery that previously required extensive cutting through body tissue can now be accomplished using less invasive techniques. Endoscopic surgery is a method of operating on internal body structures, such as knee joints or reproductive organs, by passing an instrument called an endoscope through a body opening or tiny incision. Tiny surgical instruments and a miniature video camera, allowing viewing of the area to be operated on, are attached to the endoscope.

Plastic surgery, including cosmetic surgery, has flourished in the twentieth century. Plastic surgery is the reconstruction or repair of dam-

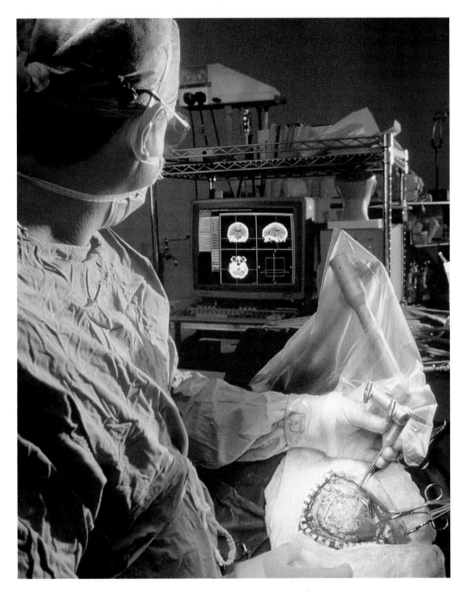

A neurosurgeon using a computer-controlled robot arm to remove a tumor from a patient's brain. *(Reproduced by permission of Photo Researchers, Inc.)*

aged tissue due to injury, birth defects, severe burns, or diseases such as cancer. Cosmetic surgery is increasingly popular for both men and women and includes facelifts, breast enlargement and reduction, nose reshaping, and liposuction (removal of fat from tissues).

A dramatic advance in recent years is fetal surgery, in which procedures such as blood transfusions or correction of a life-threatening hernia (rupture) or urinary tract obstruction are performed on the unborn fetus while the mother is under general anesthesia.

[*See also* **Plastic surgery**]

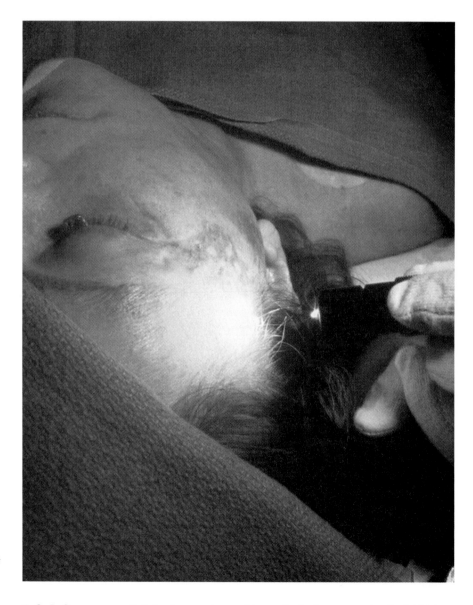

An argon laser being used to remove a birthmark. *(Reproduced by permission of Photo Researchers, Inc.)*

Symbolic logic

Symbolic logic is the branch of mathematics that makes use of symbols to express logical ideas. This method makes it possible to manipulate ideas mathematically in much the same way that numbers are manipulated.

Most people are already familiar with the use of letters and other symbols to represent both numbers and concepts. For example, many solutions to algebraic problems begin with the statement, "Let x represent. . . ." That is, the letter x can be used to represent the number of boxes of nails, the number of sheep in a flock, or the number of hours traveled by a car. Similarly, the letter p is often used in geometry to represent a point. P can then be used to describe line segments, intersections, and other geometric concepts.

In symbolic logic, a letter such as p can be used to represent a complete statement. It may, for example, represent the statement: "A triangle has three sides."

Mathematical operations in symbolic logic

Consider the two possible statements:

"I will be home tonight" and "I will be home tomorrow."

Let p represent the first statement and q represent the second statement. Then it is possible to investigate various combinations of these two statements by mathematical means. The simplest mathematical possibilities are to ask what happens when both statements are true (an AND operation) or when only one statement is true (an OR operation).

One method for performing this kind of analysis is with a truth table. A truth table is an organized way of considering all possible relationships between two logical statements, in this case, between p and q. An example of the truth table for the two statements given above is shown below. Notice in the table that the symbol $\wedge$ is used to represent an AND operation and the symbol $\vee$ to represent an OR operation:

$$
\begin{array}{cccc}
p & q & p\wedge q & p\vee q \\
T & T & T & T \\
T & F & F & T \\
F & T & F & T \\
F & F & F & F
\end{array}
$$

Notice what the table tells you. First, if "I will be home tonight" (p) and "I will be home tomorrow" (q) are both true, then the statement

"I will be home tonight and I will be home tomorrow"—(p) and (q)—also must be true. In contrast, look at line 3 of the chart. According to this line, the statement "I will be home tonight" (p) is false, but the statement "I will be home tomorrow" (q) is true. What does this tell you about $p \wedge q$ and $p \vee q$?

First, $p \wedge q$ means that "I will be home tonight" (p), *and* "I will be home tomorrow" (q). But line 3 says that the first of these statements (p) is false. Therefore, the statement "I will be home tonight *and* I will be home tomorrow" must be false. On the other hand, the condition $p \vee q$ means that "I will be home tonight *or* I will be home tomorrow." But this statement can be true since the second statement—"I will be home tomorrow"—is true.

The mathematics of symbolic logic is far more complex than can be shown in this book. Its most important applications have been in the field of computer design. When an engineer lays out the electrical circuits that make up a computer, or when a programmer writes a program for using the computer, many kinds of AND and OR decisions (along with other kinds of decisions) have to be made. Symbolic logic provides a precise method for making those decisions.

Taste

Taste is one of the five senses through which all animals interpret the world around them. (The other senses are smell, touch, sight, and hearing.) Specifically, taste is the sense for determining the flavor of food and other substances. It is one of the two chemical senses (the other being smell) and it is stimulated when taste buds on the tongue come in

Taste buds on the tongue. *(Reproduced by permission of Phototake.)*

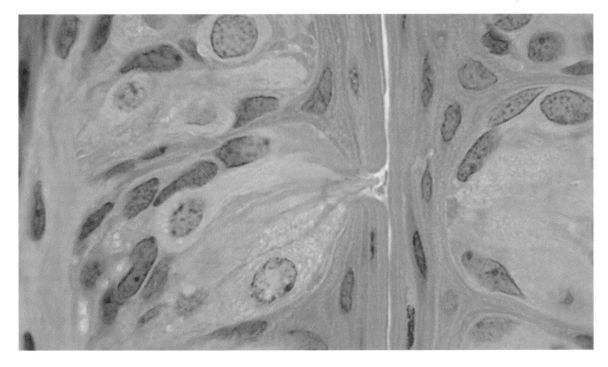

contact with certain chemicals. The sense of taste also is influenced by the smell and texture of substances, hereditary factors, culture, and familiarity with specific taste sensations.

The biology of taste

Clusters of small organs called taste buds are located in the mouth, mainly on the surface of the tongue. Taste buds (named so because under the microscope they look similar to plant buds) lie in small projections called papillae and contain taste receptors that bind to food molecules broken down by saliva. These receptors send messages along nerves to the brain, which interprets the flavor as sweet, sour, salty, or bitter.

Taste buds for all four taste groups can be found throughout the mouth, but specific kinds of buds are clustered together in certain areas. Sweetness is detected by taste buds on the tip of the tongue. The buds for sour tastes are on the sides of the tongue, and for salty toward the front. Bitter taste buds on the back of the tongue can make people gag, a natural defense mechanism to help prevent poisoning.

New taste buds are produced every three to ten days to replace the ones worn out by scalding or frozen foods. As people grow older, their

Taste regions of the tongue (left) and taste bud anatomy (right). *(Reproduced by permission of The Gale Group.)*

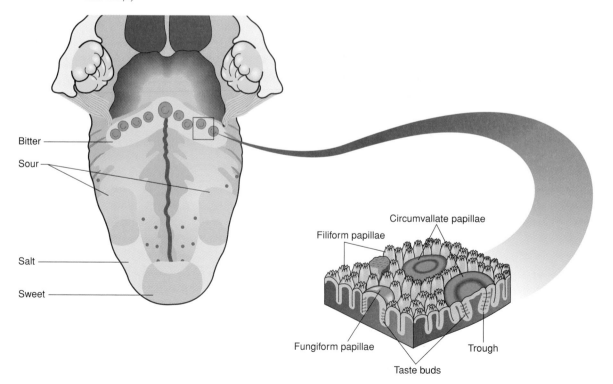

Bitter

Sour

Salt

Sweet

Circumvallate papillae

Filiform papillae

Fungiform papillae

Trough

Taste buds

taste buds are replaced at a slower rate, and more of a substance is needed to experience its full flavor. Scientists have discovered that individual tasting abilities and preferences for specific foods are partially hereditary. Some people are genetically programmed to have more taste buds than others and, as a result, taste more flavors in a particular food. Additionally, culture and familiarity with foods greatly influence taste preferences. Foods that are a tradition in certain cultures may be unappealing to those who are unfamiliar with them. A taste for a particular food usually develops as a person consumes it more frequently.

The smell, texture, and temperature of foods also affect taste. People often first experience the flavor of a food by its odor. When a person's sense of smell is decreased due to congestion from a cold or flu, they frequently experience a reduced ability to taste. Some people will not eat pears because of the fruit's gritty texture, while others would not think of drinking cold coffee.

Taste disorders

Taste disorders, in which either the sense of taste or smell is impaired, can be the result of allergies and viral or bacterial infections that produce swollen mucus membranes (behind the nose). They also may be due to a brain injury or disease that permanently damages the neural pathway through which taste and smell is transmitted. In addition, exposure to environmental toxins such as lead, mercury, and insecticides can damage taste buds and sensory cells in the nose or brain.

The inability to taste or smell not only robs an individual of certain sensory pleasures, it also can be dangerous. Without smell or taste, people cannot determine whether food is spoiled, making them vulnerable to food poisoning. Also, some psychiatrists believe that a lack of taste and smell affects the quality of a person's life and can lead to depression.

[See also **Perception**]

Telegraph

A telegraph is any system that transmits encoded information by signal across a distance. Although the word telegraph is usually associated with sending messages by means of an electric current, it was used originally to describe a visual system for sending coded messages.

Until the telephone became a workable system, the telegraph was the standard means of communication between and within metropolitan

Words to Know

Battery: A device for converting chemical energy into electrical energy.

Code: A system in which some group of symbols is used to represent words.

Electromagnet: A temporary magnet whose effect is caused by an electric current.

Semaphore: A signaling device that uses moving arms, human or mechanical, whose position indicates letters or numbers.

areas in both Europe and the United States. Telephones did not make the telegraph obsolete but rather complemented its use for many decades.

Today, telegrams and telexes still use telegraphy (the sending of messages by telegraph) but are rapidly being replaced by facsimile (fax) transmissions through telephone lines. Satellite transmission and high-frequency radio bands are used for international telegraphy.

History

The earliest forms of sending messages over distances were probably both visual and auditory. Smoke signals by day and beacon fires by night were used by the ancient people of China, Egypt, and Greece. Drumbeats extended the range of the human voice and are known to have been used to send messages, as have reed pipes and the ram's horn.

In 1791, French engineer Claude Chappe (1763–1805) and his brother Ignace (1760–1829) invented the semaphore. The semaphore is an optical telegraph system that can be used to relay messages from hilltop to hilltop. The Chappes built a series of two-arm towers between cities. Each tower was equipped with telescopes pointing in either direction and a cross at its top with extended arms that could assume seven easily seen angular positions. Together, they could signal all the letters of the French alphabet as well as some numbers. Their system was successful and soon was duplicated elsewhere in Europe. It was Claude Chappe who coined the word telegraph. He combined the Greek words *tele* meaning "distant" and *graphien* meaning "to write," to define it as "writing at a distance." The shortcomings of Chappe's system, however, were its dependence on good weather and its need for a large operating staff. Advances in electricity soon put this system out of business.

It was the invention of the battery—a source of electricity for a telegraph—by Italian physicist Alessandro Volta (1745–1827) in 1800 that made Chappe's system obsolete. The telegraph provided a means for sending messages across wires at the speed of light. Several researchers in different countries attempted to exploit the communications aspects of this discovery. The first successful device, however, was invented by two Englishmen, William Fothergill Cooke (1806–1879) and Charles Wheatstone (1802–1875). Cooke and Wheatstone designed a telegraph system in 1837 that used five needles to point to letters of the alphabet and numbers that were arranged on a panel. Their electric telegraph was immediately put to use on the British railway system.

The modern telegraph

Although Cooke and Wheatstone built the first successful telegraph, it was an American artist and inventor, Samuel F. B. Morse (1791–1872), who devised a telegraphic method that eventually was adopted worldwide. Morse made use of ideas and suggestions provided by other scientists and inventors, including those of American physicist Joseph Henry (1797–1878) and a young mechanic named Alfred Vail (1807–1859). His first public demonstration was made at Vail's shop in Morristown, New Jersey, in 1837.

The commercial success of Morse's invention was assured in 1843 when the U.S. government appropriated funds to build a pole line from Baltimore, Maryland, to Washington, D.C. On May 24, 1844, Morse sent the first telegraphic message along that system: "What hath God wrought?" The system became popular very quickly at least partly because skilled operators discovered that they could "read" a message by simply listening to the sound of the telegraph's clicking.

Operation of the telegraph

Morse's telegraph consists essentially of a source of electricity (such as a battery), an electromagnet, and an electric switch known as the key. To send a message, the operator presses down on the key. As the key comes into contact with a metal plate beneath it, an electric circuit is completed. Electricity flows out of the telegraph, into external electrical wires, to waiting receivers in other parts of the world.

At the receiver's end of the system, current flows from external wires into the receiving telegraph system. The electrical current flows through the electromagnet, creating a magnetic field. The magnetic field causes the receiver's key to be attracted to the plate beneath it. As the key comes into contact with the plate, it makes a click sound. The message received consists, therefore, of a series of clicks.

The same clicks are produced when the sender transmits the message. Each time the key is pushed down onto the plate beneath it, it makes the same click. The sender can vary the sound of the click by holding the key down for a shorter or a longer period of time. The same kind of short and long clicks are then picked up at the receiver's end.

The Morse code.   In order to use the system just described, Morse needed to have some kind of code in which short clicks (dots) and long clicks (dashes) could be used to represent letters and numbers. The code he developed is one of the most famous in the world. It consists of various combinations of dots and dashes representing letters, numbers, and symbols. For example, the combination · - represents the letter a; the combination - · · · represents the letter b; and the combination - - - - - represents the number zero.

Historical importance

The invention of the telegraph could in some ways be seen as the real beginning of our modern age. For the first time, it was possible for messages to be transmitted throughout the world. Almost coincidental with the telegraph's birth was the emergence of a new kind of journalism that depended on providing up-to-the-minute information. Reporting events as they occurred began to take precedence over a newspaper's traditional editorial role. In addition, corporations became larger and more far-flung, and nations became necessarily more interdependent. With the telegraph, information—in all its aspects and forms—began to assume the critical role it plays today.

Telephone

The word telephone comes from two Greek words, *tele,* meaning "distant," and *phone,* meaning "sound." Thus, a telephone is a device for carrying sounds over long distances. Many children are familiar with toy telephones that can be made with two tin cans joined by a taunt string or thin wire. When one person speaks into one can, sound vibrations are carried along the string or wire from the speaker's can to the listener's can. If the listener then places his or her ear next to the receiving can, the sound vibrations are converted back to an audible signal.

History

The first working telephone appears to have been invented by German inventor Johann Philipp Reis (1834–1874) in 1863. Reis constructed his telephone simply as a scientific toy, however, to demonstrate the nature of sound. He never made any attempt to convert the instrument to commercial use.

The first operational telephone was patented and produced in the United States in 1876 by American inventor Alexander Graham Bell (1847–1922). In a quirk of fate, American inventor Elisha Gray (1835–1901) filed his patent for a telephone on February 14, 1876, only two hours after Bell had filed his own patent for an essentially identical device. That two-hour difference was sufficient for Bell to receive credit as being the inventor of the telephone, although Gray deserves equal credit.

Alexander Graham Bell on the telephone at the formal opening of telephone service between New York and Chicago in 1892. *(Reproduced by permission of National Aeronautics and Space Administration.)*

Operation of the telephone

A telephone consists of four basic parts: a source of electrical current, such as a battery; conducting wires, usually made of copper; a transmitter; and a receiver. The transmitter consists of the mouthpiece into which a person speaks when placing a telephone call. The transmitter has a thin metal disk called a diaphragm inside it. Behind the diaphragm is a container that holds granules of carbon. When a person speaks into the transmitter, the diaphragm begins to vibrate. This vibration forces carbon granules into contact with each other, which varies the electrical resistance. An electric current from the source flows through the granules and into the external circuit.

The form of the current that flows out of the transmitter depends on the kinds of sound spoken into the transmitter. A loud sound presses the carbon granules together more tightly, causing the electrical resistance to drop, and a stronger electric current is produced. A quiet sound produces a weaker current. The tone of the speaker's voice also is reflected in the kind of sound waves produced and, therefore, on the kind of electric current that is created. The electric current sent out across the telephone lines, then, is a copy of the sounds made by the person's voice.

At the receiving end of the telephone line, this process is repeated in reverse order. Electric current flows into an electromagnet that pulls on the diaphragm in the receiver. The strength and nature of the electric current determines how strongly the diaphragm is pulled back and forth. As the diaphragm is pulled by the electric current, it sets up vibrations that can be detected as sound waves. Those sound waves are identical to the ones originally sent out through the transmitter.

Wireless telephone systems

The system described above requires wires to carry electrical signals from one telephone to another. As telephone usage became popular in the early part of the twentieth century, the air above urban areas became clogged with mazes of telephone wire systems. Eventually, many of these systems were brought together into large cables and buried underground.

The 1970s saw the first widespread use of wireless telephone systems in the United States. A wireless telephone system is one in which the electrical signals produced by a telephone transmitter are attached to a radio signal, similar to the one used to transmit radio broadcasts. Those radio signals can then be transmitted from one tower to another, without the need for wires. Cordless, mobile, and cellular telephones perform all the same functions as conventional telephones but use radio waves instead of wires.

The convenience and efficiency of wireless telephone communication is the reason behind the impressive growth of this service. In 1984, there were approximately 90,000 cellular telephone subscribers in the United States. By 1990, the number of subscribers had reached 4.4 million. And by the beginning of the twenty-first century, that number had ballooned to more than 13 million. The inevitable future expansion of cellular telephone communication on a global scale will be based on employing low-altitude, low-weight satellites.

At present, voice communication and data communication exist separately. As technologies become more advanced, the best of both worlds will be integrated into a multimedia telecommunications network. Multimedia will enable people to combine any media they need to send, receive, or share information in the form of speech, music, messages, text, data, images, video, animation, or even varieties of virtual reality. The emerging capabilities offered by a unified, intelligent telecommunications network will gradually transform the way people interact, work, and learn.

[*See also* **Cellular/digital technology**]

Telescope

The telescope is an instrument that gathers light or some other form of electromagnetic radiation (from radio waves to gamma rays) emitted by distant sources. The most common type is the optical telescope, which uses a collection of lenses or mirrors to magnify the visible light emitted by a distant object. There are two basic types of optical telescopes—the refractor and the reflector. The one characteristic all telescopes have in common is the ability to make distant objects appear to be closer.

The first optical telescope was constructed in 1608 by Dutch spectacle-maker Hans Lippershey (1570–1619). He used his telescope to view distant objects on the ground, not distant objects in space. The following year, Italian physicist and astronomer Galileo Galilei (1564–1642) built the first astronomical telescope. With this telescope and several following versions, Galileo made the first telescopic observations of the sky and discovered lunar mountains, four of Jupiter's moons, sunspots, and the starry nature of our Milky Way galaxy.

Words to Know

Black holes: Remains of a massive star that has burned out its nuclear fuel and collapsed under tremendous gravitational force into a single point of infinite mass and gravity.

Chromatic aberration: Blurred coloring of the edge of an image when white light passes through a lens, caused by the bending of the different wavelengths of the light at different angles.

Electromagnetic radiation: Radiation that transmits energy through the interaction of electricity and magnetism.

Gamma ray: Short-wavelength, high-energy radiation formed either by the decay of radioactive elements or by nuclear reactions.

Interferometry: In astronomy, the precise combining of light or radio waves collected by two or more instruments from one single celestial object.

Radiation: Energy transmitted in the form of subatomic particles or waves.

Radio wave: Longest form of electromagnetic radiation, measuring up to 6 miles (9.6 kilometers) from peak to peak.

Reflector telescope: Telescope that directs light from an opening at one end to a concave mirror at the far end, which reflects the light back to a smaller mirror that directs it to an eyepiece on the side of the tube.

Refractor telescope: Telescope that directs light through a glass lens, which bends the light waves and brings them to a focus at an eyepiece that acts as a magnifying glass.

Ultraviolet radiation: Electromagnetic radiation of a wavelength just shorter than the violet (shortest wavelength) end of the visible light spectrum.

X ray: Electromagnetic radiation of a wavelength shorter than ultraviolet radiation but longer than gamma rays that can penetrate solids and produce an electrical charge in gases.

Refractor telescopes

In a refractor telescope, light waves from a distant object enter the top of the telescope through a lens called an objective lens. This lens is convex—thicker at the middle than the edges. As light waves pass through it, they are bent (refracted) so that they converge (come together) at a single point, known as the focus, behind the objective lens. The distance between the objective lens and the focus is called the focal length. A second lens, the eyepiece, at the focus then magnifies the image for viewing. This is the type of telescope Galileo developed and used.

As refractor telescopes came into wider use, observers realized the instruments had a slight imperfection. Since, like a prism, a lens bends the different wavelengths (colors) that make up light through different angles, refractor telescopes produced a false color around any bright object. This defect is called chromatic aberration. Early astronomers tried to correct this problem by increasing the focal length, but the new instruments were very clumsy to use.

A solution to this problem came in 1729 when English scientist Chester Moore Hall (1703–1771) devised the achromatic lens: two lenses, made of different kinds of glass and shape, set close together. As light passes through the lenses, the false color brought about by the first lens is canceled out by the second lens. Hall went on to create the achromatic telescope in 1733. The lens itself was further developed by English optician John Dollard in 1758. His lens combined two or more lenses with varying chemical compositions to minimize the effects of aberration.

Reflector telescopes

In a reflector telescope, light waves from a distant object enter the open top end and travel down the tube until they hit a mirror at the bottom. This mirror is concave—thicker at the edges than in the middle. Because of this primary mirror's shape, the light waves are reflected back up the tube to a focus, where a small, flat secondary mirror reflects the image to an eyepiece on the side of the telescope. English physicist and mathematician Isaac Newton (1642–1727) developed the reflector telescope in 1668. English astronomer William Herschel (1738–1822) used an updated version when he discovered Uranus in 1781.

Even today, reflectors are perhaps the most prominent type of telescope. They are relatively inexpensive to build and maintain, produce little false color, and maintain a high resolution. The mirrors used in larger reflectors, however, often cause distortion due to the weight on the instrument. Newer reflectors incorporate mirrors of varying shapes (hexagonal glass segments, for example) and of lighter, more durable materials (such as Pyrex^{TM}).

Limits to ground-based telescopes

Earth's atmosphere provides an effective filter for many types of cosmic radiation. This fact is crucial for the survival of humans and other life-forms. However, since the atmosphere only allows visible light and radio waves to pass through it, celestial objects that emit other types of electromagnetic radiation cannot be viewed through telescopes on the ground. Many observatories have been constructed at high altitudes where the atmosphere is thinner—and where the glare of urban artificial light interferes less with viewing—but this improves the situation only slightly.

Space-based telescopes

One way astronomers have sought to overcome the distortion caused by the atmosphere and by city lights is by placing telescopes in space. The first of these instruments, placed in orbit around Earth during the 1970s, were small telescopes that could detect X rays, gamma rays, and

The Hubble Space Telescope (HST) seen moments after its release from the space shuttle *Discovery* on April 25, 1990. The telescope is capable of obtaining astronomical data much more accurate than that taken by ground-based telescopes. *(Reproduced by permission of National Aeronautics and Space Administration.)*

ultraviolet radiation. They discovered hundreds of previously unknown entities, including one likely black hole.

While many other space telescopes have been placed in orbit, the most well known is the Hubble Space Telescope (HST). Launched in April 1990 aboard the space shuttle *Discovery,* the HST has an 8 foot (2.4 meter) primary mirror and five major instruments for examining various characteristics of distant celestial bodies. Shortly after the HST began orbiting Earth, scientists learned that the curve in its primary mirror was off by just a fraction of a hair's width. This flaw caused light to reflect away from the center of the mirror. As a result, the HST produced blurry pictures.

In 1993, astronauts aboard the space shuttle *Endeavor* caught up with the HST and installed a group of three coin-sized mirrors around the primary mirror, which brought the light into proper focus. In 1997, another space shuttle crew conducted general repairs to the HST. Then in November 1999, the HST stopped working after its gyroscopes broke down. Without the gyroscopes, the telescope could not hold steady while focusing on stars, galaxies, and other cosmic targets. A month later, during an eight-day mission, astronauts aboard the space shuttle *Discovery* installed almost $70 million worth of new equipment on the HST, including a computer 20 times faster than the telescope's old one; new gyroscopes; batteries with voltage regulators to prevent overheating; a new guidance unit, data recorder, and radio transmitter; and steel sunshades to protect the telescope from solar damage.

Despite the need for repairs, the HST has proven to be the finest of all telescopes ever produced. The thousands of images it has captured—a comet hitting Jupiter, a nursery where stars are born, stars that belong to no galaxy, galaxies that house quasars, galaxies violently colliding—have amazed astronomers.

The future on the ground

Technological advances in the 1990s began to return astronomy to the ground. New observatories have sprung up on every continent, including Antarctica, housing telescopes that are able to capture celestial images almost as clearly as the HST. These new ground-based telescopes are far more advanced than previous ones. The cost of producing their light-gathering mirrors has been reduced, so the mirrors and the telescopes can be built even larger. Advances in photographic devices allow these telescopes to capture images in minutes instead of hours or entire nights.

The twin domes at the Keck Observatory complex on Mauna Kea in Hawaii house telescopes with mirrors roughly 32 feet (9.8 meters) in diameter. The Hobby-Eberly Telescope at the University of Texas Mc-Donald Observatory near Fort Davis, Texas, was completed on December 12, 1996. Its mirror, made up of 91 hexagonal segments, measures 36 feet (11 meters) in diameter.

Perhaps the greatest advancement is the development of interferometry. Astronomical interferometry is the art of combining light or radio waves collected by two or more telescopes from a single celestial object. The information is fed into a computer, which precisely matches up the light-wave images gathered from the telescopes, peak for peak and

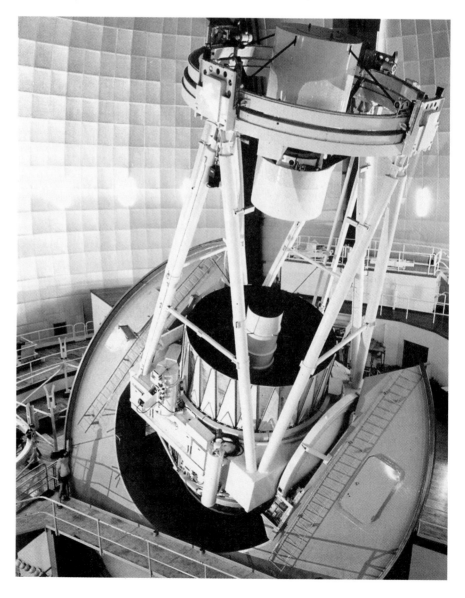

The Anglo-Australian telescope (AAT) in New South Wales, Australia. AAT was one of the first electronically controlled telescopes. *(Reproduced by permission of Photo Researchers, Inc.)*

trough for trough. After distortion is removed through mathematical analysis, the resulting image is equal in sharpness to what a single telescope of enormous size can produce.

Sometime early in the twenty-first century, the world's largest telescope will be completed. On the summit of Cerro Paranal, an 8,645-foot (2,635-meter) mountain in the Atacama Desert in northern Chile (an area considered to be the driest on Earth), stands the Paranal Observatory. The observatory houses the Very Large Telescope, which will consist of four telescopes, each containing a mirror almost 27 feet (8.2 meters) in diameter. In the language of the Mapuche, indigenous people who live in the area, the four unit telescopes are known as Antu ("Sun"), Kueyen ("Moon"), Melipal ("Southern Cross"), and Yepun ("Venus"). The four units were each operational as of the beginning of 2001, but had yet to be combined as an interferometer. Through interferometry (the precise combining of light or radio waves collected by two or more instruments from one single celestial object), the teamed instruments will have a light-gathering capacity greater than a single telescope with a mirror more than 52 feet (16 meters) in diameter.

[*See also* **Gamma ray; Infrared astronomy; Interferometry; Radio astronomy; Ultraviolet astronomy; X-ray astronomy**]

Television

The term television refers to any system for transmitting visual images at a distance. Research on such systems dates back to the 1880s, when German scientist Paul Nipkow (1860–1940) invented a device known as the Nipkow disk. This device was made of a metal or cardboard disk perforated with a series of square holes in a spiral pattern. As the disk was spun, a light was shined through the holes and onto a target. By looking through the holes, one could see the target revealed as a series of horizontal lines.

Nipkow's invention had no practical applications, but it established a model on which later television systems were based. The modern television system was invented in the 1920s at about the same time by two inventors working independently: American Philo Farnsworth (1906–1971) and Russian-born American Vladimir Zworykin (1889–1982). Of the two, Zworykin experienced the greater success in patenting and marketing his ideas.

Words to Know

Coaxial cable: A cable made of a conducting outer metal tube insulated from an inner conducting core that is used to carry telegraph, telephone, and television signals.

Electron gun: A device that gives off a stream of electrons.

Persistence: In terms of human vision, the tendency of an image to remain on the retina of the eye for a fraction of a second after the image has disappeared.

Photocell: A device that emits an electrical pulse when struck by light.

Photosensitive: Affected by light.

How television works

A television system consists primarily of two parts: picture transmission and picture reception. A television camera used to photograph a television program is similar in some ways to a still camera. Light bounces off the subject being photographed and enters the lens at the front of the television camera. The lens forms a clear image of the subject being photographed on a screen, which is located behind the lens.

Transmission. The surface of the screen contains millions of tiny particles of selenium or some other photosensitive (sensitive to light) material. These particles act like tiny photocells. That is, when struck by light, they emit a small electrical pulse. An electron gun at the back of the television camera scans back and forth, up and down across the screen at the front of the camera. As it scans, it detects electrical pulses being given off by various parts of the screen. A bright region in the scene being photographed will give off a lot of light. That light will be converted by the selenium into a relatively large electrical pulse. The electron gun will detect that electrical pulse as being greater than other pulses around it.

The electrical pulses detected by the electron gun are then amplified and sent to the broadcasting tower. In the broadcasting tower, the electrical current from the television camera is converted into radio waves and sent out through the air. The process is similar to the way in which a radio program is transmitted except the frequency is different.

Television reception.   At the receiving station, the above process is repeated in reverse order. Radio signals are received, amplified, and then fed into an electron gun in a television picture tube. The electron gun is pointed at the back of a picture tube. It travels back and forth across the picture tube tracing 525 lines on the tube 30 times every second. The back of the tube is covered with a photosensitive material that gives off light whenever it is struck by an electrical pulse. An intense beam from the electron gun (corresponding to an intense beam originally seen by the television camera) produces a strong burst of light. A weaker beam from the electron gun produces a weaker burst of light.

What the electron gun in the picture tube is producing, then, is a series of individual dots, one at a time, spread out across the screen at a very rapid pace. This mass of dots appears as a coherent picture to the human eye because of a phenomenon known as persistence. The term persistence refers to the fact that a visual image projected onto the retina of the human eye tends to remain there for a fraction of a second. Thus, what our eye sees as the electron gun scans the picture tube is a collection of millions of individual spots of light that, taken together, makes up a complete picture. That picture is identical to the one photographed originally by the television camera.

Color television

Color television did not become commercially available until the late 1950s, about 30 years after black-and-white television had been invented. The principles of color television are largely the same as those of black-and-white television. The most important difference is that three different electron guns are required for both color television cameras and color television picture tubes. The three different guns detect and project one color each: red, green, and blue. As the three guns in a television camera scan a scene simultaneously, they detect all possible combinations of the three basic colors that produce all the hues in that scene. When the three guns in a television picture tube project the electrical counterpart of that scene, they produce the same combination of hues in the original scene.

Cable and satellite television

First known as CATV (community antenna television) or simple cable, cable television was developed to deliver a clear signal to rural communities. At the time, a CATV system generally consisted of a single large antenna mounted in a high, clear area to receive signals from distant television broadcasters. Cables were fed to the houses in the community and they usually delivered two or three channels. In the mid-1960s, new technology allowed for up to twelve channels to be carried through a single cable. In order to fill these new channels, cable operators began to bring in television signals from more distant sources. This allowed viewers to watch stations from large cities and neighboring states. With access to a wider variety of stations, the demand for cable increased.

In the early 1970s, several small companies in California and on the East Coast began offering pay-per-view broadcasting: first-run films and major sporting events delivered by cable to a viewer's home for a monthly fee. The popularity of these programs caused demand to skyrocket. By 1975, the first nationwide pay-per-view cable station—Home Box Office (HBO)—was in service.

What makes cable transmission practical is its use of coaxial cable. This thick, layered cable allows transmission of a wide band of frequencies and rejects interference from automobiles and electrical appliances. As coaxial technology improved, the number of stations available to cable operators rose from twelve to more than fifty. Now, that number can be increased to almost 150.

The antennas once used to deliver a signal to a cable system are long since gone, replaced by microwave dishes often fed by communications satellites. Once a signal is delivered to a cable company in this manner, it is distributed over cable lines to customers. Broadcasts are often scrambled to prevent nonsubscribers from splicing into a cable line without paying for the service. Cable television's clear image is unaffected by poor weather conditions and most types of interference.

Beginning in the late 1970s, satellite television systems were introduced. The television signals transmitted by a satellite are quite different from the television or radio signals that are broadcast over the air. Satellite television is transmitted by microwaves. Microwaves do not behave like lower frequency radio waves that can bounce off obstructions, clouds, and the ground. Microwaves are strictly line-of-sight. In order for a satellite dish to receive a signal, there can be no obstruction between the transmitting satellite and the receiving satellite dish. Because microwaves are highly directional, the satellite dish and associated components must be properly aligned.

Currently in the United States, there are two major types of satellite television. The first is TVRO (TeleVision Receive Only). TVRO satellite systems have a large dish—6 to 12 feet (1.8 to 3.6 meters) across—that is movable. The movable dish enables a TVRO system to view programs on the many satellites that are positioned in orbit above Earth. The second type of satellite television is DBS (Direct Broadcast Satellite). DBS is broadcast by high-powered, high-frequency satellites, which make it possible for the signals to be picked up on a small dish ranging from 18 to 36 inches (46 to 91 centimeters) across. One of the big advantages of DBS systems is that the small dish does not have to move.

HDTV

Digital television refers to the transmission of pure digital television signals, along with the reception and display of those signals on a digital television set. The digital signals might be broadcast over the air or transmitted through a cable or satellite system. A decoder receives the signal and uses it, in digital form, to directly drive a digital television. A class of digital television is called high-definition television or HDTV. HDTV is high-resolution digital television (DTV) combined with dolby digital surround sound. HDTV is the highest DTV resolution in the new set of standards. Whereas traditional televisions have 525 lines of resolution, HDTV has 720 or 1080 lines of resolution.

HDTV requires new production and transmission equipment at the HDTV stations as well as new equipment for reception by the consumer. Optical fibers have proven to be an ideal method of transmitting HDTV signals. Because its transmission contains twice as much information as those of conventional television, HDTV features much greater clarity and definition in its picture. However, standard television technology cannot transmit so much information at once. Using optical fibers, the HDTV signal can be transmitted as a digital-light pulse, providing a near-flawless image. HDTV reproduction is far superior to broadcast transmission, just as music from a digital compact disc is superior to that broadcast over FM radio.

Temperature

The concept of temperature has two related, but different, interpretations. On a general level, temperature is associated with the sense of hot and cold. If you put your finger in a pan of hot water, heat energy flows from the water to your finger; you say that the water is at a higher temperature than that of your finger. If you put your finger in a glass of ice water, heat energy flows as heat away from your finger.

Words to Know

Absolute temperature scale: A temperature scale that has the lowest possible temperature—at which all molecular motion ceases—set at zero.

Absolute zero: The lowest possible temperature at which all molecular motion ceases. It is equal to −459°F (−273°C).

Kinetic energy: Energy of an object or system due to its motion.

Pyrometer: A device for obtaining temperature by measuring the amount of radiation produced by an object.

Resistance thermometer: A device for obtaining temperature by measuring the resistance of a substance to the flow of an electrical current.

Thermometer: A device for obtaining temperature by measuring a temperature-dependent property (such as the height of a liquid in a sealed tube) and relating this to temperature.

The direction of heat energy flow is the basis of one definition of temperature. Temperature is the property of objects—or more generally of systems—that determines the direction of heat energy flow when the objects are put in direct contact with each other. Energy flows as heat from objects at a higher temperature to ones at a lower temperature. When heat energy ceases to flow, the objects are at the same temperature and are said to be in thermal equilibrium.

The second definition of temperature is more rigorous. It deals with the factors that are responsible for an object's being warm or hot on the one hand or cool or cold on the other. This definition is based on the behavior of the particles (atoms, molecules, ions, etc.) of which matter is made. On this level, temperature can be defined as the total kinetic energy of the particles of which a material is made.

Kinetic energy is the motion of particles. Particles that are rotating rapidly on their axes, vibrating back and forth rapidly, or traveling rapidly through space have a large amount of kinetic energy. Particles that are moving slowly have relatively little kinetic energy.

From this perspective, a glass of warm water has a high temperature because the molecules of the water are moving rapidly. The molecules of water in a glass of cool water, by comparison, are moving more slowly.

Temperature measurement: Thermometers

Thermometers are devices that register the temperature of a substance relative to some agreed upon standard. For example, a thermometer that reads 32°F (0°C) is measuring a temperature equal to that of ice in contact with pure water.

Thermometers use changes in certain physical or electrical properties to detect temperature variations. The most common kind of thermometer consists of a liquid—usually mercury or alcohol—sealed in a narrow tube. When the thermometer is placed in contact with a substance, heat travels into or out of the thermometer. If heat leaves the thermometer, the sealed-in liquid is cooled and it contracts (takes up less space); the level of the liquid in the thermometer falls. If heat enters the thermometer, the liquid is warmed and it expands; the level of the liquid in the thermometer rises.

A resistance thermometer is based on the fact that all things resist the flow of an electric current to some degree. Furthermore, such resistance changes with temperature. In general, the higher the temperature of a substance, the more it resists the flow of an electric current. This principle can be used to measure the temperature of a substance by observing the extent to which it resists the flow of an electric current.

Another type of thermometer is known as a pyrometer. A pyrometer is a device that detects visible and infrared radiation given off by an object, then converts that information to a temperature reading.

Temperature measurement: Scales

In order to establish a scale against which temperatures can be measured, one first has to select two fixed points from which to begin. Historically, those two points have been the boiling point and freezing point of water. The two points were chosen because water is the most abundant compound on Earth, and finding its boiling and freezing points is relatively easy.

One way of making a thermometer, then, is to begin with a narrow tube that contains a liquid and is sealed at both ends. The tube is then immersed in boiling water, and the highest point reached by the liquid is marked in some appropriate way. Next, the tube is immersed in a mixture of ice and water, and the lowest point reached by the liquid is marked in a similar way. The distance between the lowest point and highest point is then divided into equal sections. The numbers assigned to the lowest and highest point on the thermometer—and the form of dividing the range between them—is what distinguishes one system of measuring temperature from another.

In the early 1700s, for example, German physicist Gabriel Daniel Fahrenheit (1686–1736) decided to assign to the freezing point of water a temperature value of 32 and to the boiling point of water a temperature value of 212. He then divided the distance between these two points into 180 equal divisions, each equal to one degree of temperature. The Fahrenheit (F) system of measuring temperature is still in use today in the United States.

A somewhat more logical system of defining the temperatures on a thermometer was suggested in 1742 by Swedish astronomer Anders Celsius (1701–1744). Celsius suggested assigning the values of 0 and 100 to the freezing point and boiling point of water and dividing the distance between these two into 100 equal parts. The Celsius system is now used throughout the scientific community and in all countries of the world except the United States and Burma.

Both Fahrenheit and Celsius temperature scales have one important inherent drawback: in both cases, negative temperatures can exist. The freezing point of carbon dioxide (dry ice), for example, is $-110°F$ ($-78.5°C$). But recall the definition of temperature as a measure of the average kinetic energy of the particles that make up a substance. What meaning can be assigned, then, to a negative temperature reading? There is no such thing as negative energy in systems with which we are familiar.

To remedy this problem, a third temperature scale was invented in 1848 by English physicist William Thomson (1824–1907). Thomson set the lowest point on the temperature scale as the lowest possible temperature, absolute zero. Absolute zero is defined as the temperature at which all motion of all particles would cease, a condition in which heat would be absent and, hence, a substance had no temperature. Theoretical calculations suggested to Thomson that the Celsius temperature corresponding to that condition was about $-273°C$ ($-459°F$). Absolute zero, then, was set at this temperature and assigned the value 0 K. The unit K in this measurement stands for Kelvin, the unit of measure in the absolute temperature system. The term Kelvin comes from William Thomson's official title, Lord Kelvin.

The relationship among the three temperature scales is as follows:

$$°C = 5/9(°F - 32)$$
$$°F = 9/5(°C) + 32$$
$$K = °C + 273$$
$$°C = K - 273$$

Thermal expansion

The term thermal expansion refers to the increase in size of an object as that object is heated. With relatively few exceptions, all objects expand when they are heated and contract when they are cooled. Perhaps the most important exception to this rule is water. Water contracts as it cools from its boiling point to about 39.2°F (4°C). At that point, it begins to expand as it cools further to its freezing point. This unusual effect explains the fact that ice is less dense than water.

General trends

Different materials expand or contract at different rates. In general, gases expand more than liquids, and liquids expand more than solids.

When an object is heated or cooled, it expands or contracts in all dimensions. However, for practical reasons, scientists and engineers often focus on two different kinds of expansion, or expansivity: linear expansivity (expansion in one direction only) and volume expansivity (expansion in all three dimensions). The amount by which any given material

Joints such as this one are used in bridges to accommodate thermal expansion. *(Reproduced by permission of JLM Visuals.)*

expands in either way is known as its coefficient of linear (or volume) expansivity.

The choice of these two variables is a practical one. Scientists and engineers often want to know the amount by which some pipe, bar, wire, or other long object will expand. For example, how much longer will a line of telephone wire be on a hot summer day when the temperature is 86°F (30°C) compared to a cold winter day when the temperature is 14°F (-10°C)? The fact is that the wire expands in all three directions, but it is only the linear direction (the length) that is of interest in a real-life situation.

Only solids have a coefficient of linear expansion. They differ from each other widely, with the coefficient of linear expansion of aluminum having a value nearly 50 times as great as that of fused quartz.

Volume expansivity also has its practical applications. Suppose that someone wants to know how much a balloon will expand as its temperature increases. The answer to that question depends on the volume expansivity of the gas used. The volume expansivity of gases ranges from a relatively low value for air to a relatively high value for carbon dioxide and sulfur dioxide.

Practical applications

A great many practical devices and systems depend on the thermal expansion of materials. An example is the bimetallic strip. A bimetallic strip consists of two metals of different thermal expansivities welded to each other. When the strip is heated, one metal expands more rapidly than the other. The strip bends in the direction of the metal with the lower thermal expansivity.

Perhaps the most common use of the bimetallic strip is in a thermostat. When a room becomes cold, the two metals in the strip contract, one more than the other. At some point, the strip bends enough to come into contact with a metal button that closes an electrical circuit, turning on the furnace. As the room warms up, the bimetallic strip begins to bend in the opposite direction. Eventually it pulls away from the contact button, the circuit is broken, and the furnace turns off.

The thermal expansion of objects in the real world often requires the attention of scientists and engineers. For example, the joints used to hold a bridge together have to be designed to provide space for expansion and contraction of the bridge deck. And railroad tracks are built so that they can slide toward and away from each other on hot and cold days, making sure that they do not bend out of shape because of overheating.

Thermodynamics

Thermodynamics is the science that deals with work and heat—and the transformation of one into the other. It is a macroscopic theory, dealing with matter in bulk, disregarding the molecular nature of materials. The corresponding microscopic theory, based on the fact that materials are made up of a vast number of particles, is called statistical mechanics.

Historical background

The origins of thermodynamics can be traced to the late eighteenth century. English-American physicist Benjamin Thomson, Count Rumford (1753–1814), became intrigued by the physical changes accompanying the boring of cannons. (Boring is the process of making a hole—in this case the barrel of the cannon—with a twisting movement.) He found that the work (or mechanical energy) involved in the boring process was converted to heat as a result of friction, causing the temperature of the cannon to rise.

Some of the fundamental relationships involved in thermodynamics were later developed by English physicist James Joule (1818–1889), who showed that work can be converted to heat without limit. Other researchers found, however, that the opposite is not true—that is, that there are limiting factors that operate in the conversion of heat to work. The research of French physicist Sadi Carnot (1796–1832), British physicist William Thomson, Lord Kelvin (1824–1907), and German physicist Rudolf Clausius (1822–1888), among others, has led to an understanding of these limitations.

The laws of thermodynamics

The most basic facts about thermodynamics can be summarized in two general laws. The first law of thermodynamics is actually nothing other than the law of conservation of energy: energy can neither be created nor destroyed. It can be converted from one form to another, but the total amount of energy in a system always remains constant.

For example, consider the simple example of heating a beaker of water with a gas flame. One can measure the amount of heat energy given off by the flame. One also can measure the increase in the heat energy of the water in the beaker, the beaker itself, and any air surrounding the beaker. Under ideal circumstances, the total amount of energy produced by the flame is equal to the total amount of energy gained by the water, the beaker, and the air.

Words to Know

Energy: The capacity for doing work.

Entropy: The amount of disorder in a system.

First law of thermodynamics: The internal energy of a system is increased by the amount of work done on the system and the heat flow to the system (Conservation of Energy).

Heat: A form of energy produced by the motion of molecules that make up a substance.

Second law of thermodynamics: All natural processes proceed in a direction that leads to an increase in entropy.

Submicroscopic level of phenomena: Phenomena that cannot be observed directly by any of the five human senses, aided or unaided.

Work: Transfer of energy by a force acting to move matter.

The first law of thermodynamics is sometimes stated in a somewhat different form because of the kinds of systems to which it is applied. Another statement is that the internal energy of a system is equal to the amount of work done on the system plus any heat added to the system. In this definition, the term work is used to describe all forms of energy *other* than heat.

The first law can be thought of as a quantitative law (involving measurement of some quantity or amount): the amount of energy lost by one system is equal to the amount of energy gained by a second system. The second law, in contrast, can be thought of as a qualitative law (involving quality or kind): the second law says that all natural processes occur in such a way as to result in an increase in entropy.

To understand this law, it is first necessary to explain the concept of entropy. Entropy means disorder. Consider the dissolving of a sugar cube in water. The sugar cube itself represents a highly ordered state in which every sugar particle is arranged in an exact position within the sugar crystal. The entropy of a sugar cube is low because there is little disorder.

But consider what happens when the sugar cube is dissolved in water. The cube breaks apart, and sugar molecules are dispersed completely throughout the water. There is no longer any order among the sugar molecules at all. The entropy of the system has increased because the sugar molecules have become completely disorganized.

The second law of thermodynamics simply says that any time some change takes place in nature, there will be more entropy—more disorganization—than there was to begin with. As a practical example, consider the process by which electricity is generated in most instances in the United States today. Coal or oil is burned in a large furnace, heating water and changing it to steam. The steam then is used to run turbines and generators that manufacture electricity. The first law of thermodynamics says that *all* of the energy stored in coal and oil must ultimately be converted to some other form: electricity or heat, for example. But the second law says that *some* of the energy from coal and oil will end up as "waste" heat, heat that performs no useful function. It is energy that simply escapes into the surrounding environment and is distributed throughout the universe.

The second law is sometimes described as the "death of the universe" law because it means that over very long periods of time, all forms of energy will be evenly distributed throughout the universe. The waste energy produced by countless numbers of natural processes will add up over the millennia until that is the only form in which energy will remain in our universe.

[*See also* **Gases, properties of; Heat; Temperature**]

Thunderstorm

A storm is any disturbance in Earth's atmosphere with strong winds accompanied by rain or snow and sometimes thunder and lightning. Storms have a generally positive effect on the environment and on human societies because they are the source of most of the precipitation on which the planet depends.

The most common violent change in the weather is the thunderstorm. In the United States, thunderstorms usually occur in the late spring and summer. Thunderstorms are rare in the parts of the country where the air tends to be colder, such as the New England states, North Dakota, and Montana. They also are rare by the Pacific Ocean, where summers are dry. The southeastern states tend to have the most thunderstorms. Some parts of Florida experience thunderstorms on a average of 100 days a year. A thunderstorm may last up to two hours, but most thunderstorms peak after about 15 to 30 minutes.

How thunderstorms form

Thunderstorms develop by the same process that forms cumulus clouds, the puffy clouds of summer skies. These clouds form when a humid air mass (air with an abundance of water vapor) near the surface rises on currents of air called updrafts. As the air mass rises through the atmosphere it expands and cools. Eventually, the rising air cools to the point where its water vapor condenses to form droplets of liquid water, releasing heat in the process into the surrounding air. This latent heat, in turn, causes the air mass to rise ever more quickly. The upward movement of air in a storm cloud has been measured at more than 50 miles (80 kilometers) per hour.

As the upward movement of air continues, more moisture condenses out of the air mass and the suspended droplets form a large cloud. Depending on atmospheric conditions, a storm cloud of this type may rise to a height of anywhere from 6 to 9 miles (10 to 15 kilometers). In the clouds of colder climates, droplets may freeze to form ice crystals, which grow as more and more water vapor condenses on them. The droplets or ice crystals only grow as long as they can be supported by the updrafts. When they grow too large they begin to fall out of the cloud as drizzle or raindrops.

If the updrafts in the cloud are vigorous enough, much larger precipitation will be formed. In a severe storm, some of the ice crystals may be dragged down by the downdrafts, then swept up again by updrafts. Ice particles may be circulated several times through the storm cloud in this manner, picking up water with each cycle. In a process called riming, raindrop water freezes onto the ice particles, eventually producing large hailstones. Hailstones continue to be recirculated through the cloud until they grow large enough to fall out under their own weight. If located in the right part of the storm, hailstones can grow to impressive sizes. Hail as large as 5.5 inches (14 centimeters) in diameter has been recorded.

Lightning and thunder

Another product of the vigorous up and down drafts in the storm cloud is lightning. Lightning is a giant spark caused by a buildup of static electrical charges. By processes that still are not fully understood, thunderstorm clouds build up a large concentration of positive electrical charges near the top of the cloud and negative electrical charges near the middle. Usually the cloud base has a smaller pocket of positive charge. These opposite charges result in huge voltage differences within the cloud and between the cloud base and the ground. The opposite charges are strongly attracted to each other and when the air between them can no longer keep them apart, a discharge takes place—a bolt of lightning. Depending upon the location of the opposite charges, lightning can occur as cloud-to-ground lightning, cloud-to-cloud lightning, or cloud-to-air lightning.

The temperature of a lightning bolt exceeds 40,000°F (22,000°C). The surrounding air is superheated, causing it to expand and then contract rapidly. This expansion and contraction produces the sound vibrations heard as thunder.

Lightning over Tucson, Arizona. *(Reproduced by permission of Photo Researchers, Inc.)*

It is possible to calculate how far away a storm is by counting the seconds between a lightning flash and a thunder clap. Since it takes thunder about 5 seconds to travel 1 mile (3 seconds to travel 1 kilometer), simply divide the counted seconds by 5 to determine the miles (by 3 to determine the kilometers). Normally, thunder cannot be heard more than 20 miles (32 kilometers) away.

[*See also* **Air masses and fronts; Cyclone and anticyclone; Tornado**]

Tides

Tides are distortions that occur in the shape of a celestial body. They are caused by the gravitational force of one or more other celestial bodies on that first body. In theory, any two bodies in the universe exert a gravitational force on each other. The most important examples of tidal forces on Earth are ocean tides, which result from the mutual attraction of the Moon and the Sun.

Greek geographer Pytheas (c. 380 B.C.–c. 300 B.C.) was perhaps the first careful observer of ocean tides. In about the third century B.C., he traveled outside the Strait of Gibraltar and observed tidal action in the Atlantic Ocean. Pytheas suggested that the pull of the Moon on Earth's oceans caused the tides. Although largely correct, his explanation was not widely accepted by scientists until the eighteenth century, when English physicist and mathematician Isaac Newton (1642–1727) first succeeded in mathematically describing the tides and what cause them.

Theories of tidal action

Although the Sun is larger than the Moon, the Moon is closer to Earth and, therefore, has a greater influence on Earth's ocean tides. The Moon's gravity pulls on the ocean water on the near side of Earth. This force causes the water, since it is able to flow, to form a slight bulge outward, making the water in that area slightly deeper.

At the same time, on the opposing side of Earth, a second tidal bulge occurs that is the same size as the first. This second bulge forms because the force of the Moon's gravity pulls the solid body of Earth away from the water on Earth's far side. The result is that two lunar tidal bulges exist on Earth at all times—one on the side of Earth facing the Moon and another directly opposite to it. These bulges account for the phenomenon known as high tide.

Words to Know

Diurnal: Occurring once every day.

Ebb tide: Period when the water level is falling; the period after high tide and before low tide.

Flood tide: The period when the water level is rising; the period after low tide and before high tide.

High tide: The event corresponding to the largest increase in water level in an area that is acted upon by tidal forces.

Low tide: The event corresponding to the largest decrease in water level in an area that is acted upon by tidal forces.

Neap tides: Period of minimum tidal range that occurs about every two weeks when the Moon and Sun are at 90-degree angles to each other (the first and third quarter moons).

Semidiurnal: Occurring twice every day.

Slack tide: Period during which the water level is neither rising nor falling.

Spring tides: Period of maximum tidal range that occurs about every two weeks when the Moon and Sun are in line with each other (at the new and full moons).

Tidal current: Horizontal movements of water due to tidal action.

Tidal range: Vertical distance in sea level between high tide and low tide during a single tidal cycle.

The formation of these two high tide bulges causes a belt of low water to form at 90-degree angles to the high tide bulges. This belt, which completely encircles Earth, produces the phenomenon known as low tide.

In addition to the lunar bulges, the Sun forms its own tidal bulges. However, due to the Sun's much greater distance from Earth, its tidal effect is approximately one-half that of the Moon.

Every 14 days, the Moon and Sun are in line with each other (new moon and full moon). Their gravitational forces combine to produce a maximum pull on Earth. The tides produced in such cases are known as spring tides. The spring high tide produces the highest high tide and the spring low tide produces the lowest low tide.

Seven days later, when the Moon and Sun are at right angles to each other (first and third quarter Moon), the two forces act in opposition to each other to produce a minimum pull on the oceans. The tides in this case are known as neap tides. The neap high tide produces the lowest high tide and the neap low tide produces the highest low tide.

The nature of tides

In most places, tides are semidiurnal, meaning there are two tidal cycles each day (a tidal cycle is one high and one low tide). The high water level reached during one of the high tide stages is usually greater than the other high tide point, and the low water level reached during one of the low tide stages is usually less than the other low tide point. This consistent difference is called the diurnal inequality of the tides.

In a few locations, tides occur only once a day, with a single high tide stage and a single low tide stage. These are known as diurnal tides. In both diurnal and semidiurnal settings, a rising tide is called the flood tide. A falling tide is called the ebb tide. The point when the water reaches its highest point at high tide, or its lowest point at low tide, is called the slack tide. At this point the water level is static, neither rising nor falling, at least for a short time.

High tide at Big Pine Key, Florida. *(Reproduced by permission of JLM Visuals.)*

As the Moon revolves around Earth, Earth also rotates on its axis. Consequently, in order to return to the same position relative to the Moon above, Earth must rotate on its axis for 24 hours and 50 minutes (a period known as a lunar day). The additional 50 minutes allows Earth to "catch up" to the Moon. As a result, on a coast with diurnal tides, each day the high tide (or low tide) will occur 50 minutes later than the day before. On a semidiurnal coast, each high tide (or low tide) will occur 12 hours and 25 minutes later than the previous high tide (or low tide).

The movement of ocean water as a result of tidal action is known as a tidal current. In open water, tidal currents are relatively weak and tend to change direction slowly and regularly throughout the day. Closer to land, however, tidal currents tend to change direction rather quickly, flowing toward land during high tide and away from land during low tide. In many cases, this onshore and offshore tidal current flows up the mouth of a river or some other narrow opening. When this occurs, the tidal current may then reach speeds as great as 9 miles (15 kilometers) an hour with crests as high as 10 feet (3 meters) or more.

Most tides rise and fall between 3 and 10 feet (1 and 3 meters). In some locations, however, the tides may be much greater. These locations are characterized by ocean bottoms that act as funnels through which ocean waters rush upward towards or downward away from the shore at

Low tide at Big Pine Key, Florida. *(Reproduced by permission of JLM Visuals.)*

very rapid speeds. In the Bay of Fundy, between Nova Scotia and New Brunswick, the difference between high and low tides (the tidal range) may be as great as 46 feet (14 meters). In comparison, some large bodies of water, such as the Mediterranean, Baltic, and Caribbean Seas, have areas with tides of less than a foot (0.3 meter). All coastal locations (as well as very large lakes) experience some variation in tidal range due to the affects of neap versus spring tides.

[*See also* **Celestial mechanics; Gravity and gravitation; Moon; Ocean**]

Time

Time is a measurement to determine the duration of an event or to indicate when an event occurred. For example, one could say that it took an object 3.58 seconds to fall, indicating how long it took for that event to occur. Or, one could say that English physicist Isaac Newton was born on December 25, 1642, telling when the event of his birth took place.

A number of units are used to measure time, including seconds, minutes, hours, days, weeks, months, and years. In the SI system (International System of Units) of measurement used in science, the standard unit of measurement is the second. The second can be subdivided (as can all SI units) into milliseconds, microseconds, and so on.

Time measurement

Humans measure time by observing some natural phenomenon that occurs very regularly. Until recently, those natural phenomena were all astronomical events: the rising and setting of the Sun, the Moon, and stars.

We know, for example, that the Sun rises and sets every day. One way to measure time is to call the time between two successive appearances of the Sun a "day." Then, an hour can be defined as 1/24 part of a day; a minute as 1/60 of an hour; and a second as 1/60 of a minute.

Solar time, which is based on the motion of the Sun, is not the only way of measuring time, however. One might keep track of the regular appearance of the full Moon. That event occurs once about every 29.5 solar days. The time between appearances of new moons, then, could be used to define a unit known as the month.

One also can use the position of the stars for measuring time. The system is the same as that used for the Sun, since the Sun itself is a star.

Words to Know

Atomic clock: A device for keeping time based on natural oscillations within atoms.

Leap time: Any adjustment made in clocks and/or calendars in order to keep them consistent with the natural event used for time measurement.

Lunar time: Any system of time measurement based on the motion of the Moon.

Sidereal time: Any system of time measurement based on the motion of the stars.

Solar time: Any system of time measurement based on the motion of the Sun.

Time reversal: The hypothesis that it may be possible to go backward in time.

All other stars also rise and set on a regular basis. Time systems based on the movement of one or more stars are known as sidereal time (pronounced seye-DEER-ee-uhl).

Although any one of these systems is a satisfactory method for measuring some unit of time, such as a day or a month, the systems may conflict with each other. It is not possible, for example, to fit 365 solar days into 12 or 13 lunar months exactly. This problem creates the need for leap years, leap centuries, and other adjustments developed to keep calendars consistent with each other. Adjustments in time-keeping systems also are necessary to correct for the fact that any natural motion—such as that of the Sun or the Moon—changes very slowly over long periods of time.

Atomic clocks

The standard of time used throughout the world today is no longer an astronomical event, but an atomic event. All atoms oscillate (vibrate back and forth) in a highly regular pattern. In a sense, this vibration is similar to the oscillation of a pendulum in a grandfather clock. The main difference is that atoms oscillate much more rapidly than do the pendulums in clocks.

In 1967, the Thirteenth General Conference on Weights and Measures decided to define a new unit of time. The Conference announced that one second would be defined as the time it takes for an atom of cesium-133 to oscillate 9,192,631,770 times.

An atomic clock, like that made of cesium-133, is preferred to older methods of measuring time based on astronomical events because it is much more accurate. The best cesium clock would be in error by 1 second no more often than once every 6,000 years.

A sundial in Death Valley, California. Sundials were the first devices used to measure time. *(Reproduced by permission of JLM Visuals.)*

Time reversal

One of the intriguing questions about time is whether it can move in two directions—forward and backward. At first thought, it would appear that time can only go forward. Science fiction stories have been written about time machines, devices for allowing people to go back into history. But thus far, no such machine has actually been built.

Yet some scientists believe that going backward in time—time reversal—may actually be possible. For more than 40 years, experiments have been conducted to see whether certain kinds of physical processes can be made to go in reverse. If that result could be obtained, it would provide some reason to believe that time reversal really is possible. At this point, however, no experiment has produced that kind of result.

[*See also* **Relativity, theory of**]

Topology

Topology is a branch of mathematics sometimes known as rubber-sheet geometry. It deals with the properties of a geometric figure that do not change when the shape is twisted, stretched, or squeezed. In topological studies, the tearing, cutting, and combining of shapes is not allowed. The geometric figure must stay intact while being studied. Topology has been used to solve problems concerning the number of colors necessary to illustrate maps, about distinguishing the characteristics of knots, and about understanding the structure and behavior of DNA (deoxyribonucleic acid) molecules, which are responsible for the transferring of physical characteristics from parents to offspring.

Topological equivalency

The crucial problem in topology is deciding when two shapes are equivalent. The term equivalent has a somewhat different meaning in topology than in Euclidean geometry. In Euclidean geometry, one is concerned with the measurement of distances and angles. It is, therefore, a form of quantitative analysis. In contrast, topology is concerned with similarities in shape and continuity between two figures. As a result, it is a form of qualitative analysis.

For example, in Figure 1 on page 1898, each of the two shapes has five points: a through e. The sequence of the points does not change from shape 1 to shape 2, even though the distance between the points changes.

Thus the two shapes in Figure 1 are topologically equivalent, even though their measurements are different.

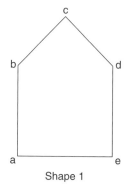 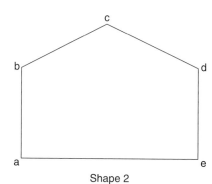

Figure 1. *(Reproduced by permission of The Gale Group.)*

Shape 1   Shape 2

Similarly, in Figure 2, each of the closed shapes is curved, but shape 3 is more circular, and shape 4 is a flattened circle, or ellipse. However, every point on shape 3 can be mapped or transposed onto shape 4. So the two figures are topologically equivalent to each other.

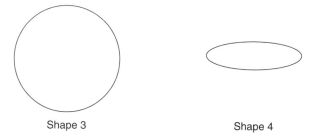

Figure 2. *(Reproduced by permission of The Gale Group.)*

Shape 3   Shape 4

Shapes 1 and 2 are both topologically equivalent to each other, as are shapes 3 and 4. That is, if each were a rubber band, it could be stretched or twisted into the same shape as the other without connecting or disconnecting any of its points. However, if either of the shapes in each pair is torn or cut, or if any of the points in each pair join together, then the shapes are not topologically equivalent. In Figure 3, neither of the shapes is topologically equivalent to any of the shapes in Figures 1 or 2, nor are shapes 5 and 6 equivalent to each other. The circles in shape 5 are fused, and the triangle in shape 6 has a broken line hanging from its apex.

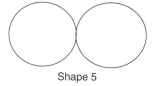 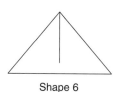

Figure 3. *(Reproduced by permission of The Gale Group.)*

Shape 5   Shape 6

Famous topologists

Topological ideas can be traced back to German mathematician Gottfried Wilhelm Leibniz (1646–1716). However, three of the most famous figures in the development of topology are later German mathematicians: Augustus Ferdinand Möbius (1790–1868), Georg Friedrich Bernhard Riemann (1826–1866), and Felix Klein (1849–1925).

Möbius is best known for his invention of the Möbius strip. You can make a Möbius strip very easily. Simply cut a long strip of paper, twist the paper once, and connect the two ends of the strip to each other. The figure that results will look like the Möbius strip shown in Figure 4. Notice that an ant crawling along the Möbius strip will never have to pass an edge to go to "the other side." In other words, there is no "other side"; the Möbius strip has only one side.

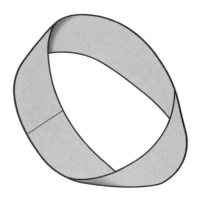

Figure 4. *(Reproduced by permission of The Gale Group.)*

Riemann developed some of the most important topological ideas about the stretching, bending, and twisting of surfaces. Unfortunately, he died at the early age of 39, before getting the chance to develop some of his ideas fully.

Klein is best known for the paradoxical figure illustrated in Figure 5, the Klein bottle. The Klein bottle is a one-sided object that has no edge. It consists of a tapered tube whose neck is bent around to enter the side of the bottle. The neck continues into the base of the bottle where it flares out and rounds off to form the outer surface of the bottle. Like the Möbius strip, any two points on the bottle can be joined by a continuous line without crossing an edge. This property gives the impression that the inside and outside of the Klein bottle are continuous.

Figure 5. *(Reproduced by permission of The Gale Group.)*

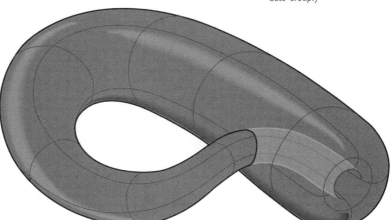

[*See also* **Geometry**]

Tornado

A tornado is a rapidly spinning column of air formed in severe thunderstorms. The rotating column, or vortex, forms inside the storm cloud (cumulonimbus), then grows downward until it touches the ground. When a tornado is visible but does not touch the ground, it is properly called a funnel cloud. A tornado in contact with a body of water is called a waterspout.

A tornado is capable of extreme damage because it packs very high wind speeds into a compact area. Tornadoes have been known to shatter buildings, drive straws through solid wood, lift locomotives from their tracks, and pull the water out of small streams. The United States experiences most of the world's tornadoes, averaging about 800 each year. Most of these tornadoes arise in the states of Texas, Oklahoma, and Kansas. On average, tornadoes are responsible for 80

Approaching tornado with distinctive funnel. *(Reproduced by permission of Photo Researchers, Inc.)*

Words to Know

Fujita Tornado Scale: A scale of six categories that rates tornado wind speed based upon the observed destruction of the storm.

Funnel cloud: A fully developed tornado vortex before it has touched the ground.

Latent heat: The heat released when water vapor condenses to form liquid water.

Vortex: A rotating column of a fluid such as air or water.

Vorticity: The tendency of an air mass to rotate.

Waterspout: Tornado in contact with a body of water.

deaths, 1,500 injuries, and millions of dollars of damage annually in the United States.

Tornado formation

Although tornadoes can occur at any time of the year, most form during the months of March through June, when conditions are right for the development of severe thunderstorms.

In a severe storm, rain that falls from a cloud causes downdrafts (sinking air) in the rear of the cloud. Meanwhile, the advancing edge of the storm has strong updrafts and humid air is pulled into the storm. As this humid air rises and cools, its water vapor condenses to form more water droplets, releasing heat in the process into the surrounding air. This latent heat, in turn, causes the air mass to rise ever more quickly, strengthening the storm.

As updrafts in a severe thunderstorm cloud get stronger, more air is pulled into the base of the cloud to replace the rising air. Some of this air may be rotating slightly since the air around the base of a thunderstorm always has a certain amount of vorticity or "spin."

As the air converges into a smaller area it begins to rotate faster due to a law of physics known as the conservation of angular momentum. This effect can be seen when an ice skater begins slowly spinning with arms outstretched. As the skater brings his or her arms inward, the skater's rate

Dust Devil

A dust devil is a relatively small, rapidly rotating wind that stirs up dust, sand, leaves, and other material as it moves across the ground. Dust devils also are known as whirlwinds or, especially in Australia, willy-willys. In most cases, dust devils are no more than 10 feet (3 meters) wide and less than 300 feet (100 meters) high.

Resembling mini-tornadoes, dust devils form most commonly on hot dry days in arid regions such as a desert. They originate when a layer of air lying just above the ground is heated and begins to rise in an updraft. Winds blowing in the area cause this rising air mass to rotate, either clockwise or counterclockwise. In some cases, wind speeds can easily exceed 50 miles (80 miles) per hour. Some large and powerful dust devils have been known to cause property damage. In the vast majority of cases, however, dust devils are too small to pose a threat to buildings or to human life.

of rotation increases dramatically. In the same way, as air converges into the strong updraft of an intense thunderstorm, its rate of spin increases. Meteorologists still are unsure whether tornadoes form deep within clouds and extend downward or form underneath the cloud and extend upward. It is possible that both situations occur.

Tornado characteristics

Tornadoes move with the thunderstorm to which they are attached at an average speed of 35 miles (56 kilometers) per hour. They have an average path length of about 5 miles (8 kilometers). The diameter of a tornado can vary from 300 feet to 1 mile (90 meters to 1.6 kilometers). Tornadoes come in a variety of shapes and sizes, and often have an ominous dark color due to the soil and other debris they pick up as they move along.

Tornado strength is classified by the Fujita Tornado Scale, or F-scale. Developed by T. Theodore Fujita of the University of Chicago, the scale measures the power and destructiveness of tornadoes. The six categories of the scale (F0 through F5) classify a tornado by the amount of damage it causes—from light to incredible—and its wind speed—from 40 to more than 300 miles (64 to more than 482 kilometers) per hour. It is estimated that 90 percent of all tornadoes have wind speeds below 115 miles (185 kilometers) per hour.

Tornado history

The deadliest tornado in United States history was the Tri-State tornado on March 18, 1925. Beginning in Missouri, the tornado stayed on the ground for almost 220 miles (350 kilometers), moving into Illinois and Indiana. In places, it left a trail of damage almost 1 mile (1.6 kilometers) wide. The Tri-State tornado plowed through nine towns and destroyed thousands of homes. When the storm was over, 695 people had lost their lives and more than 2,000 were injured.

Another historic storm was the severe tornado outbreak of April 3-4, 1974. This so-called "Super Outbreak" triggered 148 tornadoes over 13 states, devastating an area from Alabama to Michigan. More than 300 people were killed and more than 5,000 were injured. Property damage was approximately $500 million.

On May 3, 1999, a storm started near the town of Lawton in southwestern Oklahoma. By the end of the day, it had grown into a violent storm system with a reported 76 tornadoes. As the storm system tore across central Oklahoma and into Kansas, more than 40 people were killed, over 500 were injured, and more than 1,500 buildings were destroyed. One of the tornadoes in the system, classified as an F5, had a diameter of 1 mile (1.6 kilometers) at times and stayed on the ground for more than 4 hours.

Tornado prediction and tracking

The precise tracking and prediction of tornadoes is not yet a reality. Meteorologists can identify conditions that are likely to lead to severe storms and can issue warnings when atmospheric conditions are right for the development of tornadoes. They can use radar to track the path of thunderstorms that might produce tornadoes. Yet it is still not possible to detect a funnel cloud by radar and predict its path, touchdown point, and other important details. Scientific research in this area continues.

[*See also* **Atmospheric pressure; Cyclone and anticyclone; Thunderstorm**]

Touch

Touch is one of the five senses through which animals interpret the world around them. (The other senses are smell, taste, sight, and hearing.) While the organs of the other senses are located primarily in a single area (such as sight in the eyes and taste in the tongue), the sensation of touch can

Words to Know

Epidermis: The outer layer of skin.

Nerve receptor: Nerve endings or specialized cells that are in close contact with nerves.

Stimulus: Anything that causes a response.

be experienced anywhere on the body, from the top of the head to the tips of the toes.

Without the sense of touch, animals would not be able to recognize pain, which would greatly decrease their chances for survival. Research also has shown that touch is an important factor in child development, persuasion, healing, and reducing anxiety and tension.

How we feel the outside world

The sense of touch is based primarily in the outer layer of the skin called the epidermis. Nerve receptors in the epidermis respond to outside stimuli by sending impulses along nerves through the central nervous system to the brain. The brain, in turn, interprets these impulses as heat, cold, pain, or pressure.

Scientists have identified several types of touch receptors, or nerve endings. One type is associated mainly with light pressure (such as wind) and pain and occurs at the base of hairs throughout the body. Another is found in the fingertips and areas especially sensitive to touch, such as the tongue and the soles of the feet. A third type is found in deep tissues in the joints, reproductive organs, and milk glands and is extremely sensitive to pressure and rapid movement of the tissues. The skin also contains specific receptors for sensing heat and cold as well as intense pain.

These receptors also are found in greater numbers on different parts of the body. The back is the least sensitive to touch, while the lips, tongue, and fingertips are most sensitive. Most receptors for cold are found on the surface of the face while receptors for warmth usually lie deeper in the skin and are fewer in number. A light breeze on the arm or head is felt because there tend to be more sense receptors at the base of the hairs than anywhere else.

Touch and health

Numerous studies of humans and other animals have shown that touch greatly affects physical development and mental well being. Premature babies that receive regular messages gain weight more rapidly and develop faster mentally than those who do not receive the same attention. Touch also appears to be a factor in emotional stability. Difficult children often have a history of abuse and neglect. Touch provides reassurance to infants that they are loved and safe. In general, babies who are held and touched tend to be more alert and aware of their surroundings.

Touch continues to have a psychological impact throughout peoples' lives. Adults who are hospitalized or sick at home have less anxiety and tension headaches when they are regularly touched or caressed by caretakers or loved ones. Touch also has a healing power and has been shown to have the capacity to reduce rapid heartbeats and restore irregular heartbeats to normal rhythm.

Touch is a powerful persuasive force. Salespeople often use touch to establish a bond that can result in better sales. People also are more likely to respond positively to a request if it is accompanied by a slight touch on the arm or hand.

[*See also* **Perception**]

Tranquilizer

A tranquilizer is a drug that acts on the central nervous system and is used to calm, decrease anxiety, or help a person to sleep. Often called depressants because they suppress the central nervous system and slow the body down, they are used to treat mental illness as well as common anxiety and sleeplessness. Available only by prescription, they can cause dependence and certain ones can easily be abused.

Major and minor tranquilizers

There are two types or classes of tranquilizers: major tranquilizers and minor tranquilizers. The former are antipsychotic drugs and the latter are considered antianxiety drugs. Antipsychotic drugs are used to treat patients with a severe mental illness, like schizophrenia (pronounced skit-zo-FREH-nee-uh). Antianxiety drugs are given to patients with emotional problems, like anxiety. Both types of tranquilizers were first introduced in the 1950s. At the time, they revolutionized psychiatry for they seemed

Words to Know

Anxiety: A feeling of uneasiness and distress about something in the future.

Insomnia: Inability to go to sleep or stay asleep.

Psychosis: A major psychiatric disorder characterized by the inability to tell what is real from what is not real.

Schizophrenia: A serious mental illness characterized by isolation from others and thought and emotional disturbances.

to offer physicians a way to manage psychoses (pronounced sy-KOH-sees), which are severe forms of mental illness, and to make their patients emotionally calm and quiet. They also seemed to offer an alternative to people simply trying to cope or put up with the everyday anxieties, tension, and sleeplessness that many experience in their normal lives.

Major tranquilizers for psychoses

The major tranquilizers were first developed in the very early 1950s when scientists discovered that the organic compound called phenothiazine (pronounced fee-no-THY-uh-zeen) had a strong sedative effect, meaning it calmed or relaxed the person taking it. In 1952, a phenothiazine derivative called chlorpromazine (pronounced klor-PRO-muh-zeen) was seen to make highly agitated patients quiet and calm without making them unconscious. However, it also made them much less aware mentally, as they seemed to have little or no interest in anything going on around them. These calming effects led doctors to begin giving this new drug (whose trade name was Thorazine) to severely disturbed, psychotic patients, since for the first time, science had found a drug that specifically targeted the central nervous system.

About the same time, another compound called reserpine became useful as a major tranquilizer. It was found to reduce the delusions and hallucinations of schizophrenics. However, it eventually was replaced by another class of drugs since it had several physical side effects. Although antipsychotic drugs or major tranquilizers have side effects—such as increased heart rate, dry mouth, blurred vision, and constipation—they are not addictive and patients seldom build up a tolerance for them. Since they do not give the user any of the good feelings that stimulants do (instead they cause drowsiness), they do not lend themselves to recreational use. They will not make a person feel "high."

Minor tranquilizers for anxiety

Minor tranquilizers are quite different, however, and although these antianxiety drugs are called "minor," there is in fact nothing minor or mild about these drugs. Nor is there anything minor about their effects or their potential for abuse. This class of drugs is the most common type of drug today. More prescriptions are written for these compounds than for any other type of drugs. Minor tranquilizers include the well-known brand names of Valium, Librium, Xanax, and Ativan. Unlike major tranquilizers, which are used by doctors to try and manage severe psychiatric illnesses, minor tranquilizers are given fairly liberally by doctors to patients who complain about anxiety, depression, and sleep disorders. Minor tranquilizers work by reducing tension without heavily sedating the patient. Although they relax tense muscles, they produce less sleepiness during the day than major tranquilizers, although at night they do help with sleep.

Though they should be taken in prescribed doses for short periods of time, many people take these minor tranquilizers regularly, and they

Different types of tranquilizers in pill form. *(Reproduced by permission of FPG International LLC.)*

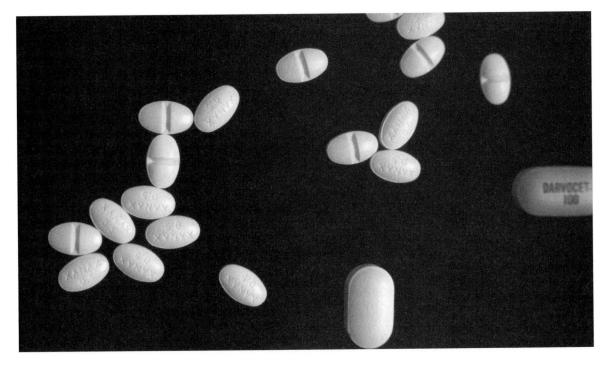

can cause dependence and tolerance. This means that the patient may experience unpleasant withdrawal symptoms if they suddenly stop taking them, and that they eventually need to take larger doses to maintain a feeling of well-being. Minor tranquilizers are the most widely abused drug in the United States and are regularly involved in suicide attempts and accidental overdoses. Called "downers" on the street, they can give a feeling of calm and relaxation (some say a "floating" sensation) that can, however, turn into more serious and unpleasant side effects. Overuse of downers can make people hostile and aggressive, and leave them with blurred vision, memory loss, disorganized thinking, headaches, and depression.

Not a cure

Whether major or minor tranquilizers, these two classes of drugs are not a cure for any of the conditions they treat. They are given by doctors to relieve symptoms that are associated with other problems. Neither type of drug should be taken with alcohol, as both are depressants and can therefore compound or exaggerate the effect of the other. People who take tranquilizers also should not drive a car or operate anything mechanical for several hours after taking the pills, since they interfere with the control of a person's movements. Although technically there are major and minor tranquilizers, the word "tranquilizer" has commonly come to refer only to the minor class of drugs that treat anxiety and insomnia—probably because they are the most frequently prescribed type of drug in the world.

[*See also* **Psychosis; Schizophrenia**]

Transformer

A transformer is an electrical device used to change the voltage in an electric circuit. It usually consists of a soft iron core with a rectangular shape. An incoming wire (the primary coil) is wrapped around one side of the core, and an outgoing wire (the secondary coil) is wrapped around the opposite side of the core. Each wire is wrapped around the core a different number of times.

A transformer works on the principle of inductance. An alternating electric current entering the transformer through the primary coil creates a magnetic field within the iron core. The strength of the magnetic field depends on the strength of the electric current.

Once the magnetic field is established in the iron core, the reverse effect occurs in the secondary coil at the opposite side of the core. The oscillating (vibrating) magnetic field within the core creates an electric current in the secondary coil. The strength of the electric current is determined by the number of times the outgoing wire is wrapped around the iron core.

A transformer can be used either to increase or decrease the voltage in a circuit. A transformer of the former type is known as a step-up transformer; one of the latter type is known as a step-down transformer.

A high-voltage transformer. *(Reproduced by permission of The Stock Market.)*

Applications

Transformers are used widely in everyday situations. The transmission of electric current from its source (such as a hydroelectric dam) to the consumer can be accomplished most efficiently at high voltages. The high-tension wires one sees overhead in the open country carry electric current at high voltage. But most household appliances operate at much lower voltages. It is necessary, therefore, to install transformers near the point where electric current enters a house or within appliances themselves.

Transistor

A transistor is a solid-state electronic device used to control the flow of an electric current. The term solid-state refers to devices that take advantage of special properties of solids. (It usually refers to devices made of semiconducting materials.) Since they were invented in the 1940s, transistors have come to revolutionize modern communications. They are found in an enormous variety of electrical devices, ranging from popular consumer items such as home computer games, pocket calculators, and portable stereos to the complex electronic systems used by business and industry.

Until World War II (1939–45), most systems of communication used vacuum tubes for the amplification and control of electrical current. However, vacuum tubes have a number of serious disadvantages. They are bulky and fragile, they consume a lot of power, and they have a tendency to overheat. The demands of radar in particular during the war encouraged scientists to look for another method of amplifying and controlling electric current in communication devices.

Semiconductors

The discovery of the transistor was announced in 1948 by three scientists from the Bell Telephone Laboratories: William Shockley (1910–1989), John Bardeen (1908–1991), and Walter Brattain (1902–1987). The key to this discovery is a class of materials known as semiconductors. Semiconductors are substances that conduct an electric current only very poorly. They fall somewhere between true conductors (such as silver, aluminum, and copper) and nonconductors (such as wool, cotton, paper, air, wood, and most plastics). The two most commonly used semiconducting elements are silicon and germanium. Some important semiconducting compounds include cadmium selenide, cadmium telluride, and gallium arsenide.

Words to Know

Amplification: Increasing the strength of some signal such as the amount of electrical current passing through a transistor.

Base: The middle slice of a transistor.

Chip: The piece of semiconducting material on which integrated circuits are etched.

Collector: One of the outer slices of a transistor.

Dopant: An impurity added to a semiconducting material.

Doping: The act of adding impurities to change semiconductor properties.

Emitter: One of the outer slices of a transistor.

Integrated circuit (IC): An electronic device that contains thousands or millions of microscopic-sized transistors etched on a single piece (chip) of material.

N-type semiconductor: An element or compound that has a slight excess of electrons.

P-type semiconductor: An element or compound that has a slight deficiency of electrons.

Resistor: Component used to introduce resistance.

Semiconductor: A substance that conducts an electric current—but only very poorly.

Solid-state: A term used for electronic devices that take advantage of special properties of solids. It usually refers to devices made of semiconducting materials.

Semiconductors fall into one of two general categories: n-type semiconductors and p-type semiconductors. The former class consists of materials that have a slight excess of electrons, while those in the latter class have a slight deficiency of electrons.

The conductivity of both n-type and p-type semiconductors can be enhanced greatly by adding very small amounts of impurities. This process is known as doping and involves the addition of roughly one atom of dopant (such as boron or phosphorus) for each ten million atoms of the base semiconductor (such as silicon or germanium).

Operation of a transistor

A typical transistor looks like a sandwich with one type of semiconductor as the slices of bread and the second type of semiconductor as the filling. For example, a thin slice of a p-type semiconductor might be placed between two thicker slices of an n-type semiconductor. The middle slice of the transistor is known as the base, while the two outer slices are called the collector and the emitter.

Suppose that this transistor is placed into an electric circuit, and current is allowed to flow through it. The current flows into the transistor through the collector, across the base, and out through the emitter.

The flow of this current can be controlled by attaching a second source of electric current to the base itself. The amount of current that flows through the transistor will be determined by this second source of electric current. If a relatively small current is allowed to flow into the base, the transistor does not permit a very large flow of current through it. If a relatively large current is allowed to flow into the base, the transistor allows a much larger flow of current through it.

For example, suppose that a particular transistor typically permits a flow of 0.01 milliamperes when the electrical flow into the base is at a minimum. Then suppose that the flow into the base is increased by a small

The development of the transistor greatly increased the complexity and sophistication of electronic devices. (Reproduced by permission of Photo Researchers, Inc.)

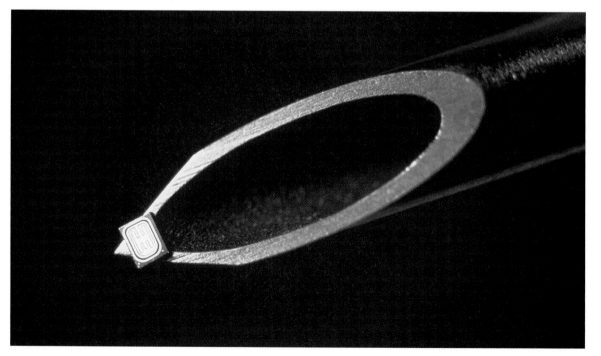

amount. That small increase will allow a much larger flow of electric current—say up to 2.5 milliamperes—through it. The transistor has been made to act, therefore, like an amplifier.

Many other kinds of transistors have been developed to perform other electronic functions. One of the greatest breakthroughs in transistor research was the invention in 1959 of the integrated circuit (IC). An integrated circuit is an electronic device that contains large numbers (usually thousands or millions) of microscopic-sized transistors etched on a single piece (chip) of material.

Transition elements

The transition elements are the elements that make up Groups 3 through 12 of the periodic table. These elements, all of which are metals, include some of the best-known names on the periodic table—iron, gold, silver, copper, mercury, zinc, nickel, chromium, and platinum among them. A number of other transition elements are probably somewhat less familiar, although they have vital industrial applications. These elements include titanium, vanadium, manganese, zirconium, molybdenum, palladium, and tungsten.

One member of the transition family deserves special mention. Technetium (element #43) is one of only two "light" elements that does not occur in nature. It was originally produced synthetically in 1937 among the products of a cyclotron reaction. The discoverers of technetium were Italian physicists Carlo Perrier and Emilio Segré (1905–1989).

The transition elements share many physical properties in common. With the notable exception of mercury, the only liquid metal, they all have relatively high melting and boiling points. They also have a shiny, lustrous, metallic appearance that may range from silver to gold to white to gray.

In addition, the transition metals share some chemical properties. For example, they tend to form complexes, compounds in which a group of atoms cluster around a single metal atom. Ordinary copper sulfate, for example, normally occurs in a configuration that includes four water molecules surrounding a single copper ion. Transition element complexes have many medical and industrial applications.

Another common property of the transition elements is their tendency to form colored compounds. Some of the most striking and beautiful chemical compounds known are those that include transition metals. Copper compounds tend to be blue or green; chromium compounds are

Words to Know

Amalgam: An alloy that contains mercury.

Basic oxygen process (BOP): A method for making steel in which a mixture of pig iron, scrap iron, and scrap steel is melted in a large steel container and a blast of pure oxygen is blown through the container.

Bessemer convertor: A device for converting pig iron to steel in which a blast of hot air is blown through molten pig iron.

Blast furnace: A structure in which a metallic ore (often, iron ore) is reduced to the elemental state.

Cast iron: A term used to describe various forms of iron that also contain anywhere from 0.5 to 4.2 percent carbon and 0.2 to 3.5 percent silicon.

Complex: A chemical compound in which a single metal atom is surrounded by two or more groups of atoms.

Ductile: Capable of being drawn or stretched into a thin wire.

Electrolytic cell: A system in which electrical energy is used to bring about chemical changes.

Electrolytic copper: A very pure form of copper.

Malleable: Capable of being rolled or hammered into thin sheets.

Open hearth process: A method for making steel in which a blast of hot air or oxygen is blown across the surface of a molten mixture of pig iron, hematite, scrap iron, and limestone in a large brick container.

Patina: A corrosion-resistant film that often develops on copper surfaces.

Pig iron: A form of iron consisting of approximately 90 percent pure iron and the remaining 10 percent of various impurities.

Slag: A by-product of the reactions by which iron is produced, consisting primarily of calcium silicate.

yellow, orange, or green; nickel compounds are blue, green, or yellow; and manganese compounds are purple, black, or green.

The discussion that follows focuses on only three of the transition elements: iron, copper, and mercury. These three elements are among the best known and most widely used of all chemical elements.

Iron

Iron is the fourth most abundant element in Earth's crust, following oxygen, silicon, and aluminum. In addition, Earth's core is believed to consist largely of iron. The element rarely occurs in an uncombined form but is usually found as a mineral such as hematite (iron[III] oxide), magnetite (lodestone, a mixture of iron[II] and iron[III] oxides), limonite (hydrated iron[III] oxide), pyrite (iron sulfide), and siderite (iron[II] carbonate).

Properties. Iron is a silver-white or gray metal with a melting point of 2,795°F (1,535°C) and a boiling point of 4,982°F (2,750°C). Its chemical symbol, Fe, is taken from the Latin name for iron, *ferrum*. It is both malleable and ductile. Malleability is a property common to most metals, meaning that a substance can be hammered into thin sheets. Many metals are also ductile, meaning that they can be drawn into a fine wire.

In a pure form, iron is relatively soft and slightly magnetic. When hardened, it becomes much more magnetic. Iron is the most widely used of all metals. Prior to its use, however, it must be treated in some way to improve its properties, or it must be combined with one or more other elements (in this case, another metal) to form an alloy. By far the most popular alloy of iron is steel.

One of the most common forms of iron is pig iron, produced by smelting iron ore with coke (nearly pure carbon) and limestone in a blast furnace. (Smelting is the process of obtaining a pure metal from its ore.) Pig iron is approximately 90 percent pure iron and is used primarily in the production of cast iron and steel.

Cast iron is a term used to describe various forms of iron that also contain carbon and silicon ranging in concentrations from 0.5 to 4.2 percent of the former and 0.2 to 3.5 percent of the latter. Cast iron has a vast array of uses in products ranging from thin rings to massive turbine bodies. Wrought iron contains small amounts of a number of other elements, including carbon, silicon, phosphorus, sulfur, chromium, nickel, cobalt, copper, and molybdenum. Wrought iron can be fabricated into a number of forms and is widely used because of its resistance to corrosion.

How iron is obtained. Iron is one of the handful of elements that was known to ancient civilizations. Originally it was prepared by heating a naturally occurring ore of iron with charcoal in a very hot flame. The charcoal was obtained by heating wood in the absence of air. There is some evidence that this method of preparation was known as early as 3000 B.C. But the secret of ore smelting was carefully guarded within the Hittite civilization of the Near East for almost 2,000 years.

Then, when that civilization fell in about 1200 B.C., the process of iron ore smelting spread throughout eastern and southern Europe. Ironsmiths were soon making ornamental objects, simple tools, and weapons from iron. So dramatic was the impact of this new technology on human societies that the period following 1200 B.C. is generally known as the Iron Age.

A major change in the technique for producing iron from its ores occurred around 1709. As trees (and therefore the charcoal made from them) grew increasingly scarce in Great Britain, English inventor Abraham Darby (c. 1678–1717) discovered a method for making coke from soft coal. Since coal was abundant in the British Isles, Darby's technique provided for a consistent and dependable method of converting iron ores to the pure metal.

The modern production of iron involves heating iron ore with coke and limestone in a blast furnace, where temperatures range from 400°F (200°C) at the top of the furnace to 3,600°F (2,000°C) at the bottom. Some blast furnaces are as tall as 15-story buildings and can produce 2,400 tons (2,180 metric tons) of iron per day.

Inside a blast furnace, a number of chemical reactions occur. One of these involves the reaction of coke (nearly pure carbon) with oxygen to form carbon monoxide. This carbon monoxide then reacts with iron ore to form pure iron and carbon dioxide. Limestone is added to the reaction mixture to remove impurities in the iron ore. The product of this reaction, known as slag, consists primarily of calcium silicate. The iron formed in a blast furnace exists in a molten form (called pig iron) that can be drawn off at the bottom of the furnace. The slag also is molten but less dense than the iron. It is drawn off from taps just above the outlet from which the molten iron is removed.

Early efforts to use pig iron for commercial and industrial applications were not very successful. The material proved to be quite brittle, and objects made from it tended to break easily. Cannons made of pig iron, for example, were likely to blow apart when they fired a shell. By 1760, inventors had begun to find ways of toughening pig iron. These methods involved remelting the pig iron and then burning off the carbon that remained mixed with the product. The most successful early device for accomplishing this step was the Bessemer converter, named after its English inventor, Henry Bessemer (1813–1898). In the Bessemer converter, a blast of hot air is blown through molten pig iron. The process results in the formation of stronger forms of iron: cast and wrought iron. More importantly, when additional elements such as manganese and chromium are added to the converter, a new product—steel—is formed.

Later inventions improved on the production of steel by the Bessemer converter. In the open hearth process, for example, a mix of molten pig iron, hematite, scrap iron, and limestone is placed into a large brick container. A blast of hot air or oxygen is then blown across the surface of the molten mixture. Chemical reactions within the molten mixture result in the formation of either pure iron or, with the addition of alloying metals such as manganese or chromium, a high grade of steel.

An even more recent variation on the Bessemer converter concept is the basic oxygen process (BOP). In the BOP, a mixture of pig iron, scrap iron, and scrap steel is melted in a large steel container and a blast of pure oxygen is blown through the container. The introduction of alloying metals makes possible the production of various types of steel with many different properties.

Uses of iron.   Alloyed with other metals, iron is the most widely used of all metallic elements. The way in which it is alloyed determines the uses to which the final product is put. Steel, for example, is a general term used to describe iron alloyed with carbon and, in some cases, with other elements. The American Iron and Steel Institute recognizes 27 standard types of steel. Three of these are designated as carbon steels that may contain, in addition to carbon, small amounts of phosphorus and/or sulfur. Another 20 types of steel are made of iron alloyed with one or more

A magnet separating the iron from an iron-sulfur mixture. *(Reproduced by permission of Phototake.)*

of the following elements: chromium, manganese, molybdenum, nickel, silicon, and vanadium. Finally, four types of stainless and heat-resisting steels contain some combination of chromium, nickel, and manganese alloyed with iron.

Steel is widely used in many types of construction. It has at least six times the strength of concrete, another traditional building material, and about three times the strength of special forms of high-strength concrete. A combination of these two materials—called reinforced concrete—is one of the strongest of all building materials available to architects. The strength of steel has made possible some remarkable feats of construction, including very tall buildings (skyscrapers) and bridges with very wide spans. It also has been used in the manufacture of automobile bodies, ship hulls, and heavy machinery and machine parts.

Metallurgists (specialists in the science and technology of metals) have invented special iron alloys to meet very specific needs. Alloys of cobalt and iron (both magnetic materials themselves) can be used in the manufacture of very powerful permanent magnets. Steels that contain the element niobium (originally called columbium) have unusually great strength and have been used, among other places, in the construction of nuclear reactors. Tungsten steels also are very strong and have been used in the production of high-speed metal cutting tools and drills. The alloying of aluminum with iron produces a material that can be used in AC (alternating current) magnetic circuits since it can gain and lose magnetism very quickly.

Metallic iron has other applications as well. Its natural magnetic properties make it suitable for both permanent magnets and electromagnets. It also is used in the production of various types of dyes, including blueprint paper and certain inks, and in the manufacture of abrasives.

Biochemical applications. Iron is essential to the survival of all vertebrates. Hemoglobin, the molecule in blood that transports oxygen from the lungs to an organism's cells, contains a single iron atom buried deep within its complex structure. When humans do not take in sufficient amounts of iron in their daily diets, they may develop a disorder known as anemia. Anemia is characterized by a loss of skin color, a weakness and tendency to faint, palpitation of the heart, and a general sense of exhaustion.

Iron also is important to the good health of plants. It is found in a group of compounds known as porphyrins (pronounced POUR-fuh-rinz) that play an important role in the growth and development of plant cells. Plants that lack iron have a tendency to lose their color, become weak, and die.

Copper

Copper is one of only two metals with a distinctive color (the other being gold). Copper is often described as having a reddish-brown hue. It has a melting point of 1,985°F (1,085°C) and a boiling point 4,645°F (2,563°C). Its chemical symbol, Cu, is derived from the Latin name for the element, *cuprum.*

Copper is one of the elements that is essential to life in tiny amounts (often referred to as trace elements), although larger amounts can be toxic. About 0.0004 percent of the weight of the human body is copper. It can be found in such foods as liver, shellfish, nuts, raisins, and dried beans.

Copper also is found in an essential biochemical compound known as hemocyanin. Hemocyanin is chemically similar to the red hemoglobin found in human blood, which has an iron atom in the center of its molecule. By contrast, hemocyanin contains an atom of copper rather than iron in its core. Lobsters and other large crustaceans have blue blood whose color is caused by the presence of hemocyanin.

History of copper. Copper was one of the first metals known to humans. One reason for this fact is that copper occurs not only as ores (compounds that must be converted to metal) but occasionally as native copper, a pure form of the element found in the ground. In prehistoric times an early human could actually find a chunk of pure copper in the earth and hammer it into a tool with a rock.

Native copper was mined and used in the Tigris-Euphrates valley (modern Iraq) as long as 7,000 years ago. Copper ores have been mined for at least 5,000 years because it is fairly easy to get the copper out of the ore. For example, if an ore of copper oxide is heated in a wood fire, the carbon in the charcoal reacts with oxygen in the oxide and converts it to pure copper metal.

Making pure copper. Extremely pure copper (greater than 99.95 percent purity) is generally called electrolytic copper because it is made by the process known as electrolysis. Electrolysis is a reaction by which electrical energy is used to bring about some kind of chemical change. The high purity is needed because most copper is used to make electrical equipment. Small amounts of impurities present in copper can seriously reduce its ability to conduct electricity. Even 0.05 percent of arsenic as an impurity, for example, will reduce copper's conductivity by 15 percent. Electric wires must be made of very pure copper, especially if the electricity is to be carried for many miles through high-voltage transmission lines.

Uses of copper.   By far the most important use of copper is in electrical wiring. It is an excellent conductor of electricity (second only to silver), it can be made extremely pure, it corrodes very slowly, and it can be formed easily into thin wires.

Copper is also an important ingredient of many useful alloys. (An alloy is a mixture of one metal with another to improve on the original metal's properties.) Brass is an alloy of copper and zinc. If the brass contains mostly copper, it is a golden yellow color; if it contains mostly zinc, it is pale yellow or silvery. Brass is one of the most useful of all alloys. It can be cast or machined into everything from candlesticks to cheap, gold-imitating jewelry (but this type of jewelry often turns human skin green—the copper reacts with salts and acids in the skin to form green copper chloride and other compounds).

Several other copper alloys include: bronze, which is mainly copper plus tin; German silver and sterling silver, which consist of silver plus copper; and silver tooth fillings, which contain about 12 percent copper.

Probably the first alloy ever to be made and used by humans was bronze. Archaeologists broadly divide human history into three periods. The Bronze Age (c. 4000–3000 B.C.) is the second of these periods, occurring after the Stone Age and before the Iron Age. During the Bronze Age, both bronze and pure copper were used for making tools and weapons.

Copper sample from northern Michigan. *(Reproduced by permission of JLM Visuals.)*

Because it resists corrosion and conducts heat well, copper is widely used in plumbing and heating applications. Copper pipes and tubing are used to distribute hot and cold water through houses and other buildings. Copper's superior ability to conduct heat also makes it useful in the manufacture of cooking utensils such as pots and pans. An even temperature across the pan bottom is important for cooking so food doesn't burn or stick to hot spots. The insides of the pans must be coated with tin, however, to keep excessive amounts of copper from seeping into the food.

Copper corrodes only slowly in moist air—much more slowly than iron rusts. First, it darkens in color because of the formation of a thin layer of black copper oxide. Then, as the years go by, the copper oxide is converted into a bluish-green patina (a surface appearance that comes with age) of basic copper carbonate. The green color of the Statue of Liberty, for example, was formed in this way.

Mercury

Mercury, the only liquid metal, has a beautiful silvery color. Its chemical symbol, Hg, comes from the Latin name of the element, *hydrargyrum,* for "liquid silver." Mercury has a melting point of $-38°F$ $(-70°C)$ and a boiling point of $673°F$ $(352.5°C)$. Its presence in Earth's crust is relatively low compared to other elements, equal to about 0.08 parts per million. Mercury is not considered to be rare, however, because it is found in large, highly concentrated deposits.

Nearly all mercury exists in the form of a red ore called cinnabar, or mercury (II) sulfide. Sometimes shiny globules of mercury appear among outcrops of cinnabar, which is probably the reason that mercury was discovered so long ago. The metal is relatively easy to extract from the ore. In fact, the modern technique for extracting mercury is nearly identical in principle to the method used centuries ago. Cinnabar is heated in the open air. Oxygen in the air reacts with sulfur in the cinnabar, producing pure mercury metal. The mercury metal vaporizes and is allowed to condense on a cool surface, from which it can be collected.

Mercury does not react readily with air, water, acids, alkalis, or most other chemicals. It has a surface tension six times greater than that of water. Surface tension refers to the tendency of a liquid to form a tough "skin" on its surface. The high surface tension of mercury explains its tendency not to "wet" surfaces with which it comes into contact.

No one knows exactly when mercury was discovered, but many ancient civilizations were familiar with this element. As long ago as Roman times, people had learned to extract mercury from ore and used it to purify gold and silver. Ore containing gold or silver would be crushed and treated with mercury, which rejects impurities, to form a mercury alloy, called an amalgam. When the amalgam is heated, the mercury vaporizes, leaving pure gold or silver behind.

Toxicity.　Mercury and all of its compounds are extremely poisonous. The element also has no known natural function in the human body. Classified as a heavy metal, mercury is difficult for the body to eliminate. This means that even small amounts of the metal can act as a cumulative poison, collecting over a long period of time until it reaches a dangerous level.

Humans can absorb mercury through any mucous membrane and through the skin. Its vapor can be inhaled, and mercury can be ingested in foods such as fish, eggs, meat, and grain. In the body, mercury affects the nervous system, liver, and kidneys. Symptoms of mercury poisoning include tremors, tunnel vision, loss of balance, slurred speech, and unpredictable emotions. (Tunnel vision is a narrowing of the visual field so

Droplets of mercury, the only liquid metal. *(Reproduced by permission of Photo Researchers, Inc.)*

that peripheral vision—the outer part of the field of vision that encompasses the far right and far left sides—is completely eliminated.) The phrase "mad as a hatter" owes it origin to symptoms of mercury poisoning that afflicted hatmakers in the 1800s, when a mercury compound was used to prepare beaver fur and felt materials.

Until recently, scientists thought that inorganic mercury was relatively harmless. As a result, industrial wastes containing mercury were routinely discharged into large bodies of water. Then, in the 1950s, more than 100 people in Japan were poisoned by fish containing mercury. Forty-three people died, dozens more were horribly crippled, and babies born after the outbreak developed irreversible damage. It was found that inorganic mercury in industrial wastes had been converted to a much more harmful organic form known as methyl mercury. As this substance works its way up the food chain, its quantities accumulate to dangerous levels in larger fish. Today, the dumping of mercury-containing wastes has been largely banned, and many of its industrial uses have been halted.

Uses.   Mercury is used widely in a variety of measuring instruments and devices, such as thermometers, barometers, hydrometers, and pyrometers. It also is used in electrical switches and relays, in mercury arc lamps, and for the extraction of gold and silver from amalgams. A small amount is still used in the preparation of amalgams for dental repairs.

The largest single use of mercury today, however, is in electrolytic cells, in which sodium chloride is converted to metallic sodium and gaseous chlorine. The mercury is used to form an amalgam with sodium in the cells.

[*See also* **Alloy**]

Transplant, surgical

A surgical transplant involves removing organs or tissues from one person and replacing them with corresponding ones from another part of that person's body or from another person. The idea of surgical transplantation dates back several centuries, but it has become a practical medical approach only in the last few decades of the twentieth century. The main reason is that the body naturally rejects foreign tissue placed inside it. Only since the mid-twentieth century have doctors begun to learn more about the body's immune system and how to suppress it's natural rejection response.

Words to Know

Graft: Bone, skin, or other tissue that is taken from one place on the body (or, in some cases, from another body) and then transplanted to another place, where it begins to grow again.

Immune system: The body's natural defense system that guards against foreign invaders and that includes lymphocytes.

Immunosuppressant: Something used to reduce the immune system's ability to function, like certain drugs or radiation.

Lymphocytes: A type of white blood cell that is involved in the body's immune response.

Radiation therapy: Use of radioactive substances to kill cancer cells in the human body.

The history of transplants

The idea of transplanting animal or human parts dates back for many centuries. In the sixteenth century, a transplantation technique was developed for replacing noses lost during battle or due to syphilis (an infectious disease contracted through sexual contact). The technique involved using skin from the upper inner arm and then grafting (transplanting) and shaping it onto the nose area.

During the nineteenth century, advances in surgery (like the development of antiseptic surgery to prevent infection and anesthetics to the lessen pain) increased the success rates of most surgical procedures. However, transplantation of organs failed as surgeons had no knowledge of how to "reconnect" the organ to the new body. Transplant surgery did not move ahead until doctors developed techniques for reconnecting blood vessels in the early twentieth century.

Studies in rejection

The next major advance in transplantation did not occur for more than 40 years. Although kidney transplants were attempted, the recipient's body always rejected the organ. Researchers experimenting with transplants began to suspect that the body's rejection of the implanted organ was an immune system response to foreign tissue. During World War

II (1939–45), British biologist Peter Medawar (1915–1987) became interested in skin graft problems while working with severely burned soldiers. He soon proved that the rejection was due to the immune system, which attacked the foreign tissues or organs as foreign invaders, much the same way it works to ward of viruses and other disease.

The first successful human kidney transplant took place at Loyola University in Chicago, Illinois, in 1950. In the years following, however, most transplants resulted in rejection (only those between identical twins were successful). As a result, scientists began to focus on controlling the immune system so it would accept the transplant.

Advances lead to successes

By the early 1960s, doctors discovered how to match donor and recipient tissue more closely. They also began to use a combination of radiation (to destroy certain cells) and drugs to suppress the immune system, in effect shutting it down to prevent rejection. These antirejection drugs are called immunosuppressants. As a result of this therapy, the first successful human pancreas transplant took place in 1966. The following year, Thomas Starzl (1926–) of the University of Colorado performed the first successful liver transplant. (Because of its complicated blood supply, the liver remains difficult to transplant.)

In 1967, Christiaan Barnard (1922–), a South African surgeon, received worldwide notoriety for achieving the first successful heart transplant. Barnard took the heart of a young woman and implanted it in Louis Washansky, a 55-year-old grocer. Washansky survived only 18 days. Barnard's second patient, dentist Philip Blaiberg, lived for 17 months.

The next major advance came in 1972 with the discovery of cyclosporine, an extremely effective immunosuppressant. This drug has proven to be the most effective medicine used to combat the body's own immune system. It has increased survival rates for transplant patients, especially in heart and liver operations.

Because transplantation of both lungs succeeds better than transplanting a single lung, and because most patients with lung disease also have serious heart deterioration, heart-lung transplants are sometimes performed. The first successful operation of this type was carried out in 1981 at Stanford University Medical Center by Bruce Reitz (1944–) and Norman Shumway (1923–).

In September 1998, in a landmark operation, a team of microsurgeons from four countries spent fourteen hours delicately attaching the forearm and hand from a dead Frenchman to Clint Hallam. The only other reported hand transplant before this took place in Ecuador in 1964, but it had failed because potent immunosuppressant drugs had not yet been developed. The Hallam transplant, however, was doomed from the beginning. Before the operation, Hallam had told doctors he had lost his hand in an industrial accident. The truth was that it had been severed in an accident in a prison in his native New Zealand. After the operation, Hallam agreed to adhere to a physical therapy program to train his new hand and to a regimen of immunosuppressant drugs. But he did neither. Finally, in February 2001, because Hallam's body was rejecting the transplant, a doctor who had helped attach the hand amputated it.

The lesson doctors learned from this transplant, though, were not lost. Between the end of 1998 and the beginning of 2001, nine other people received new hands in six countries. All were reported doing well. Three of those patients even received right and left hands in double transplants.

Current state of transplantation

Doctors have successfully transplanted hearts, kidneys, livers, lungs and other tissues for many years, but problems still remain. Many grafts do not survive permanently. Graft-versus-host rejection, in which lymphocytes in the transplanted tissue attack the foreign host tissue, is diffi-

A comparison of the old and new hearts of Dylan Stork, the smallest heart transplant recipient in the world. Dylan weighed 5.5 pounds (2.5 kilograms) at the time of the operation. *(Reproduced by permission of Photo Researchers, Inc.)*

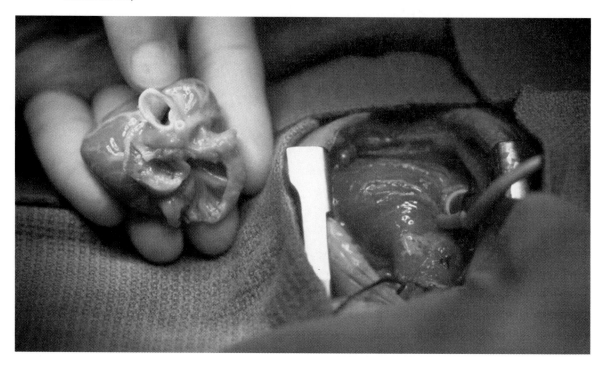

cult to control. (Lymphocytes are white blood cells, the body's main in-fection-fighting agents.) Cyclosporine is very expensive and has serious side effects, including possible kidney damage, elevated blood pressure, seizures, and other nervous system disorders.

Research on how to selectively control the immune system continues. Another problem facing the field of transplantation is the extreme shortage of available donors. Although transplantation is now a relatively common operation with thousands of surgical transplants performed in medical centers throughout the world each year, many people who need a transplant do not receive one. Nearly 20,000 people die in the United States each year who would have been suitable organ donors. But only about 3,000 of these organs are ever donated and harvested.

[See also **Antibody and antigen; Immune system; Surgery**]

Tree

A tree is a woody perennial plant that has a single trunk arising from the ground (typically without branches near the base) and that usually grows to 20 feet (6 meters) or more in height. Branches and twigs grow from the trunk of a tree to form its characteristic leafy crown. Trees are the dominant plants in the world's forests, providing critical habitats for the other species that live there. Trees also provide many products that are important to humans, such as fruits, nuts, timber, and medicine.

Trees may be classified into two major groups: deciduous and ever-green (conifer). Deciduous trees shed their broad leaves at the end of the growing season—typically each fall. Examples of deciduous trees are maples, oaks, and elms. Evergreen or coniferous trees typically have needle-shaped leaves that remain for several years before being replaced. Pines, firs, and spruces are examples of evergreens.

Structure of a tree trunk

Bark is the protective external covering of the stems (roots, trunk, and branches) of trees. The waterproof outer layer is known as cork. Composed of dead cells, cork can be as thick as several inches or more and serves to protect the internal living tissues from insects, animals, fungi, fire, and dehydration (the loss of water).

Underneath the cork is a layer of living tissue called the phloem (pronounced FLOW-em). Phloem cells are elongated cells that transport plant nutrients, such as the carbohydrates made during photosynthesis, from the leaves to all other parts of the plant.

When young, all trees have smooth bark. As trees mature, the outer surface of their bark begins to change in appearance, varying greatly among different species. For example, the bark of a mature American beech is distinctively grey and smooth while the bark of a mature sugar maple is rough and scaly, with deep fissures (long narrow cracks).

Beneath the layers of bark is the cambium layer, a living sheath or covering of cells. On its outside face, the cambium produces phloem cells.

A birch tree. *(Reproduced by permission of Photo Researchers, Inc.)*

Words to Know

Bark: Protective external covering of the stems (roots, trunk, and branches) of trees and other woody plants.

Cambium: Plant tissue that produces phloem and xylem cells.

Cork: Waterproof outer layer of bark composed of dead cells.

Growth ring: Layer of wood produced in a single growing season.

Heartwood: Dead central portion of wood in a tree.

Perennial: Any plant that lives, grows, flowers, and produces seeds for three or more consecutive years.

Phloem: Plant tissue consisting of elongated cells that transport carbohydrates and other nutrients.

Photosynthesis: Process by which light energy is captured from the Sun by pigment molecules in plants and algae and converted to food.

Sapwood: Newly formed, outer layer of wood between the heartwood and bark that contains the living elements of the wood.

Xylem: Plant tissue consisting of thick-walled cells that transport water and mineral nutrients.

On its inside face, it produces xylem (pronounced ZEYE-lem) cells. These thick-walled cells carry water and mineral nutrients from the roots to the farthest branches. The broad layer of xylem tissue is known as the sapwood.

Finally, the heartwood is in the center of the tree. As a tree ages and increases in diameter, dead xylem cells are used to store waste products, such as resin and other compounds. These waste-filled xylem cells form the heartwood. Typically darker than the sapwood, the heartwood is very stiff and serves to strengthen the tree.

Tree growth

The periodic formation of layers of xylem cells results in the diameter growth of trees. New sapwood is created during each growing season, but within two to three years these cells become part of the heartwood.

In most trees growing in a climate with definite seasons, the cambium produces wide, thin-walled cells in the spring, narrow thick-walled cells in the summer, and few or no cells in the autumn and winter. This seasonal cell production results in the formation of annual growth rings. The bristle-cone pine is the world's longest-lived tree species. One specimen of this species has about 5,000 growth rings, indicating it is at least 5,000 years old.

Within a given growth ring, the large cells of springwood and the small cells of summerwood are often readily seen with the naked eye. Light, temperature, soil moisture, and other environmental factors affect the growth of trees, and therefore the width of their growth rings.

Human use of trees

Humans use trees as a source of food, building materials, and paper. Almond, coconut, cherry, prune, peach, pear, and many other tree species are grown in orchards for their fruits and nuts. The wood of many trees is a valuable construction material because it is relatively inexpensive, easy to cut, and very strong relative to its weight. Many species of pine and other conifers are important sources of softwoods, while deciduous trees are important sources of hardwoods.

The heartwood, at the center of a tree. *(Reproduced by permission of Field Mark Publications.)*

Chemicals in the bark of specific trees are used for medicinal or commercial purposes. Quinine, found in the bark of the South American cinchona tree, has been used for many years to treat malaria. More recently, anticancer chemicals have been discovered in the bark of the Pacific yew. Tannic acid, extracted from the bark of North American oak, hemlock, and chestnut trees, is used in tanning (the process of turning animal hides into leather).

The bark of certain trees is itself used to create products. The light, spongy outer bark of the European cork oak is used for bottle stoppers and in life rafts, insulation, and flooring. The bark of certain conifers, such as Douglas-fir and redwood, is used as a mulch in landscaping.

[*See also* **Forestry; Forests; Rain forest**]

Trigonometry

Trigonometry is a branch of mathematics concerned with the relationship between angles and their sides and the calculations based on them. First developed during the third century B.C. as a branch of geometry focusing on triangles, trigonometry was used extensively for astronomical measurements. The major trigonometric functions—including sine, cosine, and tangent—were first defined as ratios of sides in a right triangle. Since trigonometric functions are a natural part of any triangle, they can be used to determine the dimensions of any triangle given limited information.

In the eighteenth century, the definitions of trigonometric functions were broadened by being defined as points on a unit circle. This development allowed the construction of graphs of functions related to the angles they represent, which were periodic. Today, using the periodic (regularly repeating) nature of trigonometric functions, mathematicians and scientists have developed mathematical models to predict many natural periodic phenomena.

Trigonometric functions

The principles of trigonometry were originally developed around the relationship among the sides of a right triangle and its angles. The basic idea was that the unknown length of a side or size of an angle could be determined if the length or magnitude of some of the other sides or angles were known. Recall that a triangle is a geometric figure made up of

▼ Words to Know

Adjacent side: The side of a right triangle that forms one side of the angle in question.

Angle: A geometric figure created by two lines drawn from the same point.

Cosine: A trigonometric function that relates the ratio of the adjacent side of a right triangle to its hypotenuse.

Geometry: A branch of mathematics originally developed and used to measure common features on Earth, such as lines, circles, angles, triangles, squares, trapezoids, spheres, cones, and cylinders.

Hypotenuse: The longest side of a right triangle that is opposite the right angle.

Opposite side: The side of a right triangle that is opposite the angle in question.

Periodic function: A function that changes regularly over time.

Radian: A unit of angular measurement that relates the radius of a circle to the amount of rotation of the angle. One complete revolution is equal to 2π radians.

Right triangle: A triangle that contains a 90-degree or right angle.

Sine: A trigonometric function that represents the ratio of the opposite side of a right triangle to its hypotenuse.

Tangent: A trigonometric function that represents the ratio of the opposite side of right triangle to its adjacent side.

Trigonometric function: An angular function that can be described as the ratio of the sides of a right triangle to each other.

Vertices: The point where two lines come together, such as the corners of a triangle.

three sides and three angles, the sum of the angles equaling 180 degrees. The three points of a triangle, known as its vertices, are usually denoted by capital letters.

The longest side of a right triangle, which is directly across the right angle, is known as the hypotenuse. The sides that form the right angle are the legs of the triangle. For either acute angle (less than 90 degrees) in the triangle, the leg that forms the angle with the hypotenuse is known as the adjacent side. The side across from this angle is known as the opposite side. Typically, the length of each side of the right triangle is denoted by a lowercase letter.

Three basic functions—the sine (sin), cosine (cos), and tangent (tan)—can be defined for any right triangle. Those functions are defined as follows:

$\sin \theta$ = length of opposite side ÷ length of hypotenuse, or $^a/_c$

$\cos \theta$ = length of adjacent side ÷ length of hypotenuse, or $^b/_c$

$\tan \theta$ = length of opposite side ÷ length of adjacent side, or $^a/_b$

Three other functions—the secant (sec), cosecant (csc), and cotangent (cot)—can be derived from these three basic functions. Each is the inverse of the basic function. Those inverse functions are as follows:

$$\sec \theta = 1/\sin \theta = c/a$$

$$\csc \theta = 1/\cos \theta = c/b$$

$$\cot \theta = 1/\tan \theta = b/a$$

Periodicity of trigonometric functions

One of the most useful characteristics of trigonometric functions is their periodicity. The term periodicity means that the function repeats itself over and over again in a very regular fashion. For example, suppose that you graph the function $y = \sin \theta$. In order to solve this equation, one must express the size of the angle θ in radians. A radian is a unit for measuring the size of the angle in which 1 radian equals $180/\pi$. (The symbol π [pi] is the ratio of the circumference of a circle to its diameter, and it is always the same, 3.141592+, no matter the size of the circle.)

Applications

The use of trigonometry has expanded beyond merely solving problems dealing with right triangles. Some of the most important applications today deal with the periodic nature of trigonometric functions. For example, the times of sunsets, sunrises, and comet appearances can all be calculated by using trigonometric functions. Such functions also can be used to describe seasonal temperature changes, the movement of waves in the ocean, and even the quality of a musical sound.

[*See also* **Function; Pythagorean theorem**]

Tumor

A tumor is an abnormal growth of tissue. Also known as a neoplasm (meaning "new formation"), a tumor can be either benign (not serious or harmful) or malignant (cancerous or deadly). Either type may require therapy to remove it or reduce its size.

It is not known what triggers a tumor's abnormal growth. The body normally creates cells only at a rate needed to replace those that die or to aid an individual's growth and development. The growth of a tumor, however, is unregulated by normal body control mechanisms.

A comparison of benign and malignant tumor characteristics. *(Reproduced by permission of The Gale Group.)*

Benign tumors are generally self-contained and localized and have a well-defined perimeter.

They grow slowly, expanding outward from a central mass.

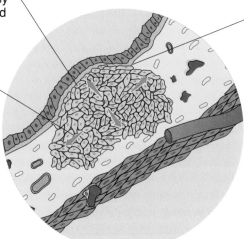

They are dangerous when they compress surrounding tissues. A benign tumor near a blood vessel could restrict the flow of blood; in the abdomen it could impair digestion; in the brain it could cause paralysis.

Malignant tumors are not self-contained, and usually do not compress surrounding tissues. Their growth is an irregular invasion of adjacent cells.

Although they may grow slowly, they are also capable of very rapid growth.

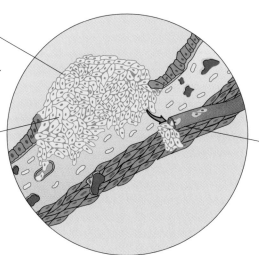

They are not localized; in a process called metastasis they shed cells that travel through the bloodstream and infect tissues at other locations. They can even establish malignant growth in a different type of tissue; a breast cancer can spread to bone tissue, for example.

▼ Words to Know

Benign: A slow-growing, self-contained tumor that is not seriously harmful.

Biopsy: The surgical removal of a small part of a tumor, which is then studied under a microscope to determine whether it is benign or malignant.

Chemotherapy: Use of powerful chemicals to kill cancer cells in the human body.

Malignant: A usually fast-growing, often fatal tumor that invades surrounding tissue and sheds cells that spread throughout the body, creating new tumors.

Metastasis: Spreading of a cancerous growth by shedding cells that grow in other locations.

Radiation therapy: Use of radioactive substances to kill cancer cells in the human body.

Benign and malignant tumors

A benign tumor is a well-defined growth with smooth boundaries that simply grows in diameter. This can be harmful if the tumor compresses the surrounding tissue against a hard surface in the body. A benign brain tumor that compresses brain tissue against the skull or the bony floor of the cranium can result in paralysis, loss of hearing or sight, dizziness, and other ailments. A tumor growing in the abdomen can compress the intestine and interfere with digestion. It also can prevent the proper functioning of the liver or pancreas. The benign tumor usually grows at a relatively slow pace and may stop growing for a time when it reaches a certain size.

A malignant tumor may grow quite rapidly and can be fatal. It usually has irregular boundaries and invades the surrounding tissue instead of pressing it aside. Most important, this cancer also sheds cells that travel through the bloodstream, starting new tumor growth at other locations in the body. This process is called metastasis (pronounced me-TAS-ta-sis). The cancerous cells can establish a cancer in tissue that is different from the original cancer. A breast cancer could spread to bone tissue or to liver tissue.

Medical approaches

Benign tissue is distinctly different from cancer tissue. However, it is difficult to determine whether a tumor is benign or malignant without surgically removing a sample of it and studying the tissue under the microscope. This sampling is called a biopsy (pronounced BY-op-see).

A benign tumor can be removed surgically if it is in a location that a surgeon can reach. A tumor growing in an unreachable area of the body can be treated using radiation (by which the patient is administered radioactive substances that target a specific area and destroy cells there). Another method is to insert thin probes into the tumor and freeze it with liquid nitrogen. This operation is called cryosurgery (pronounced cry-o-SUR-jer-ee).

A malignant tumor may be removed surgically. However, if the tumor has been growing for some time and has begun to metastasize or spread, the patient also may require treatment with powerful chemicals

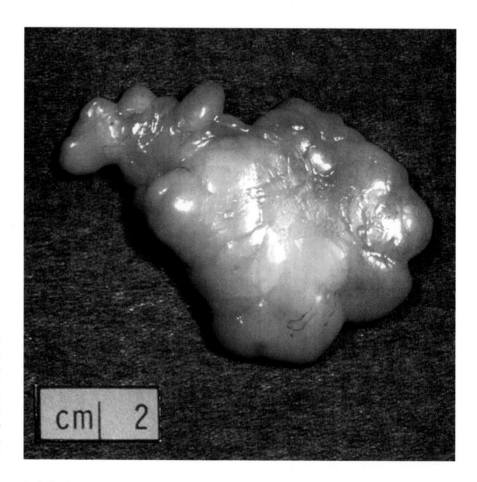

A benign tumor extracted from an individual. Such a tumor is not harmful unless its growth compresses surrounding tissue, preventing the tissue from functioning normally. *(Reproduced by permission of Photo Researchers, Inc.)*

to kill any stray cells. This treatment is called chemotherapy (pronounced key-moe-THER-a-pee).

[*See also* **Cancer**]

Tunneling

Tunneling is a phenomenon in which a tiny particle penetrates an energy barrier that it could not, according to the classical laws of science, pass across. One way of describing this process, also known as the tunnel effect, is shown in Figure 1. Notice that the y-axis in this graph represents energy, while the x-axis represents position. The graph shows that in order for the particle to move from left to right, it must surmount an "energy barrier." In other words, the particle must absorb enough energy to climb over the barrier.

An everyday example of this phenomenon is rolling a ball over a small hill. Suppose you stand on one side of the hill and want to roll the ball to a friend on the other side of the hill. You can do so only if you roll the ball hard enough for it to climb up your side of the hill. If you

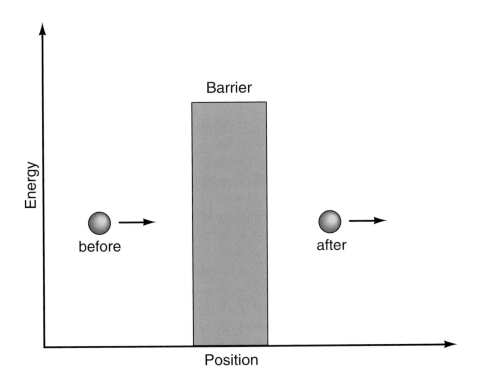

Figure 1. A particle before and after tunneling. It approaches from the left with far less energy than it would need to pass over the energy barrier. *(Reproduced by permission of The Gale Group.)*

Words to Know

Energy barrier: An obstacle somewhat similar to a physical wall, such that any object must either possess an energy greater than that of the barrier or be able to tunnel through the barrier in order to pass the barrier.

Macroscopic: Not needing a microscope to be seen; readily observed by any one of the human senses.

Quantum mechanics: A system of physical principles that arose in the early twentieth century to improve upon those developed earlier by Isaac Newton, specifically with respect to submicroscopic phenomena.

don't push the ball with enough force, it goes only part way up the hill and then rolls back down to you.

The tunnel effect would mean in this example that you might give the ball only a slight nudge—not enough to get it over the hill. But after the slight nudge, the ball would suddenly appear on the other side of the hill, right in front of your friend. You might be tempted to say that the ball had "tunneled through" the hill rather that going over it. In fact, that analogy explains the way in which the tunneling phenomenon got its name.

In fact, you would never observe an effect like this with a ball, a friend, and a hill. Tunneling occurs only with particles the size of atoms and smaller. The physical laws that describe very small particles such as these are somewhat different from the laws we use to describe large-scale everyday events and objects. The physical laws of very small particles are included in the field of science known as quantum mechanics.

One of the interesting discoveries resulting from quantum mechanics is that tunneling can occur with very tiny particles. The chance that the particle can get from position A to position B in Figure 1 is not zero. That probability may be very small (one chance out of one million, for example), but it is something greater than zero.

The interesting point is that once the probability of tunneling is greater than zero, than we know that it probably will occur from time to time. When that happens, we observe physical phenomena that do not and cannot be observed at the macroscopic level.

Applications

One of the first applications of tunneling was an atomic clock based on the tunneling frequency of the nitrogen atom in an ammonia (NH_3) molecule. In this molecule, the nitrogen atom tunnels back and forth across the energy barrier presented by the hydrogen atoms in a pattern that is reliable and easily measured. This characteristic made it ideal for use as one of the earliest atomic clocks.

A current and rapidly growing application of tunneling is Scanning Tunneling Microscopy (abbreviated STM). This technique can produce high-resolution images that accurately map the surface of a material. Some of the best STM pictures may actually show us what individual atoms look like. As with many high-tech tools, the operation of a scanning tunneling microscope is fairly simple in principle, while its actual construction is quite challenging.

The working part of a tunneling microscope is an incredibly sharp metal tip. This tip is electrically charged and held near the surface of an object that is to be imaged. The energy barrier in this case is the gap between the tip and the sample. When the tip gets sufficiently close to the sample surface, the energy barrier becomes thin enough that a noticeable number of electrons begin to tunnel from the tip to the object. Classically, the technique could never work because the electrons would not pass from the tip to the sample until the two actually touched. The number of tunneling electrons, measured by highly sensitive equipment, can eventually yield enough information to create a picture of the sample surface.

Another application of tunneling has resulted in the tunnel diode. The tunnel diode is a small electronic switch that can process electronic signals much faster than any ordinary physical switch. At peak performance, it can switch on and then off again ten billion times in a single second.

[See also **Quantum mechanics**]

Ultrasonics

The term ultrasonics applies to sound waves that vibrate at a frequency higher than the frequency that can be heard by the human ear (or higher than about 20,000 hertz).

Sound is transmitted from one place to another by means of waves. The character of any wave can be described by identifying two related properties: its wavelength (indicated by the Greek letter lambda, λ) or its frequency (f). The unit used to measure the frequency of any wave is the hertz (abbreviation: Hz). One hertz is defined as the passage of a single wave per second.

Ultrasonics, then, deals with sound waves that pass a given point at least 20,000 times per second. Since ultrasonic waves vibrate very rapidly, additional units also are used to indicate their frequency. The kilohertz (kHz), for example, can be used to measure sound waves vibrating at the rate of 1,000 (kilo means 1,000) times per second, and the unit megahertz (MHZ) stands for a million vibrations per second. Some ultrasonic devices have been constructed that produce waves with frequencies of more than a billion hertz.

Production of ultrasonic waves

The general principle involved in generating ultrasonic waves is to cause some dense material to vibrate very rapidly. The vibrations produced by this material than cause air surrounding the material to begin vibrating with the same frequency. These vibrations then spread out in the form of ultrasonic waves.

↓ Words to Know

Hertz (Hz): The unit of frequency; a measure of the number of waves that pass a given point per second of time.

Kilohertz (kHz): One thousand hertz.

Megahertz (MHZ): One thousand kilohertz, or one million hertz.

Piezoelectric: A material that becomes electrically charged when compressed, generating an electric current.

Ultrasound: Another term for ultrasonic waves; sometimes reserved for medical applications.

Wavelength: The distance between one part of a wave and the next identical part of the wave.

In most applications, ultrasonic waves are generated by applying an electric current to a special kind of crystal known as a piezoelectric crystal. The crystal converts electrical energy into mechanical energy, which, in turn, causes the crystal to vibrate at a high frequency. In another technique, a magnetic field is applied to a crystal, causing it to emit ultrasonic waves.

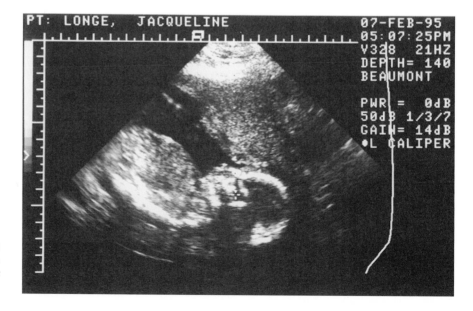

An ultrasound image of a fetus at 20 weeks. *(Reproduced by permission of Jackie Longe.)*

Applications

There are numerous practical applications for ultrasonics. The first widespread use was in underwater exploration. Ultrasonic waves proved to be an excellent method for determining the depth of water. Ultrasonics also are used to map the shape of lake and ocean floors. Submarines use ultrasonic waves to maintain secret contact with each other.

In industry, ultrasonic waves have been used in the testing of machinery and machine parts. Using a narrow beam of ultrasound, engineers can look inside metal parts in much the same way that doctors use X rays to examine the human body. With ultrasonic technology, flaws in machinery can be detected and repaired without having to take them apart.

Similar ultrasonic methods have been used to diagnose problems in the human body. As an ultrasonic beam passes through the body, it encounters different types of tissue such as flesh, bone, and organs. Each type of tissue causes the ultrasonic beam to reflect in a different way. By studying these reflections, physicians can accurately map the interior of the body. Unlike X rays, there is no risk of harmful overexposure with ultrasonics. Therefore, they have become a useful alternative to X rays for diagnosis and are often used on sensitive organs, such as kidneys, as well as to monitor the progress of pregnancies.

Because they can vibrate the particles through which they pass, ultrasonic waves are often used to shake, or even destroy, certain materials. An example of this procedure is ultrasonic emulsification. In this technique, two liquids that normally do not mix with each other (such as oil and water) are made to vibrate until they are blended. This technique is also used to remove air bubbles from molten metals before casting so that the finished piece will be free of cavities. Doctors use ultrasound to break up kidney stones and gallstones, thus avoiding invasive (cutting through the skin with a knife) surgery.

Ultrasonic vibration also can be used to kill bacteria in milk and other liquids. Some inventors are attempting to perfect an "ultrasonic laundry," using high-frequency vibrations to shake dirt and other particles out of clothing.

Ultraviolet astronomy

Matter in the universe emits radiation (energy in the form of subatomic particles or waves) from all parts of the electromagnetic spectrum. The electromagnetic spectrum is the range of wavelengths produced by the

Words to Know

Electromagnetic radiation: Radiation that transmits energy through the interaction of electricity and magnetism.

Gamma rays: Short-wavelength, high-energy radiation formed either by the decay of radioactive elements or by nuclear reactions.

Infrared radiation: Electromagnetic radiation of a wavelength shorter than radio waves but longer than visible light that takes the form of heat.

Quasars: Extremely bright, starlike sources of radio waves that are the oldest known objects in the universe.

Radiation: Energy transmitted in the form of subatomic particles or waves.

Radio waves: Longest form of electromagnetic radiation, measuring up to 6 miles (9.7 kilometers) from peak to peak.

Ultraviolet radiation: Electromagnetic radiation of a wavelength just shorter than the violet (shortest wavelength) end of the visible light spectrum.

Wavelength: The distance between two troughs or two peaks in any wave.

X rays: Electromagnetic radiation of a wavelength just shorter than ultraviolet radiation but longer than gamma rays that can penetrate solids and produce an electrical charge in gases.

interaction of electricity and magnetism. The electromagnetic spectrum includes light waves, radio waves, infrared radiation, ultraviolet radiation, X rays, and gamma rays.

Ultraviolet astronomy is the study of celestial matter that emits ultraviolet radiation. Ultraviolet waves are just shorter than the violet end (shortest wavelength) of the visible light spectrum. This branch of astronomy has provided additional information about stars (including the Sun), galaxies, the solar system, the interstellar medium (the "empty" space between celestial bodies), and quasars.

An ultraviolet telescope is similar to an optical telescope, except for a special coating on the lens. Due to Earth's ozone layer, which filters out most ultraviolet rays, ultraviolet astronomy is impossible to conduct on the ground. In order to function, an ultraviolet telescope must be placed on a satellite orbiting beyond Earth's atmosphere.

Information collected by ultraviolet telescopes

Beginning in the 1960s, a series of ultraviolet telescopes have been launched on spacecraft. The first such instruments were the eight Orbiting Solar Observatories placed into orbit between 1962 and 1975. These satellites measured ultraviolet radiation from the Sun. The data collected from these telescopes provided scientists with a much more complete picture of the solar corona, the outermost part of the Sun's atmosphere.

The Orbiting Astronomical Observatories (OAO) were designed to provide information on a variety of subjects, including thousands of stars, a comet, a nova in the constellation Serpus, and some galaxies beyond

ROSAT Iroentgensatellit satellite prior to its launch on June 1, 1990. This German/United Kingdom/ United States (NASA) satellite is capable of detecting both X rays and extreme ultraviolet light. *(Reproduced by permission of Photo Researchers, Inc.)*

the Milky Way. Between 1972 and 1980, OAO Copernicus collected information on many stars as well as the composition, temperature, and structure of interstellar gas.

The most successful ultraviolet satellite to date was the International Ultraviolet Explorer (IUE) launched in 1978. The IUE was a joint project of the United States, Great Britain, and the European Space Agency. With very sensitive equipment, the IUE studied planets, stars, galaxies, nebulae, quasars, and comets. It recorded especially valuable information from novae and supernovae. Although intended to function for only three to five years, the IUE operated until September 30, 1996, making it the longest-lived astronomical satellite.

The IUE was succeeded by the Extreme Utraviolet Explorer (EUEV), which was launched on June 7, 1992. The EUEV was designed to extend the spectral coverage of the IUE by being able to observe much shorter wavelengths. A third ultraviolet satellite, the Far Ultraviolet Spectroscopic Explorer (FUSE), was launched on June 24, 1999. This satellite also was designed to look farther into the ultraviolet (meaning to shorter wavelengths) than the IUE. With FUSE, astronomers hope to study high-energy processes in stars and galaxies in addition to exploring conditions in the universe as they existed only shortly after the big bang (theory that explains the beginning of the universe as a tremendous explosion from a single point that occurred 12 to 15 billion years ago).

[*See also* **Electromagnetic spectrum; Galaxy; International Ultra violet Explorer; Telescope**]

Uniformitarianism

In geology, uniformitarianism is the belief that Earth's physical structure is the result of currently existing forces that have operated uniformly (in the same way) since Earth formed roughly 4.5 billion years ago. Mountains rise, valleys deepen, and sand grains collect now the same way they uplifted, eroded, and deposited over these millions of years. The activities of the present are a key to those of the past.

Early theories of Earth's formation were based on a literal reading of the Biblical book of Genesis. In the mid-sixteenth century, Irish Catholic bishop James Ussher (1581–1656) counted the ages of Biblical characters and calculated Earth to be only 6,000 years old. Bound by tradition (and even by law) to work within this short time frame, scientists of the time had to explain the placement and composition of rocks with more acceptable theories like catastrophism—the belief that Earth changes suddenly during cataclysmic earthquakes, floods, or eruptions.

In 1785, Scottish geologist James Hutton (1726–1797) electrified the geologic community when he presented a theory on the formation of Earth that contradicted the Bible-based one. The major elements contained in his *Theory of the Earth* were later termed "uniformitarianism." Hutton maintained that:

1. The fossilized strata (horizontal layers of material) of Earth, originating from the bottom of the sea, were formed by natural processes driven by heat energy from Earth's core.

2. The present continents' shapes indicated that they had once belonged to a singular landmass. Hutton added that the current disintegration and erosion of surface rock would lead to the formation of future continents.

3. These processes that shaped Earth were natural and operated very slowly, and most of this activity predated humankind by much more than a few days.

Eventually, the scientific community embraced uniformitarianism because it explained a majority of geological mysteries and did not rely on any kind of divine intervention to bring about change.

Modern uniformitarianism differs slightly from its original version. It agrees that the laws of nature operate the same way today as they did millions of years ago, with one exception: the processes that shape Earth operate the same as they always have, but the speed and intensity of those processes may vary. Volcanoes erupt as they have all along (as shown in rocks), but there were times of greater volcanic activity than today. Land erodes now as it did millions of year ago, but land eroded faster when there were no plants to stop rocks and soil from washing into the seas.

Uniformitarianism allows us to interpret the events of the past in rocks; it allows us to write the history of Earth. In addition to allowing the interpretation of the past, uniformitarianism allows for the prediction of the future. Understanding how and when rivers flood, what causes earthquakes and where they are likely to occur, or how and when a volcano will erupt can limit damage from these events. Although short-term prediction still eludes geologists, long-range forecasting of such disasters can ultimately saves lives and property.

[*See also* **Catastrophism**]

Units and standards

A unit of measurement is some specific quantity that has been chosen as the standard against which other measurements of the same kind are made. For example, the meter is the unit of measurement for length in the metric system. When an object is said to be 4 meters long, that means that the object is four times as long as the unit standard (1 meter).

The term standard refers to the physical object on which the unit of measurement is based. For example, for many years the standard used in measuring length in the metric system was the distance between two scratches on a platinum-iridium bar kept at the Bureau of Standards in Sèvres, France. A standard serves as a norm against which other measuring devices of the same kind are made. The meter stick in a school classroom or home is thought to be exactly one meter long because it was made from a permanent model kept at the manufacturing plant that was originally copied from the standard meter in France.

All measurements consist of two parts: a scalar (numerical) quantity and the unit designation. In the measurement 8.5 meters, the scalar quantity is 8.5 and the unit designation is meters.

History

The need for units and standards developed at a point in human history when people needed to know how much of something they were buying, selling, or exchanging. A farmer might want to sell a bushel of wheat, for example, for ten dollars, but he or she could do so only if the unit "bushel" were known to potential buyers. Furthermore, the unit "bushel" had to have the same meaning for everyone who used the term.

The measuring system that most Americans know best is the British system, with units including the foot, yard, second, pound, and gallon. The British system grew up informally and in a disorganized way over many centuries. The first units of measurement probably came into use shortly after the year 1215. These units were tied to easily obtained or produced standards. The yard, for example, was defined as the distance from King Henry II's nose to the thumb of his outstretched hand. (Henry II of England reigned from 1154 to 1189.)

The British system of measurement consists of a complex, irrational (meaning, in this case, not sensibly organized) collection of units whose only advantage is its familiarity. As an example of the problems it poses, the British system has three different units known as the quart. These are

Words to Know

British system: A collection of measuring units that has developed haphazardly over many centuries and is now used almost exclusively in the United States and for certain specialized types of measurements.

Derived units: Units of measurements that can be obtained by multiplying or dividing various combinations of the nine basic SI units.

Metric system: A system of measurement developed in France in the 1790s.

Natural units: Units of measurement that are based on some obvious natural standard, such as the mass of an electron.

SI system: An abbreviation for Le Système International d'Unités, a system of weights and measures adopted in 1960 by the General Conference on Weights and Measures.

the British quart, the U.S. dry quart, and the U.S. liquid quart. The exact size of each of these "quarts" differs.

In addition, a number of different units are in use for specific purposes. Among the units of volume in use in the British system (in addition to those mentioned above) are the bag, barrel (of which there are three types—British and U.S. dry, U.S. liquid, and U.S. petroleum), bushel, butt, cord, drachm, firkin, gill, hogshead, kilderkin, last, noggin, peck, perch, pint, and quarter.

The metric system

In an effort to bring some rationality to systems of measurement, the French National Assembly established a committee in 1790 to propose a new system of measurement with new units and new standards. That system has come to be known as the metric system and is now the only system of measurement used by all scientists and in every country of the world except the United States and the Myanmar Republic. The units of measurement chosen for the metric system were the gram (abbreviated g) for mass, the liter (L) for volume, the meter (m) for length, and the second (s) for time.

A specific standard was chosen for each of these basic units. The meter was originally defined as one ten-millionth the distance from the

North Pole to the equator along the prime meridian. As a definition, this standard is perfectly acceptable, but it has one major disadvantage: a person who wants to make a meter stick would have difficulty using that standard to construct a meter stick of his or her own.

As a result, new and more suitable standards were selected over time. One improvement was to construct the platinum-iridium bar standard mentioned above. Manufacturers of measuring devices could ask for copies of the fundamental standard kept in France and then make their own copies from those. As you can imagine, the more copies of copies that had to be made, the less accurate the final measuring device would be.

The most recent standard adopted for the meter solves this problem. In 1983, the International Conference on Weights and Measures defined the meter as the distance that light travels in $^{1}/_{299,792,458}$ second. The standard is useful because it depends on the most accurate physical measurement known—the second—and because anyone in the world is able, given the proper equipment, to determine the true length of a meter.

Le Système International d'Unités (the SI system)

In 1960, the metric system was modified somewhat with the adoption of new units of measurement. The modification was given the name of Le Système International d'Unités, or the International System of Units. This system is more commonly known as the SI system.

Nine fundamental units make up the SI system. These are the meter (abbreviated m) for length, the kilogram (kg) for mass, the second (s) for time, the ampere (A) for electric current, the kelvin (K) for temperature, the candela (cd) for light intensity, the mole (mol) for quantity of a substance, the radian (rad) for plane angles, and the steradian (sr) for solid angles.

Derived units

Many physical phenomena are measured in units that are derived from SI units. For example, frequency is measured in a unit known as the hertz (Hz). The hertz is the number of vibrations made by a wave in a second. It can be expressed in terms of the basic SI unit as s^{-1}. Pressure is another derived unit. Pressure is defined as the force per unit area. In the SI system, the unit of pressure is the pascal (Pa) and can be expressed as kilograms per meter per second squared, or $kg/m/s^2$. Even units that appear to have little or no relationship to the nine fundamental units can, nonetheless, be expressed in these terms. The absorbed dose, for example, indicates that amount of radiation received by a person or object. In the metric system, the unit for this measurement is the gray. One gray can be defined in terms of the fundamental units as meters squared per second squared, or m^2/s^2.

Many other commonly used units can also be expressed in terms of the nine fundamental units. Some of the most familiar are the units for area (square meter: m^2), volume (cubic meter: m^3), velocity (meters per second: m/s), concentration (moles per cubic meter: mol/m^3), density (kilogram per cubic meter: kg/m^3), luminance (candela per square meter: cd/m^2), and magnetic field strength (amperes per meter: A/m).

A set of prefixes is available that makes it possible to use the fundamental SI units to express larger or smaller amounts of the same quantity. Among the most commonly used prefixes are milli- (m) for one-thousandth; centi- (c) for one-hundredth; micro- (μ) for one-millionth; kilo- (k) for one thousand times; and mega- (M) for one million times. Thus, any volume can be expressed by using some combination of the fundamental unit (liter) and the appropriate prefix. One million liters, using this system, would be a megaliter (ML), and one millionth of a liter would be a microliter (μL).

Natural units

One characteristic of all of the above units is that they have been selected arbitrarily (by individual preference or convenience rather than by law). The committee that established the metric system could, for example, have defined the meter as one one-hundredth the distance between Paris and Sèvres. It was completely free to choose any standard it wanted to.

Some measurements, however, suggest "natural" units. In the field of electricity, for example, the charge carried by a single electron would appear to be a natural unit of measurement. That quantity is known as the elementary charge (e) and has the value of $1.6021892 \times 10^{-19}$ coulomb. Other natural units of measurement include the speed of light (c: 2.99792458×10^8 m/s), the Planck constant ($\hbar$: 6.626176×10^{-34} joule per hertz), the mass of an electron (m_e: $0.9109534 \times 10^{-30}$ kg), and the mass of a proton (m_p: $1.6726485 \times 10^{-27}$ kg). As you can see, each of these natural units can be expressed in terms of SI units, but they often are used as basic units in specialized fields of science.

Unit conversions between systems

For many years, an effort has been made to have the metric system, including SI units, adopted worldwide. As early as 1866, the U.S.

Congress legalized the use of the metric system. More than a hundred years later, in 1976, Congress adopted the Metric Conversion Act, declaring it the policy of the nation to increase the use of the metric system in the United States.

In fact, little progress has been made in that direction. Indeed, elements of the British system of measurement continue in use for specialized purposes throughout the world. All flight navigation, for example, is expressed in terms of feet, not meters. As a consequence, it is still necessary for an educated person to be able to convert from one system of measurement to the other.

In 1959, English-speaking countries around the world met to adopt standard conversion factors between British and metric systems. To convert from the pound to the kilogram, for example, it is necessary to multiply the given quantity (in pounds) by the factor 0.45359237. A conversion in the reverse direction, from kilograms to pounds, involves multiplying the given quantity (in kilograms) by the factor 2.2046226. Other relevant conversion factors are 1 inch equals 2.54 centimeters and 1 yard equals 0.9144 meter.

[*See also* **Metric system**]

Uranus

Uranus, the seventh planet from the Sun, was probably struck by a large object at some point in its history. The collision knocked the planet sideways, giving it a most unique orbit. Unlike the other planets, whose axes are generally upright on their orbits, Uranus rotates on its side with its axis in the plane of its orbit.

It takes the planet slightly more than 84 Earth years to complete one revolution around the Sun and almost 18 Earth hours to complete one rotation about its axis. Because Uranus's poles—and not its equator—face the Sun, each pole is in sunlight for 42 continuous Earth years.

Discovery of the planet

Uranus was discovered in 1781 by German astronomer William Herschel (1738–1822) during a survey of the stars and planets. At first, Herschel thought he had spotted a comet, but the object's orbit was not as elongated as a comet's would normally be. It was more circular, like that of a planet. Six months later, Herschel became convinced that this body was indeed a planet. The new planet was given two tentative names before astronomers decided to call it Uranus, the mythological father of Saturn.

Uranus is about 1.78 billion miles (2.88 billion kilometers) from the Sun, more than twice as far from the Sun as Saturn, its closest neighbor. Thus, the discovery of Uranus doubled the known size of the solar system.

Uranus is 31,800 miles (51,165 kilometers) in diameter at its equator, making it the third largest planet in the solar system (after Jupiter and Saturn). It is four times the size of Earth. Similar to Jupiter, Saturn, and Neptune, Uranus consists mostly of gas. Its pale blue-green, cloudy atmosphere is made of 83 percent hydrogen, 15 percent helium, and small amounts of methane and hydrocarbons. Uranus gets its color because the atmospheric methane absorbs light at the red end of the visible spectrum and reflects light at the blue end. Deep down into the planet, a slushy mixture of ice, ammonia, and methane surrounds a rocky core.

Voyager 2 mission to Uranus

Most of what is known about Uranus was discovered during the 1986 *Voyager 2* mission to the planet. The *Voyager 2* space probe left Earth in August 1977. It first visited Jupiter in July 1979, then Saturn in August 1981.

Unlike other gas giants, Uranus doesn't reveal many atmospheric features in visible light. However, latitudinal (side-to-side) atmospheric bands do exist, as can be seen in the enhanced image on the right. Because Uranus rotates nearly on its side, atmospheric bands that cross the planet's surface appear as concentric circles in the photo. *(Reproduced by permission of National Aeronautics and Space Administration.)*

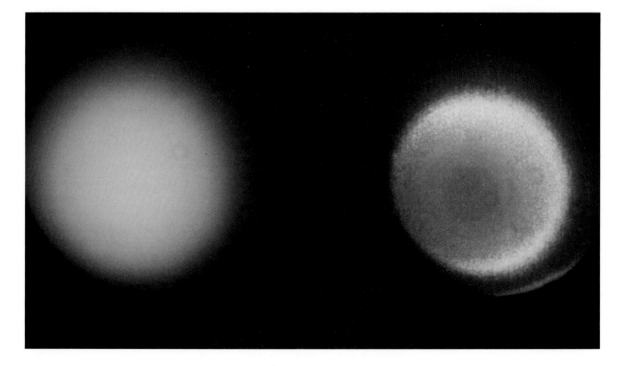

Voyager 2 collected information on Uranus during the first two months of 1986. At its closest approach, on January 24, it came within 50,600 miles (81,415 kilometers) of the planet. Among its most important findings were ten previously undiscovered moons (bringing the total to fifteen) and two new rings (bringing the total to eleven). *Voyager* also made the first accurate determination of Uranus's rate of rotation and found a large and unusual magnetic field. Finally, it discovered that despite greatly varying exposure to sunlight, the planet is about the same temperature all over: about −346°F (−210°C).

Uranus's moons

Before *Voyager 2*'s visit, scientists believed Uranus had just five moons: Titania, Oberon, Umbriel, Ariel, and Miranda. After a rash of discoveries in the late 1990s, it is now known that Uranus has a complex system of twenty-one natural satellites, each with distinctive features (many of the moons are named for characters in plays by English dramatist William Shakespeare) The five previously discovered moons of Uranus range in diameter from about 980 miles (1,580 kilometers) to about 290 miles (470 kilometers). The largest of the newly discovered moons is 99 miles (160 kilometers) in diameter, just larger than an asteroid. The smallest is a mere 12.5 miles (20 kilometers) wide. The moons

All the known rings of Uranus. *(Reproduced by permission of National Aeronautics and Space Administration.)*

fall into three distinct classes: the original five large ones; the eleven small, very dark inner ones uncovered by *Voyager 2;* and the five newly discovered much more distant ones.

Voyager 2 determined that the five largest moons are made mostly of ice and rock. While some are heavily cratered and others have steep cliffs and canyons, a few are much flatter. This discovery suggests varying amounts of geologic activity on each moon, such as lava flows and the shifting of regions of lunar crust.

Uranus's rings

The original nine rings of Uranus were discovered only nine years before *Voyager 2*'s visit. It is now known that Uranus has eleven rings plus ring fragments consisting of dust, rocky particles, and ice. The eleven rings lie between 23,500 and 31,700 miles (38,000 and 51,000 kilometers) from the planet's center. The extremely dark rings range in size from less than 1 mile to 60 miles (0.5 to 95 kilometers) wide.

[*See also* **Solar system**]

Vaccine

A vaccine is a substance made of weakened or killed disease germs designed to make a body immune to (safe against) that particular infectious disease. Effective vaccines change the immune system (the body's natural defense system against disease and infection) so it acts as if it has already developed a disease. The vaccine prepares the immune system and its antibodies (disease-fighting chemicals) to react quickly and effectively when threatened by disease in the future. The development of vaccines against diseases ranging from polio to smallpox is considered among the great accomplishments of medical science.

Smallpox

The first effective vaccine was developed against smallpox, a fast-spreading disease characterized by high fever and sores on the skin that killed many of its victims and left others permanently disfigured. The disease was so common in ancient China that newborns were not named until they survived the disease. The development of the vaccine (which was injected with a needle) in the late 1700s followed centuries of innovative efforts to fight smallpox.

English physician Edward Jenner (1749–1823) observed that people who were in contact with cows did not develop smallpox. Instead, they developed cowpox, an illness similar to smallpox but one that was not a threat to human life.

In 1796, Jenner injected a healthy eight-year-old boy with cowpox. The boy became moderately ill, but soon recovered. Jenner then injected the boy twice with the smallpox virus, and the boy did not get sick. Jenner discovered that exposure to the cowpox virus spurred the boy's immune system. The cowpox antigen stimulated the production of antibodies specific to that disease. (An antigen is a substance that stimulates the production of an antibody when introduced into the body.) The antigen conditioned the immune system to move faster and more efficiently against smallpox in the future. Jenner called the procedure vaccination, from the Latin word *vaccinus,* meaning "of cows." In 1979, world health authorities declared the eradication of smallpox, the only infectious disease to be completely eliminated.

Rabies and poliomyelitis

The next advancement in the study of vaccines came almost 100 years after Jenner's discovery. In 1885, French microbiologist Louis Pasteur (1822–1895) saved the life of Joseph Meister, a nine-year-old who had been attacked by a rabid dog, by using a series of experimental rabies vaccinations. Rabies attacks the nervous system and can cause odd behavior, paralysis, and death. Pasteur's rabies vaccine, the first human vaccine created in a laboratory, was made from a mild version of the live virus. (Pasteur had weakened the virus by drying it over potash.)

While the viruses that cause poliomyelitis (more commonly known as polio) appear to have been present for centuries, the disease emerged with a vengeance in the early 1900s. Polio wastes away the skeletal muscles and thus brings about paralysis and often permanent disability and deformity. At the peak of the epidemic, in 1952, polio killed 3,000 Americans and 58,000 new cases of polio were reported. In 1955, American microbiologist Jonas Salk (1914–1995) created a vaccine for polio. When the vaccine was declared safe after massive testing with schoolchildren, the vaccine and its creator were celebrated. The Salk vaccine contained the killed versions of the three types of polio virus that had been identified in the 1940s.

In 1961, an oral polio vaccine developed by Russian-born American virologist Albert Sabin (1906–1993) was licensed in the United States. The Sabin vaccine, which used weakened, live polio virus, quickly overtook the Salk vaccine in popularity in the United States. Because it is taken by mouth, the Sabin vaccine is more convenient and less expensive to administer than the Salk vaccine. It is currently administered to all healthy children. In the early 1990s, health organizations reported that polio was close to extinction in the Western Hemisphere.

Contemporary vaccines

Effective vaccines have limited many life-threatening infectious diseases. In the United States, children starting kindergarten are required to be immunized against polio, diphtheria, tetanus, measles, and several other

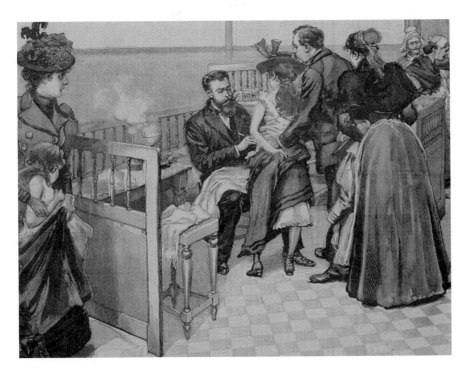

An engraving showing patients being vaccinated against rabies at the Pasteur Institute in Paris, France. Louis Pasteur (1822–1895) developed a rabies virus that was milder and had a shorter incubation (development) period than the wild virus. A person bitten by a rabid animal would be inoculated with the Pasteur virus and rapidly develop immunity to the wild strain. The first human patient was successfully treated in 1885. *(Reproduced by permission of Photo Researchers, Inc.)*

diseases. Other vaccinations are used only by people who are at risk for a disease, who are exposed to a disease, or who are traveling to an area where a disease is common. These include vaccinations for influenza, yellow fever, typhoid, cholera, and hepatitis A.

Internationally, the challenge of vaccinating large numbers of people is immense. Although more than 80 percent of the world's children were immunized by 1990, no new vaccines have been introduced extensively since then. More than 4 million people, mostly children, die needlessly every year from preventable diseases. Worldwide each year, measles kills 1.1 million children, whooping cough kills 350,000, tetanus kills 500,000, and yellow fever kills 30,000. Another 8 million people each year die from diseases for which vaccines are still being developed. While some researchers seek new vaccines, others continue to look for ways to distribute existing vaccines to those in desperate need.

[*See also* **AIDS (acquired immunodeficiency syndrome); Disease; Poliomyelitis**]

Vacuum

The term vacuum has two different meanings. In its strictest sense, a vacuum is a region of space completely lacking any form of matter. The term represents absolute emptiness. One problem with this definition is that it describes an ideal condition that cannot exist in the real world. No one has ever discovered a way to make a perfect vacuum of this kind.

For that reason, the term vacuum also is used to describe regions of space from which the greatest possible amount of matter has been removed. In most cases, a vacuum is a container from which all gases have been removed as completely as possible.

Actually, the closest thing to a perfect vacuum is outer space. Astronomers believe that the space between stars consists in some cases of no more than a single atom or molecule per cubic kilometer. No vacuum produced on Earth comes even close to this condition.

The usual procedure for making a vacuum is with a vacuum pump. The pump, which consists of a piston (a sliding valve) in a cylinder, is attached to a closed container. With each stroke of the pump, some of the gas in the container is removed. The longer the pump operates, the better the vacuum produced in the container. To achieve the very best vacuums, however, special types of equipment are necessary.

Vacuums have many applications in scientific research, industry, and everyday life. Perhaps the most common example of the use of a vacuum is the household vacuum cleaner. The fan in a vacuum cleaner continually removes air from a canister, creating a partial vacuum. Atmospheric pressure outside the vacuum cleaner pushes air into the canister, taking along with it dust and dirt stirred up by the brush at the front of the vacuum cleaner.

Another common application of vacuums is a thermos bottle. A thermos bottle consists of two bottles, one nested inside the other. The space between the two bottles consists of a vacuum. In the absence of air, heat does not pass between the two bottles very easily. Hot liquids inside the container retain their heat, and cold liquids stay cold because heat cannot pass into them.

Vacuum tube

A vacuum tube is a hollow glass cylinder from which as much air as possible has been removed. The cylinder also contains two metal electrodes: the cathode, or negative electrode, and the anode, or positive electrode. Current flows within a vacuum tube from the cathode, which has an excess of electrons, to the anode, which has a deficiency of electrons.

Vacuum tubes were a subject of great interest among both scientists and inventors at the end of the nineteenth century. Among scientists, vacuum tubes were used to study the basic nature of matter. Among inventors, vacuum tubes were used as a means of controlling the flow of electric current within an electrical system.

One of the first practical vacuum tubes was invented by English electrical engineer John Ambrose Fleming (1849–1945). Fleming's device permitted the flow of electric current in one direction (from cathode to anode) but not in the other (from anode to cathode). It was, therefore, one of the first devices that could be used to control the direction of flow of electric current. Because it consisted of two parts, Fleming's invention is called a diode. Fleming himself referred to the device as a thermionic valve because, like a water valve, it controlled the flow of electricity.

In 1906, American inventor Lee de Forest (1873–1961) discovered a way to improve the efficiency with which vacuum tubes operate. He installed a third element in the diode: a metal screen between the anode and cathode. This modification of the diode was given the name triode because it consists of three parts rather than two.

Words to Know

Anode: Also known as target electrode; the positively charged electrode in an X-ray tube.

Cathode: The negatively charged electrode in an X-ray tube.

Cathode-ray tube (CRT): A form of vacuum tube in which a beam of electrons is projected onto a screen covered with a fluorescent material in order to produce a visible picture.

Electrode: A material that will conduct an electrical current, usually a metal, used to carry electrons into or out of an electrochemical cell.

Transistor: A device capable of amplifying and switching electrical signals.

Applications

For more than half a century, the vacuum tube had an enormous number of applications in research and communications. They were used in radio receivers as well as in early digital computers. Incorporated into photo tubes, they were used in sound equipment, making it possible to record and retrieve audio from motion picture film. In the form of cathode-ray tubes, they were used to focus an electron beam, leading to the invention of oscilloscopes (which measure changes in voltage over time), televisions, and cameras. As microwave tubes, they were used in radar, early space communication, and microwave ovens. When modified as storage tubes, they could be used to store and retrieve data and, thus, were essential in the advancement of computers.

Despite their many advantages, vacuum tubes had many drawbacks. They are extremely fragile, have a limited life, are fairly large, and require a lot of power to operate. The successor to the vacuum tube, the transistor, invented by Walter Brattain, John Bardeen, and William Shockley in 1948, overcame these drawbacks. After 1960, small, lightweight, low-voltage transistors became commercially available and replaced vacuum tubes in most applications. With the creation of microscopic vacuum tubes (microtubes) in the 1990s, however, vacuum tubes are again being used in electronic devices.

[*See also* **Cathode-ray tube; Superconductor; Transistor**]

Variable star

Variable stars are stars that vary in brightness over time. In most cases, these changes occur very slowly over a period of months or even years. In some cases, however, the changes take place in a matter of hours.

The category variable stars encompasses several different types of stars that vary in brightness for entirely different reasons. Examples include red giants, eclipsing binaries, Cepheid variables, and RR Lyrae.

The most common variables, with the longest bright-dim cycles, are red giants. Red giants are stars of average size (like the Sun) in the final stages of life. During the last several million years of its multibillion-year lifetime, a red giant will puff up and shrink many times. It becomes alternately brighter and dimmer, generally spending about one year in each phase until it completely runs out of fuel to burn.

The apparent variable behavior of a second group of stars, eclipsing binaries, is caused by a very different process. A binary star is a double star system in which two stars orbit each other around a central point of gravity. An eclipsing binary occurs when the plane of a binary's orbit is nearly edgewise to our line of sight (that is, from a viewpoint on Earth). Each star is then eclipsed by the other as they complete their orbits.

A special class of variables, discovered by American astronomer Henrietta Swan Leavitt (1868–1921), consists of blinking yellow supergiants called Cepheid (pronounced SEF-ee-id) variables. They are so named because they were first found in the constellation Cepheus. The pulsing of Cepheids seems to be caused by the expansion and contraction of their surface layers. They become brighter (expansion) and dimmer (contraction) on a regular cycle (lasting 3 to 50 days). For this reason, astronomers use Cepheids as a way of measuring distances in space. If two Cepheids have the same cycle of variation, then the brighter one is closer to Earth.

Similar to Cepheids but older are a group of stars known as RR Lyrae stars. They are so named because one of the first stars of this type was discovered in the constellation Lyra. RR Lyrae are usually found in densely packed groups called globular clusters. Because of their age, RR Lyrae stars are relatively dim. They also have very short light variation cycles, lasting usually less than one day.

▼ Words to Know

Cepheids: Pulsating yellow supergiant stars that can be used to measure distance in space.

Eclipsing binaries: Double star system in which the orbital plane is nearly edgewise to a viewpoint on Earth, meaning that each star is eclipsed (partially or totally hidden) by the other as they revolve around a common point of gravity.

Globular clusters: Tight grouping of stars found near the edges of the Milky Way.

Red giants: Stage in which an average-sized star (like the Sun) spends the final 10 percent of its lifetime; its surface temperature drops and its diameter expands to 10 to 1,000 times that of the Sun.

RR Lyrae: A class of giant pulsating stars that have light variation periods of about a day.

Supergiant: Largest and brightest type of star, which has more than fifteen times the mass of the Sun and shines over one million times more brightly.

Two American astronomers have been instrumental in tracking variable stars. Leavitt, in a search of the southern skies in the early 1900s, discovered about 2,400 variable stars. In 1939, Helen Sawyer Hogg (1905–1993) created the first complete listing of the known 1,116 variable stars in the Milky Way galaxy. In 1955, she updated this catalogue, adding 329 new variables, one-third of which she discovered herself.

[*See also* **Binary star; Red giant; Star**]

Venus

Venus, the second planet from the Sun, is the closest planet to Earth. It is visible in the sky either three hours after sunset or three hours before sunrise, depending on the season. This pattern prompted early astronomers to refer to the planet as the "evening star" or the "morning star." Venus is named for the Roman goddess of love and beauty. Throughout history, the planet has been thought of as one of the most beautiful objects in the sky.

Venus and Earth have long been considered sister planets. The reason for this comparison is that they are similar in size, mass, and age. The diameter of Venus at its equator is about 7,500 miles (12,000 kilometers). The planet revolves around the Sun at an average distance of 67 million miles (107 million kilometers). It takes Venus about 225 Earth days to complete one revolution. The planet spins extremely slowly on its axis, taking about 243 Earth days to complete one rotation. Like Uranus and Pluto, Venus spins on its axis in the opposite direction to which it orbits the Sun.

Space probes to Venus

Beginning in 1961, both the United States and the former Soviet Union began sending space probes to explore Venus. The probes revealed that Venus is an extremely hot, dry planet, with no signs of life. Its atmosphere is made primarily of carbon dioxide with some nitrogen and trace amounts of water vapor, acids, and heavy metals. Its clouds are laced with sulfur dioxide.

Venus provides a perfect example of the greenhouse effect. Heat from the Sun penetrates the planet's atmosphere and reaches the surface. The heat is then prevented from escaping back into space by atmospheric carbon dioxide (similar to heat in a greenhouse). The result is that Venus has a surface temperature of 900°F (482°C), even hotter than that of Mercury, the closet planet to the Sun.

The surface of Venus is obscured by a dense layer of clouds composed of sulfuric acid droplets. The cloud cover creates a greenhouse effect (not allowing heat to escape the atmosphere) that results in surface temperatures of more than 900°F (482°C), higher than that of Mercury. *(Reproduced by permission of National Aeronautics and Space Administration.)*

Under Venus's atmosphere, the U.S. and Soviet space probes found a rocky surface covered with volcanoes (some still active), volcanic features (such as lava plains), channels (like dry riverbeds), mountains, and medium- and large-sized craters.

Magellan. The U.S. probe *Magellan* mapped the entire Venusian surface from 1990 to 1994. The *Magellan* radar data showed that Venus is remarkably flat, and that some 80 percent of the planet's surface is covered by smooth volcanic plains, the result of many lava outflows. *Magellan* also revealed the existence of two large continent-like features on Venus. These features are known as Ishtar Terra (named after the Babylonian goddess of love) and Aphrodite Terra (named after the Greek goddess of love). Ishtar Terra, which measures some 620 miles (1,000 kilometers) by 930 miles (1,500 kilometers), lies in Venus's northern hemisphere. It has the form of a high plateau ringed with mountains. The largest mountain in the region, Maxwell Montes, rises to a height of 7 miles (11 kilometers). Aphrodite Terra is situated just to the south of the Venusian equator and is some 10,000 miles (16,000 kilometers) long by 1,200 miles (2,000 kilometers) wide. It is a region dominated by mountainous highlands and several large volcanoes.

Astronomers analyzing *Magellan*'s data have concluded that about 500 to 800 million years ago, lava surfaced and covered the entire planet,

An artist's impression of one of the three continent-sized highland regions of Venus, Beta Regio, which consists of two huge volcanoes rising above the plains. Both are about 2.5 miles (4 kilometers) high and appear to be on a north-south fault line connecting them with other possibly volcanic features in the south. They have smooth surfaces and are shaped like Hawaiian volcanoes. *(Reproduced by permission of National Aeronautics and Space*

giving it a fresh, new face. One indication of this event is the presence of volcanic craters and other formations on the surface that lack the same weathered appearance of that of older formations.

[*See also* **Solar system**]

Vertebrates

Vertebrates are any animals that have a backbone or spinal column. These animals are so named because nearly all adults have vertebrae, bone or segments of cartilage forming the spinal column. The five main classes of vertebrates are fish, amphibians, birds, reptiles, and mammals.

Vertebrates are the most complex of Earth's animal life-forms. The earliest vertebrates were marine, jawless, fishlike creatures with poorly developed fins. First appearing on Earth more than 500 million years ago, they probably fed on algae (single-celled or multicellular plants and plant-like animals), small animals, and decaying organic matter. The evolution of jaws, limbs, internal reproduction organs, and other anatomical changes over millions of years allowed vertebrates to move from ocean habitats to those on land.

A numbat, or banded anteater, is native to western Australia and is just one of many species of vertebrates that inhabit the planet. (*Reproduced by permission of John Cancalosi.*)

All vertebrates have an internal skeleton of bone and cartilage or just cartilage alone. In addition to a bony spinal column, all have a bony cranium surrounding the brain. Vertebrates have a heart with two to four chambers, a liver, pancreas, kidneys, and a number of other internal organs. Most have two pairs of appendages that have formed as either fins, limbs, or wings.

[*See also* **Amphibians; Birds; Fish; Invertebrates; Mammals; Reptiles**]

Video recording

Video recording is the process by which visual images are recorded on some form of magnetic recording device such as tape or a video disc. In magnetic recording, an unrecorded tape is wrapped around a rotating drum that carries the tape through a series of steps before it leaves as a recorded tape.

The actual recording of the tape occurs on a cylindrical device known as the head. The head consists of a coil of wire wrapped around a core made of ferrite (iron oxide). When a camera is focused on a scene, the visual images it receives are converted to an electrical signal within the camera. That electrical signal passes into the recording head.

When the electrical signal reaches the recording head, it passes through the wire coil. When an electrical current passes through a metal coil, it creates a magnetic field. The strength of the magnetic field (called a flux) created depends on the strength of the electric current passing through the coil of wire. The strength of the electric current, in turn, depends on the intensity of the light received by the video camera. If the camera sees a bright spot, it produces a strong electric current, and the strong electric current produces a strong magnetic flux. When the camera sees a dim spot, it produces a weak electric current, and that weak electric current produces a weak magnetic flux.

The strength of the magnetic flux produced by the head is recorded on the magnetic tape that passes over it. The magnetic tape consists of millions of tiny pieces of iron oxide, like very tiny specks of flour. When the tape passes through a magnetic field, the iron oxide particles line themselves up in the direction of the magnetic field. If the field is very strong, all of the particles will line up in the same direction. If the field is very weak, only a small fraction of the particles will be aligned in the same direction. The brightness or dimness of the scene being photographed, then, is eventually translated into many or few iron oxide particles being lined up on the recording tape.

Video disk recording

Magnetic tape is satisfactory for recording visual images under most circumstances. However, it does have certain disadvantages. One disadvantage is the time it takes to locate and play back any given portion of the recorded image. An alternative to using tape for recording images is a video disk.

A video disk is similar to a sound recording disk. It is a round, flat object covered with a thin layer of iron oxide. An incoming electrical signal is fed into recording heads posed above the rotating disk. As the signal is recorded on the disk, the recording heads move outward in a series of concentric circles away from the middle of the disk. Recording continues until the disk is filled.

[*See also* **DVD technology; Magnetic recording/audiocassette**]

Virtual reality

Virtual reality is an artificial environment that is created and maintained by a computer and that is at least partly shaped and determined by the user. A virtual reality system allows the user to "leave" the real world and step into a world whose sensory inputs (sights, sounds, smells, etc.) are provided not by natural objects but by computer-created means. The things that happen in that virtual world can then be manipulated to a large extent by the user.

Components

In its most basic form, virtual reality systems consist of a computer and software—known as the reality engine—and input and output sensors. A sensor is a device that responds to some physical stimulus. A human eye, for example, is a sensor that responds to light rays.

In standard computer technology, input devices are the familiar keyboard, mouse, knobs, and joysticks; output devices include the printer and video display. Virtual reality input/output devices include head- and ear-mounted equipment for hearing and seeing and gloves for controlling the virtual world. The fourth "component" is the user, who directs the chosen environment and reacts to it.

▼ Words to Know

Cathode-ray tube (CRT): A form of vacuum tube in which a beam of electrons is projected onto a screen covered with a fluorescent material in order to produce a visible picture.

Ergonomics: The study of the way humans and objects interact with each other.

Haptic: Relating to the sense of touch.

Light-emitting diode (LED): A device made of semiconducting materials that emits light when an electric current is applied to it.

Liquid crystal display (LCD): A way of displaying visual information by using liquid crystals that emit light when exposed to electric current.

Pixel: One of the small individual elements of which a visual image consists.

Reality engine: The hardware and software used in virtual reality systems.

Virtual: Something that is representative or the essence of a thing but not the actual thing.

The reality engine. The reality engine employs both computer hardware and software to create the virtual world. Reality engines are based largely on the same components that make up a personal computer (PC), although much more computing power is required for the reality engine than is available in a standard PC.

One key to virtual reality is creating a world that appears real. The images created by the computer and software are extremely complex compared to the relatively simple line-based graphics associated with computer games. Virtual reality images are made with tiny dotlike segments of a picture known as pixels, or picture elements. Each pixel itself is made up of hundreds of thousands of dots. The more pixels there are per inch, the better or more realistic the image will be.

Creating realistic images that can be manipulated is known as realization. These images can be either opaque, in which all the viewer sees is the virtual world, or see-through, in which the virtual image is projected or superimposed onto the outer world.

Sound enriches the virtual world. The experience of soaring through the air in a simulated cockpit is more realistic if the user hears the roar of the engines. Sound also enhances participation in the virtual world by providing the user with audio cues. For example, the user may be directed to look for the virtual airplane flying overhead.

To incorporate the total experience, the reality engine also may use haptic enhancement. Haptic experiences are those that involve the participant's senses of touch and pressure. Haptic cues, however, are complex and expensive and have been used primarily for military and research applications.

Headsets. Head-mounted display (HMD) units use a small screen or screens (one for each eye) that are worn in a helmet or a pair glasses. Unlike a movie, where the director controls what the viewer sees, the HMD allows viewers to look at an image from various angles or change their field of view by simply moving their heads.

HMD units usually employ cathode-ray tube (CRT) or liquid crystal display (LCD) technology. CRTs incorporate optic systems that reflect an image onto the viewer's eye. Although more bulky and heavy than LCD displays, CRT systems create images that have extremely high resolutions, making a scene seem that much more realistic. In addition, CRT images can be semireflective, allowing the viewer to see the outside world as well. Such units have practical applications since the user can operate a machine or other device while viewing the virtual world.

Although LCD technology has lagged behind CRT in picture quality, LCD systems are slimmer, lighter, and less expensive, making them better suited for home use. These units use liquid crystal monitors to display two slightly different images that the brain processes into a single three-dimensional view. Initial efforts to market this technology to home users failed because of poor LCD image quality. But rapid advances in LCD technology have improved the images, and higher quality LCD-based units have become available for home use.

Audio units. Sound effects in virtual reality rely on a prerecorded sound set that is difficult to alter once the reality engine begins to generate audio. The audio portion of virtual reality is transmitted through small speakers placed over each ear. Audio cues may include voices, singing, the sound of bubbling water, thudlike noises of colliding objects—in short, any sound that can be recorded.

Three-dimensional (or omnidirectional) sound further enhances the virtual reality experience. Sounds that seem to come from above, below, or either side provide audio cues that mimic how sounds are heard in the real world. Three-dimensional sound is achieved through the use of highly complex filtering devices. This technology must take into account factors like interaural time difference (which ear hears the sound first) and interaural amplitude difference (which ear hears the sound louder). The most complex human hearing dynamic is called head-related transfer functions (HRTF). HRTF accounts for how the eardrum and inner ear process sound waves, taking into consideration the various frequencies at which these waves travel as well as how waves are absorbed and reflected by other objects. HRTF audio processing enables the listener not only to locate a sound source but also to focus in on a specific sound out of a multitude of sounds, like distinguishing the call of a hot dog vendor out of a noisy crowd at a baseball game.

Gloves.   Gloves in virtual reality allow the user to interact with the virtual world. For example, the user may pick up a virtual block, turn it over in a virtual hand, and set it on a virtual table. Wired with thin fiber-optic cables, some gloves use light-emitting diodes (LEDs) to detect the amount of light passing through the cable in relation to the movement of the hand or joint. The computer then analyzes the corresponding information and projects this moving hand into the virtual reality. Magnetic tracking systems also are used to determine where the hand is in space in relation to the virtual scene.

Some gloves use haptic enhancement to provide a sense of touch and feel. In haptic enhancement, the reality engine outputs the tactile experience, which may include force, heat, and texture. Tactile experiences are created by remeasuring a pattern of forces, which is programmed into the reality engine and then relayed back to the user when the appropriate object is touched. Virtual reality gloves may use either air pressure (such as strategically placed inflated air pockets in the glove) or vibrating transducers placed next to the skin (such as a voice coil from a stereo speaker or alloys that change shape through the conduction of electrical currents) to simulate tactile experience.

Tools under development.   Many other virtual reality tools are in the phases of research and development. Remote control robotic or manipulator haptic devices are being tested for industry and medicine. Special wands with sensors, joysticks, and finger sensors such as picks and rings will eventually be as common to virtual reality technology as microwaves are to cooking. The technology to control the virtual world through voice commands also is rapidly advancing.

Perhaps the most impressive technology under development is the whole body suit. These suits would function similarly to the gloves, creating a virtual body that could take a stroll through a virtual world and feel a virtual windstorm.

Applications

The potential for virtual reality as an entertainment medium is apparent. Instead of manipulating computerized images of two boxers or a car race, the virtual playground allows the user to experience the event. Disney World's Epcot Center houses a virtual reality system that propels the user on a magic carpet ride like the one featured in the popular animated film *Aladdin*. Although most entertainment applications are primarily visually based, virtual reality players of the future also may experience a variety of tactile events. For example, in a simulated boxing match, virtual reality users would bob and weave, throw and land punches, and—unless they were very adept—take a few punches themselves.

Virtual reality also has practical applications in the realms of business, manufacturing, and medicine. The National Aeronautics and Space Administration (NASA) has developed a virtual wind tunnel to test aerodynamics shape. Virtual reality holds promise for discovering the most efficient manufacturing conditions by allowing planners to evaluate the actual physical motions and strength needed to complete a job. The

A virtual reality system. *(Reproduced by permission of The Stock Market.)*

McDonnell-Douglas Corporation is using virtual reality to explore the use of different materials and tools in building the F-18 E/F aircraft.

The study of people in relation to their environments, also known as ergonomics, also may be revolutionized by trials in cyberspace. Engineers at the Volvo car company use virtual reality to test various designs for the dashboard configuration from the perspective of the user. In medicine, virtual reality systems are being developed to help surgeons plan and practice delicate surgical procedures. Philip Green, a researcher at SRI International, is developing a telemanipulator, a special remote-controlled robot, to be used in surgery. Using instruments connected to a computer, doctors will be able to perform an operation in cyberspace, while the computer sends signals to direct the telemanipulator. Virtual reality may even have applications in psychiatry. For example, someone with acrophobia (a fear of heights) may be treated by practicing standing atop virtual skyscrapers or soaring through the air like a bird.

[*See also* **Cathode-ray tube**]

Virus

A virus is a small, infectious agent that is made up of a core of genetic material surrounded by a shell of protein. The genetic material (which is responsible for carrying forward hereditary traits from parent cells to offspring) may be either deoxyribonucleic acid (DNA) or ribonucleic acid (RNA). Viruses are at the borderline between living and nonliving matter. When they infect a host cell, they are able to carry on many life functions, such as metabolism and reproduction. But outside a host cell, they are as inactive as a grain of sand.

Viruses cause disease by infecting a host cell and taking over its biochemical functions. In order to produce new copies of itself, a virus must use the host cell's reproductive "machinery." The newly made viruses then leave the host cell, sometimes killing it in the process, and proceed to infect other cells within the organism.

Viruses can infect plants, bacteria, and animals. The tobacco mosaic virus, one of the most studied of all viruses, infects tobacco plants. Animal viruses cause a variety of diseases, including AIDS (acquired immuno deficiency syndrome), hepatitis, chicken pox, smallpox, polio, measles, rabies, the common cold, and some forms of cancer.

Viruses that affect bacteria are called bacteriophages, or simply phages (pronounced FAY-jez). Phages are of special importance because

Words to Know

Adult T cell leukemia (ATL): A form of cancer caused by the retrovirus HTLV.

AIDS (acquired immunodeficiency syndrome): A set of life-threatening, opportunistic infections that strike people who are infected with the retrovirus HIV.

Bacteriophage: A virus that infects bacteria.

Capsid: The outer protein coat of a virus.

DNA (deoxyribonucleic acid): Genetic material consisting of a pair of nucleic acid molecules intertwined with each other.

Envelope: The outermost covering of some viruses.

Gene: Unit of heredity contained in the nucleus of cells that is composed of DNA and that carries information for a specific trait.

Host cell: The specific cell that a virus targets and infects.

HIV (human immunodeficiency virus): The retrovirus that causes AIDS.

Human T cell leukemia virus (HTLV): The retrovirus that causes ATL.

Infectious: Relating to a disease that is spread primarily through contact with someone who already has the disease.

Lysogenic cycle: A viral replication cycle in which the virus does not destroy the host cell but coexists within it.

Lytic cycle: A viral replication cycle in which the virus destroys the host cell.

Metabolism: The sum of all the physiological processes by which an organism maintains life.

Orthomyxovirus: Group of viruses that causes influenza in humans and animals.

Proteins: Complex chemical compounds that are essential to the structure and functioning of all living cells.

Retrovirus: A type of virus that contains a pair of single stranded RNA molecules joined to each other.

Reverse transcriptase: An enzyme that makes it possible for a retrovirus to produce DNA from RNA.

Ribonucleic acid (RNA): Genetic material consisting of a single strand of nucleic acid.

they have been studied much more thoroughly than have viruses. In fact, much of what we now know about viruses is based on the study of phages. Although there are both structural and functional differences between the two, they share many characteristics in common.

Structure of viruses

Although viral structure varies considerably among different types of viruses, all viruses share some common characteristics. All viruses contain either RNA or DNA surrounded by a protective protein shell called a capsid. The genetic material in a virus may take one of four forms: a double strand of DNA, a single strand of DNA, a double strand of RNA, or a single strand of RNA. The size of the genetic material of viruses is often quite small. Compared to the 100,000 genes that exist within human DNA, viral genes number from 10 to about 200 genes.

Viruses exist in one of three forms, as shown in Figure 1. They are named on the basis of their general shape as rodlike, icosahedral (having 20 sides), or spherical. Some viruses also have an outer covering known as an envelope that surrounds the capsid. The outer surface of some kinds of viral particles contain threadlike "spikes" that are often used in helping a virus invade a host cell (for example, the spherical virus in Figure 1).

Viral infection

A virus remains totally inactive until it attaches itself to and infects a host cell. Once that happens, the virus may follow one of two paths. First, the virus may insert its genetic material (it is always DNA in this case) into the DNA of the host cell. The combined host-viral DNA is then

Figure 1. The three forms of viruses. Viruses are shaped either like rods or spheres or have twenty sides (are icosahedral). *(Reproduced by permission of The Gale Group.)*

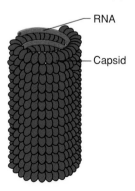

RNA

Capsid

Rod-like virus

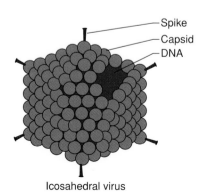

Spike
Capsid
DNA

Icosahedral virus

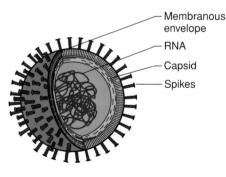

Membranous envelope

RNA

Capsid

Spikes

Spherical virus

carried along in the host cell as it lives and reproduces, generation after generation. Viruses that follow this pathway are said to be temperate or lysogenic viruses. At some point in the host cell's life, the viral DNA may be extracted (taken out) from the host DNA and follow the second pathway.

The second pathway available to viruses is called the lytic cycle. In the lytic cycle, the virus first attaches itself to the surface of the host cell. It then makes a hole in the cell membrane and injects its genetic material (DNA or RNA). The viral capsid is left behind outside the cell.

The next step depends on the nature of the viral genetic material, whether that material is single stranded or double stranded DNA or RNA. The end result of any one of the processes is that many additional copies of the viral capsid and the viral genetic material are made. These capsids and genetic material are then assembled into new viral particles. The single collection of genetic material originally injected into the host cell has been used to make dozens or hundreds of new viral particles.

When these particles have been assembled, they burst through the cell membrane. In the act, the host cell is destroyed. The new viral particles are then free to find other host cells and to repeat the process.

Retroviruses

Retroviruses make up an unusual group of viruses. Their genetic material consists of two single strands of RNA linked to each other. Retroviruses also contain an essential enzyme known as reverse transcriptase.

The unusual character of retroviruses is that they have evolved a method for manufacturing protein beginning with RNA. In nearly all living organisms, the pattern by which protein is manufactured is as follows: DNA in the cell's nucleus carries directions for the production of new protein. The coded message in DNA molecules is copied into RNA molecules. These RNA molecules then direct the manufacture of new protein. In retroviruses, that process is reversed: viral RNA is used to make new viral DNA. The viral DNA is then incorporated into host cell DNA, where it is used to direct the manufacture of new viral protein.

The first retrovirus discovered was the Rous sarcoma virus (RSV) that infects chickens. It was named after its discoverer, the American pathologist Peyton Rous (1879–1970). Other animal retroviruses are the simian immunodeficiency virus (SIV), which attacks monkeys, and the feline leukemia virus (FELV), which causes feline leukemia in cats. The first human retrovirus was discovered in 1980 by a research team headed by American virologist Robert Gallo (1937–). Called human T cell leukemia virus (HTLV), this virus causes a form of leukemia (cancer of the blood) called adult T cell leukemia. In 1983–84, another human retrovirus was discovered. This virus, the human immunodeficiency virus (HIV), is responsible for AIDS.

The common cold and influenza

Two of the most common viral diseases known to humans are the common cold and influenza. The common cold, also called acute coryza or upper respiratory infection, is caused by any one of some 200 different viruses, including rhinoviruses, adenoviruses, influenza viruses, parainfluenza viruses, syncytial viruses, echoviruses, and coxsackie viruses. Each virus has its own characteristics, including its favored method of transmission and its own gestation (developmental) period. All have been implicated as the agent that causes the runny nose, cough, sore throat, and sneezing that advertise the presence of the common cold. According to experts, more than a half billion colds strike Americans every year, an average of two infections for each man, woman, and child in the United States. In spite of intense efforts on the part of researchers, there are no cures, no preventative treatments, and very few treatments for the common cure.

Viruses that cause the common cold can be transmitted from one person to another by sneezing on the person, shaking hands, or handling an object previously touched by the infected person. Oddly, direct contact with an infected person, as in kissing, is not an efficient way for the virus to spread. In only about 10 percent of contacts between an infected and uninfected person does the latter get the virus.

Contrary to general opinion, walking around in a cold rain will not necessarily cause a cold. Viruses like warm, moist surroundings, so they thrive indoors in the winter. However, being outdoors in cold weather can dehydrate the mucous membranes in the nose and make them more susceptible to infection by a rhinovirus. The viruses that cause colds mutate with regularity. Each time a virus is passed from one person to the next, it may change slightly, so it may not be the virus the first person had.

The common cold differs in several ways from influenza, commonly known as the flu. Cold symptoms develop gradually and are relatively mild. The flu has a sudden onset and has more serious symptoms that usually put the sufferer to bed. The flu lasts about twice as long as the cold. Also, influenza can be fatal, especially to elderly persons. Finally, the number of influenza viruses is more limited than the number of cold viruses, and vaccines are available against certain types of flu.

Influenza. Influenza is a highly contagious illness caused by a group of viruses called the orthomyxoviruses. Infection with these viruses leads to an illness usually characterized by fever, muscle aches, fatigue (tiredness), and upper respiratory obstruction and inflammation. Children and young adults usually recover from influenza within 3 to 7 days with no complications. However, influenza can be a very serious disease among older adults, especially those over 65 with preexisting conditions such as heart disease or lung illnesses. Most hospitalizations and deaths from influenza occur in this age group. Although an influenza vaccine is avail-

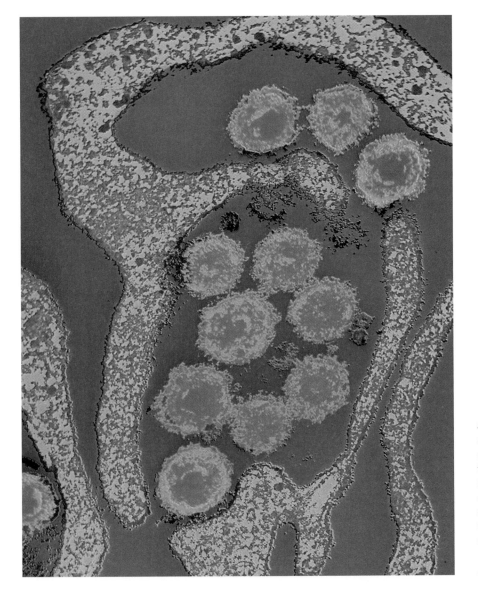

A transmission electron micrograph of Human Herpes Virus type 6 (HHV6) infecting a cell. HHV6 has been found to be the cause of the childhood disease roseola infantum, characterized by sudden fever, irritability, and a skin rash. *(Reproduced by permission of Photo Researchers, Inc.)*

able, it does not offer complete protection against the disease. The vaccine has been shown only to limit the complications that may occur due to influenza.

Three types of orthomyxoviruses cause illness in humans and animals: types A, B, and C. Type A causes epidemic influenza, in which large numbers of people become infected during a short period of time. Flu epidemics caused by Type A orthomyxoviruses include the worldwide outbreaks of 1918, 1957, 1968, and 1977. Type A viruses infect both humans and animals and usually originate in Asia, where a large population of ducks and swine incubate the virus and pass it to humans. (Incubate means to provide a suitable environment for growth, in this case within the animals' bodies.) Asia also has a very large human population that provides a fertile ground for viral replication.

Type B influenza viruses are not as common as type A viruses. Type B viruses cause outbreaks of influenza about every two to four years. Type C viruses are the least common type of influenza virus and cause irregular and milder infections.

An important characteristic of all three kinds of influenza viruses is that they frequently mutate. Because they contain only a small amount of genetic material, flu viruses mutate frequently. The result of this frequent mutation is that each flu virus is different, and people who have become immune to one flu virus are not immune to other flu viruses. The ability to mutate frequently, therefore, allows these viruses to cause frequent outbreaks.

The most common complication of influenza is pneumonia, a disease of the lungs. Pneumonia may be viral or bacterial. The viral form of pneumonia that occurs with influenza can be very severe. This form of pneumonia has a high mortality rate. Bacterial pneumonia may develop when bacteria accumulate in the lungs. This type of pneumonia occurs five to ten days after onset of the flu. Because it is bacterial in origin, it can be treated with antibiotics.

Flu is treated with rest and fluids. Maintaining a high fluid intake is important, because fluids increase the flow of respiratory secretions, which may prevent pneumonia. A new antiviral medication is prescribed for people who have initial symptoms of the flu and who are at high risk for complications. This medication does not prevent the illness, but reduces its duration and severity.

A flu vaccine is available that is formulated each year against the current type and strain of flu virus. The vaccine would be most effective in reducing attack rates if it were effective in preventing influenza in schoolchildren. However, in vaccine trials, the vaccine has not been shown to be effective in flu prevention in this age group. In certain populations, particularly the elderly, the vaccine is effective in preventing serious complications of influenza and thus lowers mortality.

[*See also* **AIDS (acquired immunodeficiency syndrome); Cancer; Disease; Immune system; Nucleic acid; Poliomyelitis; Vaccine**]

Vitamin

Vitamins are complex organic compounds that occur naturally in plants and animals. People and other animals need these compounds in order to maintain life functions and prevent diseases. About 15 different vitamins are necessary for the nutritional needs of humans. Only minute amounts are required to achieve their purpose, yet without them life cannot be maintained. Some vitamins, including vitamins A, D, E, and K, are fat soluble and are found in the fatty parts of food and body tissue. As such they can be stored in the body. Others, the most notable of which are vitamin C and all the B-complex vitamins, are water soluble. These vitamins are found in the watery parts of food and body tissue and cannot be stored by the body. They are excreted in urine and must be consumed on a daily basis.

History

Vitamins were not discovered until early in the twentieth century. Yet it was common knowledge long before that time that substances in certain foods were necessary for good health. Information about which foods were necessary developed by trial and error—with no understanding of why they promoted health. Scurvy, for example, had long been a dreaded disease of sailors. They often spent months at sea and, due to limited ways of preserving food without refrigeration, their diet consisted of dried foods and salted meats. In 1746, English naval captain and surgeon James Lind (1716–1794) observed that 80 out of his 350 seamen came down with scurvy during a 10-week cruise. He demonstrated that this disease could be prevented by eating fresh fruits and vegetables during these long periods at sea. Because they lasted a long time, limes became the fruit of choice. In 1795, lemon juice was officially ordered as part of the seaman's diet. The vitamin C found in both limes and lemons prevented scurvy in sailors.

In 1897, Dutch physician Christian Eijkman (1858–1930) found that something in the hulls of rice (thiamine, a B vitamin) not present in the

Words to Know

Antioxidant: A substance that can counteract the effects of oxidation.

Beriberi: A disease caused by a deficiency of thiamine and characterized by nerve and gastrointestinal disorders.

Carbohydrate: A compound consisting of carbon, hydrogen, and oxygen found in plants and used as a food by humans and other animals.

Deficiency diseases: Diseases caused by inadequate amounts in the diet of some substance necessary for good health and the prevention of disease.

Fat-soluble vitamins: Vitamins such as A, D, E, and K that are soluble in the fatty parts of plants and animals.

Pellagra: A disease caused by a deficiency of niacin and characterized by severe skin problems and diarrhea.

Proteins: Large molecules that are essential to the structure and functioning of all living cells.

Scurvy: A disease caused by a deficiency of vitamin C, which causes a weakening of connective tissue in bone and muscle.

Water-soluble vitamins: Vitamins such as C and the B-complex vitamins that are soluble in the watery parts of plant and animal tissues.

polished grains prevented the disease beriberi (a disease that affects the nerves, the digestive system, and the heart). Soon after, British biochemist Frederick G. Hopkins (1861–1947) fed a synthetic diet of fats, carbohydrates, proteins, and minerals (but no vitamins) to experimental rats. The rats showed poor growth and became ill, leading Hopkins to conclude that there were some "accessory food factors" necessary in the diet. Eijkman and Hopkins shared the 1929 Nobel Prize in physiology and medicine for their important work on vitamins.

Finally, in 1912, Polish American biochemist Casimir Funk (1884–1967) published a paper on vitamin-deficiency diseases. He coined the word vitamine from the Latin *vita,* for "life," and *amine,* because he thought that all of these substances belonged to a group of chemicals known as amines. The e was later dropped when it was found that not all vitamins contained an amine group. Funk identified four vitamins (B_1 or thiamine, B_2, C, and D) as substances necessary for good health and the prevention of disease.

Since that time additional vitamins have been isolated from foods, and their relationship to specific diseases have been identified. All of these accessory food factors have been successfully synthesized in the laboratory. There is no difference in the chemical nature of the natural vitamins and those that are made synthetically, even though advertisements sometimes try to promote natural sources (such as vitamin C from rose hips) as having special properties not present in the synthesized form.

Nature of vitamins

Vitamins belong to a group of organic compounds required in the diets of humans and other animals in order to maintain good health: normal growth, sustenance, reproduction, and disease prevention. In spite of their importance to life, they are necessary in only very small quantities. The total amount of vitamins required for one day weigh about one-fifth of a gram. Vitamins have no caloric value and are not a source of energy.

Vitamins cannot be synthesized by the cells of an animal but are vital for normal cell function. Certain plants manufacture these substances, and they are passed on when the plants are eaten as food. Not all vitamins are required in the diets of all animals. For example, vitamin C is necessary for humans, monkeys, and guinea pigs but not for animals able to produce it in their cells from other chemical substances. Nevertheless, all higher animals require vitamin C, and its function within organisms is always the same.

Vitamins were originally classified into two broad categories according to their solubilities in water or in fat. As more vitamins were discovered, they were named after letters of the alphabet. Some substances once thought to be vitamins were later removed from the category when it was found that they were unnecessary or that they could be produced by an animal. Four of the better known vitamins, A, D, E, and K, are fat soluble. Other vitamins such as vitamin C and the B-complex vitamins are water soluble.

This difference in solubility is extremely important to the way the vitamins function within an organism and in the way they are consumed. Fat-soluble vitamins lodge in the fatty tissues of the body and can be stored there. It is, therefore, not necessary to include them in the diet every day. Because these vitamins can be stored, it also is possible (when consumed in excess) for them to build up to dangerous levels in the tissues and cause poisoning.

The Food and Drug Administration publishes a set of nutritional recommendations called the U.S. Recommended Dietary Allowances (USRDA) patterned on the needs of the average adult. These recommendations are based on the best information available but are less than perfect; most of the research upon which they are determined is done on experimental animals. Because the amounts of vitamins required are so small, precise work is very difficult.

A person who eats a balanced diet with plenty of fresh fruits and vegetables should receive adequate amounts of all the vitamins. Many vitamins, however, are very sensitive to heat, pressure cooking, cold, and other aspects of food preparation and storage and can be inactivated or destroyed.

A controversy about vitamins exists among experts regarding the dose needed to fight off some common diseases. According to these experts, the USRDA are really *minimum* requirements, and higher doses will keep a person healthier. Thus, many people worldwide take vitamin supplements as insurance that they are getting all they need. Overdosage on vitamins, especially the fat-soluble ones, can cause serious side effects, however, and in some cases they even interfere with the proper function of other nutrients.

Vitamin A

Vitamin A is present in animal tissue, mainly in liver, fish oil, egg yolks, butter, and cheese. Plants do not contain vitamin A, but they do contain beta carotene, which is converted to vitamin A in the intestine and then absorbed by the body. Beta carotene occurs most commonly in dark green leafy vegetables and in yellowish fruits and vegetables such as carrots, sweet potatoes, cantaloupe, corn, and peaches. The bodies of healthy adults who have an adequate diet can store several years' supply of this vitamin. But young children, who have not had time to build up such a large reserve, suffer from deprivation more quickly if they do not consume enough of the vitamin.

Vitamin A is necessary for proper growth of bones and teeth, for the maintenance and functioning of skin and mucous membranes, and for the ability to see in dim light. There is some evidence that it can help prevent cataracts and cardiovascular disease and, when taken at the onset of a cold, can ward it off and fight its symptoms. One of the first signs of a deficiency of this vitamin is night blindness, in which the rods of the eye (necessary for night vision) fail to function normally. Extreme cases of vitamin A deficiency can lead to total blindness. Other symptoms include dry and scaly skin, problems with the mucous linings of the digestive tract and urinary system, and abnormal growth of teeth and bones.

Vitamin A is stored in the fatty tissues of the body and is toxic in high doses. As early as 1596, Arctic explorers experienced vitamin A poisoning. In this region of extreme conditions, the polar bear was a major source of their food supply, and a quarter pound of polar bear liver contains about 450 times the recommended daily dose of vitamin A. Excessive amounts of vitamin A cause chronic liver disease, peeling of the skin of the entire body, bone thickening, and painful joints. However, it is nearly impossible to ingest beta carotene in toxic amounts since the body will not convert excess amounts to toxic levels of vitamin A.

Vitamin D

Vitamin D is often called the sunshine vitamin. It is produced when compounds that occur naturally in animal bodies are exposed to sunlight. Thus, it is difficult to suffer a vitamin D deficiency if one gets enough sunshine. One form of vitamin D is often added to milk as an additive. Storage and food preparation do not seem to affect this vitamin.

Vitamin D lets the body utilize calcium and phosphorus in bone and tooth formation. Deficiency of this vitamin causes a bone disease called rickets. This disease is characterized by bone deformities (such as bowlegs, pigeon breast, and knobby bone growths on the ribs where they join the breastbone) and tooth abnormalities. In adults, bones become soft and porous as calcium is lost.

Excessive amounts of vitamin D cause nausea, diarrhea, weight loss, and pain in the bones and joints. Damage to the kidneys and blood vessels can occur as calcium deposits build up in these tissues.

Vitamin E

Vitamin E is present in green leafy vegetables, wheat germ and other plant oils, egg yolks, and meat. The main function of this vitamin is to act as an antioxidant, particularly for fats. (When oxidized, fats form a very reactive substance called peroxide, which is often very damaging to cells. Vitamin E is more reactive than the fatty acid molecule and, therefore, takes its place in the oxidizing process.) Because cell membranes are partially composed of fat molecules, vitamin E is vitally important in maintaining the nervous, circulatory, and reproductive systems and in protecting the kidneys, lungs, and liver.

All of the symptoms of vitamin E deficiency are believed to be due to the loss of the antioxidant protection it offers to cells. This protective effect also keeps vitamin A from oxidizing to an inactive form. And when vitamin E is lacking, vitamin A deficiency also frequently occurs. However, because vitamin E is so prevalent in foods, it is very difficult to suffer from a deficiency of this vitamin unless no fats are consumed in the diet. When it does occur, the symptoms include cramping in the legs, muscular dystrophy, and fibrocystic breast disease.

According to some current theories, many of the effects of aging are caused by the oxidation of fat molecules in cells. If this is true, then consuming extra vitamin E might counteract these effects because of its antioxidant properties.

Vitamin K

Vitamin K is found in many plants (especially green leafy ones like spinach), in liver, and in the bacteria of the intestine. Nearly all higher animals must obtain the vitamin K they need from these sources. Although the exact method by which vitamin K works in the body is not understood, it is known that vitamin K is vital to the formation of prothrombin—one of the chemicals necessary for blood clotting—found in the liver.

When vitamin K deficiency develops, it is rarely due to an incomplete diet. Instead, it results from liver damage and the blood's inability to process the vitamin. The deficiency is characterized by the inability of the blood to clot, and it manifests in unusual bleeding or large bruises under the skin or in the muscles. Newborn infants sometimes suffer from brain hemorrhage due to a deficiency of vitamin K.

Vitamin B

What was once thought to be vitamin B was later found to be only one of many B vitamins. Today, more than a dozen B vitamins are known, and they are frequently referred to as vitamin B-complex. Thiamine was the first of these vitamins to be identified. All of the B vitamins are water soluble.

Each of the B vitamins acts by combining with another molecule to form an organic compound known as a coenzyme. A coenzyme then works with an enzyme to perform vital activities within the cell. The function of enzymes within a cell vary, but all are somehow related to the release of energy. The most common members of this group of vitamins include vitamin B_1 (thiamine), vitamin B_2 (riboflavin), vitamin B_6 (pyridoxine), vitamin B_{12} (cobalamin), biotin, folate (also folacin or folic acid), niacin, and pantothenic acid.

Vitamin B_1 is present in whole grains, nuts, legumes, pork, and liver. It helps the body release energy from carbohydrates. More than 4,000 years ago, the Chinese described a disease we know today as beriberi, which is caused by a deficiency of thiamine. The disease affects the nervous and gastrointestinal system and causes nausea, fatigue, and mental confusion. Thiamine is found in the husks or bran of rice and grains. Once the grain is milled and the husks removed, rice is no longer a source of this vitamin. Manufacturers today produce enriched rice and flour by adding thiamine back into the milled products.

Vitamin B_2 helps the body release energy from fats, proteins, and carbohydrates. It can be obtained from whole grains, organ meats, and green leafy vegetables. Lack of this vitamin causes severe skin problems. Vitamin B_6 is important in the building of body tissue as well as in protein metabolism and the synthesis of hemoglobin. A deficiency can cause depression, nausea, and vomiting. Vitamin B_{12} is necessary for the proper functioning of the nervous system and in the formation of red blood cells. It can be obtained from meat, fish, and dairy products. Anemia, nervousness, fatigue, and even brain degeneration can result from vitamin B_{12} deficiency.

Niacin is required to release energy from glucose. It is present in whole grains (but not corn), meat, fish, and dairy products. Inadequate amounts of this vitamin cause a disease called pellagra, which is characterized by skin disorders, weak muscles, diarrhea, and loss of appetite. Pellagra was once common in Spain, Mexico, and the southeastern United States, where a large component of the diet consisted of corn and corn products. The niacin in corn exists as part of a large, fibrous molecule that cannot be absorbed by the blood or used by the body. However, after it was discovered that treating corn with an alkaline solution (such as lime water) releases the niacin from the larger molecule and makes it available for the body to use, pellagra became much less common.

Pantothenic acid helps release energy from fats and carbohydrates and is found in large quantities in egg yolk, liver, eggs, nuts, and whole grains. Deficiency of this vitamin causes anemia. Biotin is involved in the release of energy from carbohydrates and in the formation of fatty acids. It is widely available from grains, legumes (peas or beans), egg yolk, and liver. A lack of biotin causes dermatitis (skin inflammation).

Vitamin C

Because of its association with the common cold, vitamin C (also known as ascorbic acid) is probably the best known of all the vitamins.

Most animals can synthesize this vitamin in the liver, where glucose is converted to ascorbic acid. Humans, monkeys, guinea pigs, and the Indian fruit bat are exceptions and must obtain the vitamin from their diets. The vitamin is easily oxidized, and food storage or food processing and preparation frequently destroy its activity. Soaking fruits and vegetables in water for long periods also removes most of the vitamin C. Citrus fruits, berries, and some vegetables like tomatoes and peppers are good sources of vitamin C.

The exact function of vitamin C in the body is still not well understood, but it is believed to be necessary for the formation of collagen, an important protein in skin, cartilage, ligaments, tendons, and bone. It also plays a role in the body's absorption, use, and storage of iron. Vitamin C is an antioxidant and is therefore believed to offer protection to cells much as vitamin E does. An increasing body of evidence suggests that a greatly increased amount of vitamin C in the diet lessens the risk of heart disease and cancer.

Polarized light micrograph of crystals of ascorbic acid, or vitamin C. The vitamin is found almost exclusively in fruits (particularly citrus) and vegetables. *(Reproduced by permission of Photo Researchers, Inc.)*

A deficiency of vitamin C causes a disease called scurvy. Scurvy weakens the connective tissue in bones and muscles, causing bones to become very porous and brittle and muscles to weaken. As the walls of the circulatory system become affected, sore and bleeding gums and bruises result from internal bleeding. Anemia can occur because iron, which is critical to the transport of oxygen in the blood, cannot be utilized. Vitamin C is metabolized (broken down) very slowly by the body, and deficiency diseases do not usually manifest themselves for several months.

Linus Pauling (1901–1994), the winner of two Nobel Prizes (one for chemistry and one for peace), believed that massive doses of vitamin C could ward off the common cold and offer protection against some forms of cancer. While scientific studies have been unable to confirm this theory, they do suggest that vitamin C can at least reduce the severity of the symptoms of a cold. Some studies also suggest that vitamin C can lessen the incidence of heart disease and cancer. If this is true, it could be that the antioxidant properties of the vitamin help protect cells from weakening and breaking down much as vitamin E does. In fact, vitamins A, C, and E all play similar roles in the body, and it is difficult to distinguish among their effects.

[*See also* **Malnutrition; Nutrition**]

Vivisection

Vivisection (pronounced vih-vih-SEK-shun) literally means the dissection or cutting of a living animal. The term has come to apply to any and all types of experiments on live animals, and it is a term to which many scientists object. People who believe that humans have no right to perform any type of experiments on animals are sometimes called antivivisectionists, although they can be more properly described as animal rights activists.

Early history

Humans have been using animals for their own purposes probably from the earliest times, and some would say that the notion that people are more important than animals is taught in the Bible. The Greeks said that since animals could not think as humans did, they were a lesser form of life, and this notion was continued by Christians who said that since animals had no souls, they were not really important. With the beginning of modern science in the seventeenth century, animals were used as an easy way of understanding our own bodies. That is, a doctor would cut open a pig or a sheep and study its internal organs as a way of learning more about human anatomy. But cutting into a dead animal's body is different than performing an experiment on a living subject.

Scientific use of animals

By the nineteenth century, doctors were regularly using cows, sheep, and goats to study diseases. The French microbiologist Louis Pasteur (1822–1895) pioneered the use of vaccines by testing them on healthy animals. His unvaccinated animals died when they were exposed to certain diseases. Other great physiologists (scientists who study how the body functions) like Russian Ivan Pavlov (1849–1936) and Frenchman Claude Bernard (1813–1878) operated on dogs and left their surgical cuts open in order to better understand how their organs worked. Both men made major medical discoveries because of this. After World War II (1939–45), the use of animals in laboratories of all types grew enormously. Increasingly, dogs, cats, rats, mice, monkeys, and many other types of animals were needed by scientists for many different purposes. Animals were used for biological and medical research, as well as for the education and training of doctors and veterinarians; they were used to develop and test vaccines and new drugs; and they were used for the testing of commercial products such as cosmetics.

The case for experimentation

The use of animals for experimentation has become a sensitive issue, and the opposing sides in this debate can both make persuasive arguments. Many of those in favor say simply that people are more important than animals, and that while it is unfortunate that animals must sometimes suffer and die, it is worth it if humans lives are saved by this research. They argue that two-thirds of all the Nobel Prizes for medicine or physiology awarded since 1902 have been discoveries made involving the use of animals. Those who argue that animals also should be used for medicine and product testing say that these tests are essential if our drugs and products are to be safe. In fact, the U.S. Food and Drug Administration, the government agency responsible for that safety, actually requires animal tests for certain medicines and eye-care products. Finally, the dead bodies of animals are used in schools to teach biology, and many high school students dissect frogs or even an unborn pig or a rabbit in biology class. There is no doubt that the use of all sort of animals in all sorts of laboratories requires that millions of animals be used experimentally.

The case against experimentation

People who are against such use argue that this is not just "use" of an animal but rather, it is abuse. The case against animal research states that nearly everything about the system of animal experimentation is bad for the animals. They state that certain animals are bred only for this

Many people oppose vivisections, considering it animal cruelty. *(Reproduced by permission of The Corbis Corporation [Bellevue].)*

purpose, and most are kept caged in stressful environments. They are subjected to all manner of cruel and sometimes painful procedures, and in the end they are disposed of. Animal rights activists say that such research really does not save human lives since scientists cannot really compare the reactions of an animal with those of a human being. They also argue that new techniques can provide scientists with alternatives to testing animals.

Opposition to vivisection has been organized since the last quarter of the nineteenth century when a strong antivivisection movement in England resulted in the Cruelty to Animals Act of 1876. Nearly 100 years later, the modern animal rights movement helped get the Animal Welfare Act of 1966 passed in the United States. These and later laws regulate the conditions under which animals may be used in laboratories, yet most who oppose them would say that they do not go far enough. The most active group in America, called People for the Ethical Treatment of Animals (PETA), has a motto saying, "Animals are not ours to eat, wear, experiment on, or use in entertainment."

Although the numbers of animals used for experiments is dropping, animal research is still big business and, some would argue, an essential and very important business. The debate between the scientific community and those who oppose vivisection involves some very difficult questions. Animal rights activists believe that those who use animals experimentally, even though responsibly, should realize that their work treats animals as objects who have no rights. It also inflicts stress, fear, pain, and a lack of freedom on its subjects. Experimenters would counter this by saying that their work is essential to our way of life and to human health and well-being, and that there is no real substitute for animal experimentation. In the end, animal testing is a moral dilemma that each person must come to terms with on his or her own.

Volcano

A volcano is a hole in Earth's surface through which magma (called lava when it reaches Earth's surface), hot gases, ash, and rock fragments escape from deep inside the planet. The word volcano also is used to describe the cone of erupted material (lava and ash) that builds up around the opening.

Volcanic activity is the main process by which material from Earth's interior reaches its surface. Volcanoes played a large part in the formation of Earth's atmosphere, oceans, and continents. When Earth was new, the superheated gases within it (including carbon dioxide) streamed out through countless volcanoes to form the original atmosphere and oceans.

Words to Know

Caldera: Large circular depression formed when an empty magma chamber causes the collapse of the volcano above it.

Chemosynthesis: Process by which the energy from certain chemical reactions, rather than light (as in photosynthesis), is used by some organisms to manufacture food.

Hot spot: An upwelling of heat from beneath Earth's crust.

Ignimbrite: Rock formation that results from a large pyroclastic flow.

Lava: Magma at Earth's surface.

Magma: Molten rock deep within Earth that consists of liquids, gases, and particles of rocks and crystals.

Photosynthesis: Process by which light energy is captured from the Sun by pigment molecules in plants and algae and converted to food.

Pyroclastic flow: A dense wave of superheated air and rock that moves as a fluid from an erupting volcano, sometimes crossing thousands of square miles of landscape.

Seafloor spreading: Spreading of the seafloor outward at ridges where two oceanic plates are diverging.

Seamount: Large, submarine volcano.

Tuff: Fused hard rock formed from a large pyroclastic flow.

Volcanoes are found both on land and under the oceans (where they are called seamounts). Geologists label volcanoes by their periods of activity. If a volcano is erupting, it is called active. If a volcano is not presently erupting but might at some future date, it is called dormant. If a volcano has stopped erupting forever, it is called extinct. Generally, volcanoes are labeled extinct when no eruption has been noted in recorded history.

How volcanoes form

According to the geologic theory called plate tectonics, Earth's crust is broken into various rigid plates that "float" on the surface of the planet. The plates move in response to intense pressure created underneath by the movement of currents carrying heat energy from the center of the

Hydrothermal Vents

Hydrothermal vents are cracks in the ocean floor or chimney-like structures extending from the ocean floor up to 150 feet (45 meters) high. Due to nearby volcanic activity, these vents release hot mineral-laden water into the surrounding ocean. Temperature of this fluid is typically around 660°F (350°C).

Often, the fluid released is black due to the presence of very fine sulfide mineral particles (iron, copper, zinc, and other metals). As a result, these deep-ocean hot springs are called black smokers. Hydrothermal vents usually occur at midocean ridges where new seafloor is created.

Hydrothermal vents are surrounded by unusual forms of sea life, including giant clams, tube worms, and unique types of fish. These organisms live off bacteria that thrive on the energy-rich chemical compounds transported by hydrothermal fluids. This is the only environment on Earth supported by a food chain that does not depend on the energy of the Sun or photosynthesis. The energy source is chemical, not solar, and is called chemosynthesis.

planet to the surface. This pressure causes plates to move toward or away from each other (and also past each other in a horizontal motion).

Volcanoes form on land near coastal areas when a continental (land) plate and an oceanic plate converge or move toward each other. Since the oceanic plate is denser, it subducts or sinks beneath the continental plate. As the rock of this subducted oceanic plate is pushed farther and farther beneath the continent's surface, extremely high temperatures and pressure melt the rock. This creates hot, buoyant magma that then rises toward the surface. When the magma reaches the crust, it collects in a magma reservoir or chamber. When pressure inside the reservoir exceeds that of the overlying rock, magma is forced upward through cracks in Earth's crust.

Seamounts (underwater volcanoes) form when oceanic plates both converge (move toward each other) and diverge (move away from each other). When oceanic plates converge, one sinks beneath the other, creating a deep-sea trench. Rising magma from the subducted plate then rises to form volcanoes along the trench. When oceanic plates diverge, magma seeps upward at the ridge between the plates to create new seafloor (a process called seafloor spreading). Volcanoes form on either side of the ridge.

Hot spots are special areas where volcanoes form apart from plates converging or diverging. Hot spots are a common term for thermal plumes of magma welling up through the crust far from the edges of plates. As a plate drifts over a hot spot, magma from Earth's interior rises and volcanic activity takes place. Some famous hot spots are Hawaii, Yellowstone National Park (United States), Iceland, Samoa, and Bermuda.

Volcanic eruptions

Volcanoes erupt different material, and they each have their own style of erupting. These varied eruptions result from the differences in magma that each volcano contains. Magma that is low in gas and silica (silicon dioxide, a compound found widely in rocks and minerals) yields a gentle flow of thin, quickly spreading lava. In contrast, magma that is rich in gas and silica gives rise to violent explosions: the thick, tarlike magma may plug up the volcanic vent, blocking the upward movement of the magma until built-up pressure blows away the overlying rock. Geologists classify volcanic eruptions according to four chief forms or phases: Hawaiian, Strombolian, Vulcanian, and Peleean.

In a Hawaiian phase, runny lava gushes out in a fountain without any explosive eruptions. In a Strombolian phase (named after the Stromboli volcano on an island north of Sicily), thick lava is emitted in continuous

Ropelike, twisted lava such as this is called pahoehoe. *(Reproduced by permission of JLM Visuals.)*

but mild explosions. Lava arcs and steam-driven clouds of ash shower the dome with molten drizzle. A Vulcanian phase occurs when a magma plug has blocked the volcanic vent. The resulting explosive eruption hurls tons of almost solid magma into the sky, and a vapor cloud forms over the crater. The most violent eruption is the Peleean, named after Mount Pelee on the Caribbean island of Martinique. Fine ash, thick lava, and glowing, gas-charged clouds are emitted, traveling downhill at a tremendous speed.

Fierce rains often accompany eruptions because of the release of steam from the volcano, which then condenses in the atmosphere to form clouds. Volatile gases in the magma also fly into the atmosphere upon eruption. These include hydrogen sulfide, fluorine, carbon dioxide, and radon. A dense wave of ash, superheated gases, and rock that moves as a fluid from an erupting volcano is known as a pyroclastic flow. Flows travel downhill at speeds more than 60 miles (100 kilometers) per hour, filling existing valleys with the fluid mixture. This material deflates as it cools. The rock formation that results is called an ignimbrite (pronounced IG-nim-bright), and the fused rock is called tuff. Ignimbrites can cover hundreds of square miles of landscape, such as the Mitchell Mesa Tuff of West Texas.

When a volcano erupts such a large volume of material, often emptying its magma chamber, the central part of the cone is left unsupported. As a result, the crater and walls of the vent collapse into the hollow chamber, creating a large circular depression known as a caldera across the summit. The famous Crater Lake in southern Oregon formed in this way.

Volcanic structures

The size and shape of a volcano is dependent on the history and type of its eruptions. Based on this, geologists classify volcanoes into four shapes: cinder cones, composite cones, shield volcanoes, and lava domes.

Cinder cones are built of lava fragments. They have slopes of 30 to 40 degrees and seldom exceed 1,640 feet (500 meters) in height. Sunset Crater in Arizona and Parícutin in Mexico are examples of cinder cones.

Composite cones (or stratovolcanoes) are made up of alternating layers of lava, ash, and solid rock. They are characterized by slopes of up to 30 degrees at the summit, tapering off to 5 degrees at the base. Mount Fuji in Japan and Mount St. Helens in Washington are composite cone volcanoes.

Shield volcanoes are built primarily by a series of lava flows that pile one on top of another. Their slopes are seldom more than 10 degrees at the summit and 2 degrees at the base. The Hawaiian Islands are clusters of shield volcanoes. Mauna Loa (on the island of Hawaii) is the world's largest active volcano, rising 13,680 feet (4,170 meters) above sea level. Kenya's Mount Kilamanjaro, the tallest mountain in Africa, is a shield volcano.

Lava domes are made of thick, pasty lava squeezed like toothpaste from a tube. Examples of lava domes are Lassen Peak and Mono Dome in California.

Volcanic catastrophes

Numerous volcanoes erupt around the world every century, usually in sparsely populated areas. Even so, volcanoes have threatened human civilization throughout history and will do so as long as people live on Earth's often violent surface.

An ash fall from Mount Vesuvius buried the Roman city of Pompeii in A.D. 79. The volcano, which sent a column of hot ash 12 miles (19 kilometers) into the sky, struck down the people where they lived, preserving the shapes of their bodies where they fell in the ash. The nearby city of Herculaneum was covered by a pyroclastic flow that destroyed it in seconds. Pompeii remained buried until 1748, when construction workers first unearthed parts of the ancient city—much of it appearing as it did on the morning Vesuvius erupted.

A volcanic cinder cone and lava flow in northern Arizona. *(Reproduced by permission of The Stock Market.)*

On August 27, 1883, the volcanic island of Krakatoa in Indonesia erupted, blowing an ash cloud 50 miles (80 kilometers) high then collapsing into a caldera. The collapse was heard almost 2,500 miles (4,020 kilometers) away. Resulting tidal waves reaching 130 feet (40 meters) killed 36,000 people in coastal Java and Sumatra. Spectacularly weird sky phenomena from this eruption included brilliant green sunrises and moonrises in the equatorial latitudes, followed by day-long blue sunlight and bright green sunsets.

On the morning of May 18, 1980, Mount St. Helens in Washington erupted with the force of more than 500 atomic bombs—one of the largest volcanic explosions in North American history. The blast, which sent a mushroom-shaped ash plume 12 miles (20 kilometers) high, reduced the summit (peak) by more than 1,300 feet (400 meters). Sixty people and countless animals were killed, and every tree within 15 miles (24 kilometers) was flattened. Ensuing landslides carried debris for nearly 20 miles (32 kilometers).

The July 22, 1980, eruption of Mount St. Helens in southern Washington State. *(Reproduced by permission of John McCann.)*

Volcanic benefits

The eruption of volcanoes through geologic time built the continents. The soil of some of the world's richest farmland draws its fertility from minerals provided by nearby volcanoes. The heat of magma boils water into steam that spins the turbines of geothermal power stations. Geothermal stations now light electric power grids in Iceland, Italy, New Zealand, and a other places. Enough heat flows from the world's volcanic regions and midoceanic ridges to power industrial civilization for several hundred million years. This power source awaits only the development of feasible geothermal technology.

[*See also* **Island; Ocean; Plate tectonics; Rocks**]

Volume

Volume is the amount of space occupied by an object or a material. Volume is said to be a derived unit, since the volume of an object can be known from other measurements. In order to find the volume of a rectangular box, for example, one only needs to know the length, width, and depth of the box. Then the volume can be calculated from the formula, $V = l \cdot w \cdot d$.

The volume of most physical objects is a function of two other factors: temperature and pressure. In general, the volume of an object increases with an increase in temperature and decreases with an increase in pressure. Some exceptions exist to this general rule. For example, when water is heated from a temperature of 32°F (0°C) to 39°F (4°C), it decreases in volume. Above 39°F, however, further heating of water results in an increase in volume that is more characteristic of matter.

Units of volume

The term unit volume refers to the volume of "one something": one quart, one milliliter, or one cubic inch, for example. Every measuring system that exists defines a unit volume for that system. Then, when one speaks about the volume of an object in that system, what he or she means is how many times that unit volume is contained within the object. If the volume of a glass of water is said to be 35.6 cubic inches, for example, what is meant is that 35.6 cubic inch unit volumes could be placed into that glass.

The units in which volume is measured depend on a variety of factors, such as the system of measurement being used and the type of

Words to Know

British system: A system of measurement long used in many parts of the world but now used commonly only in the United States among the major nations of the world.

Displacement method: A method for determining the volume of an irregularly shaped solid object by placing it in a measured amount of water or other liquid and noting the increase in volume of the liquid.

Metric system: A system of measurement used by all scientists and in common practice by almost every nation of the world.

Unit volume: The basic size of an object against which all other volumes are measured in a system.

material being measured. For example, volume in the British system of measurement may be measured in barrels, bushels, drams, gills, pecks, teaspoons, or other units. Each of these units may have more than one meaning, depending on the material being measured. For example, the precise size of a barrel ranges anywhere from 31 to 42 gallons, depending on federal and state statutes. The more standard units used in the British system, however, are the cubic inch or cubic foot and the gallon.

Variability in the basic units also exists. For example, the quart differs in size depending on whether it is being used to measure a liquid or dry volume and whether it is a measurement made in the British or customary U.S. system. As an example, 1 customary liquid quart is equivalent to 57.75 cubic inches, while 1 customary dry quart is equivalent to 67.201 cubic inches. In contrast, 1 British quart is equivalent to 69.354 cubic inches.

The basic unit of volume in the metric system is the liter (abbreviated as L), although the cubic centimeter (cc or cm^3) and milliliter (mL) are also widely used as units for measuring volume. The fundamental relationship between units in the two systems is given by the fact that 1 U.S. liquid quart is equivalent to 0.946 liter or, conversely, 1 liter is equivalent to 1.057 customary liquid quarts.

The volume of solids

The volumes of solids are relatively less affected by pressure and temperature changes than are the volumes of most liquids and all gases.

For example, heating a liter of iron from 0°C to 100°C causes an increase in volume of less than 1 percent. Heating a liter of water through the same temperature range causes an increase in volume of less than 5 percent. But heating a liter of air from 0°C to 100°C causes an increase in volume of nearly 140 percent.

The volume of a solid object can be determined in one of two general ways, depending on whether or not a mathematical formula can be written for the object. For example, the volume of a cube can be determined if one knows the length of one side. In such a case, $V = s^3$, or the volume of the cube is equal to the cube of the length of any one side (all sides being equal in length). The volume of a cylinder, on the other hand, is equal to the product of the area of the base multiplied by the height of the cylinder.

Many solid objects have irregular shapes for which no mathematical formula exists. One way to find the volume of such objects is to subdivide them into recognizable shapes for which formulas do exist (such as many small cubes) and then approximate the total volume by summing the volumes of individual subdivisions. This method of approximation can become exact by using calculus.

Another way is to calculate the volume by water displacement, or the displacement of some other liquid. Suppose, for example, that one wishes to calculate the volume of an irregularly shaped piece of rock. One way to determine that volume is first to add water to some volume-measuring instrument, such as a graduated cylinder. The exact volume of water added to the cylinder is recorded. Then, the object whose volume is to be determined is also added to the cylinder. The water in the cylinder will rise by an amount equivalent to the volume of the object. Thus, the final volume read on the cylinder less the original volume is equal to the volume of the submerged object.

This method is applicable, of course, only if the object is insoluble in water. If the object is soluble in water, then another liquid, such as alcohol or cyclohexane, can be substituted for the water.

The volume of liquids and gases

Measuring the volume of a liquid is relatively straightforward. Since liquids take the shape of the container in which they are placed, a liquid whose volume is to be found can simply be poured into a graduated container, that is, a container on which some scale has been etched. Graduated cylinders of various sizes ranging from 10 milliliters to 1 liter are commonly available in science laboratories for measuring the volumes of liquids. Other devices, such as pipettes and burettes (small measuring tubes), are available for measuring exact volumes, especially small volumes.

The volume of a liquid is only moderately affected by pressure, but it is often quite sensitive to changes in temperature. For this reason, volume measurements made at temperatures other than ambient (the surrounding) temperature are generally so indicated when they are reported, as V = 35.89 milliliters (35°C).

The volume of gases is very much influenced by temperature and pressure. Thus, any attempt to measure or report the volume of the gas must always include an indication of the pressure and temperature under which that volume was measured. Indeed, since gases expand to fill any container into which they are placed, the term volume has meaning for a gas *only* when temperature and pressure are indicated.

Waste management

Waste management is the handling of discarded materials. The term most commonly applies to the disposition of solid wastes, which is often described as solid waste management. One form of waste management involves the elimination of undesirable waste products by methods such as landfilling and incineration. But recycling and composting, which transform waste into useful products, also are forms of waste management.

The term waste can apply to a wide variety of materials, including discarded food, leaves, newspapers, bottles, construction debris, chemicals from a factory, candy wrappers, disposable diapers, and radioactive materials. Civilization has always produced waste. But as industry and technology have evolved and the world's population has grown, waste management has become an increasingly difficult and complex problem.

A primary objective of waste management today is to protect the public and the environment from potential harmful effects of waste. Some waste materials are normally safe but can be hazardous if not managed properly. One gallon (3.75 liters) of used motor oil, for example, can contaminate one million gallons (3,750,000 liters) of water.

Who manages waste? Every individual, business, and industry must make decisions and take some responsibility regarding its own waste. On a larger scale, government agencies at the local, state, and federal levels enact and enforce waste management regulations. These agencies also educate the public about proper waste management. In addition, local government agencies may provide disposal or recycling services themselves, or they may hire private companies to perform those functions.

↓ Words to Know

Biosolids: Another name for sewage sludge.

Cremators: Primitive devices for incinerating municipal wastes.

Dump (or open dump): An area in which wastes are simply deposited and left to rot or decay.

Hazardous wastes: Wastes that are poisonous, flammable, or corrosive, or that react with other substances in a dangerous way.

Incineration: The burning of solid waste as a disposal method.

Landfilling: A land disposal method for solid waste in which garbage is covered every day with several inches of soil.

Leachate: The liquid that filters through a dump or landfill.

Recycling: The use of waste materials, also known as secondary materials or recyclables, to produce new products.

Resource recovery plant: An incinerator that uses energy produced by the burning of solid wastes for some useful purpose.

Source reduction: Reduction in the quantity or the toxicity of material used for a product or packaging; a form of waste prevention.

Tailings: Piles of mine wastes.

Waste prevention: A waste management method that involves preventing waste from being created, or reducing waste.

Waste-to-energy plant: An incinerator that uses energy produced by the burning of solid wastes for some useful purpose.

Forms of waste

Most solid wastes can be subdivided into one of three major categories: municipal solid wastes; agricultural, mining, and industrial wastes; and hazardous wastes. Municipal solid waste is what most people think of as garbage, refuse, or trash. It is generated by households, businesses (other than heavy industry), and institutions such as schools and hospitals.

Although we may be very conscious of municipal wastes, they actually represent only a small fraction of all solid wastes produced annually. Indeed, more than 95 percent of the 4.5 billion tons of solid waste generated in the United States each year come from agriculture, mining, and industry. These forms of solid waste are less visible to the ordinary person because they are usually generated at remote mining sites or in the fields.

Mining nearly always generates substantial waste, whether the material being mined is coal, clay, sand, gravel, building stone, or metallic ore. Early mining techniques concentrated on the removal of ores with the highest concentration of the desired mineral. Because modern methods of mining are more efficient, they can extract the desired minerals from veins that are less rich. However, much more waste is produced in the process.

Many of the plant and animal wastes generated by agriculture remain in the fields or rangelands. These wastes can be beneficial because they return nutrients to the soil. But modern techniques of raising large numbers of animals in small areas generate great volumes of animal waste, or manure. Waste in such quantities must be managed carefully, or it can contaminate groundwater or surface water.

An employee at a hazardous waste collection site in Santa Cruz County, California, sorting through household hazardous waste items. *(Reproduced by permission of Photo Researchers, Inc.)*

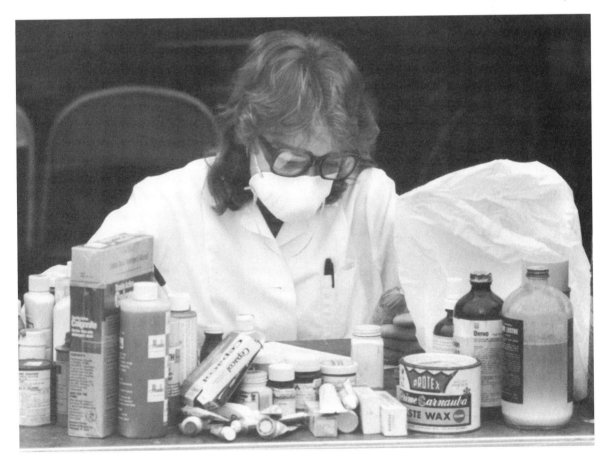

Hazardous waste

Hazardous wastes are materials considered harmful or potentially harmful to human health or the environment. Wastes may be deemed hazardous because they are poisonous, flammable, or corrosive, or because they react with other substances in a dangerous way.

Industrial operations have produced large quantities of hazardous waste for hundreds of years. Some hazardous wastes, such as mercury and dioxins, may be released as gases. Many hazardous industrial wastes are in liquid form. One of the greatest risks is that these wastes will contaminate water supplies.

Pesticides used in farming may contaminate agricultural waste. Because of the enormous volumes of pesticides used in agriculture, the proper handling of unused or waste pesticides is a daunting challenge for modern waste management. Certain mining techniques also utilize toxic chemicals. Piles of mining waste, known as tailings, may contain hazardous

Hazardous waste being disposed of in special drums. *(Reproduced by permission of Field Mark Publications.)*

substances. When these substances react with the oxygen in the air, toxic acids may form and may be washed into the groundwater by rain.

Hazardous wastes come from the home as well. Many common household products contain toxic chemicals. Examples include drain cleaner, pesticides, glue, paint, paint thinner, air freshener, and nail polish. Twenty years ago, most people dumped these products in the garbage, even if the containers were not empty. But local governments do not want them in the garbage. They also do not want residents to pour leftover household chemicals down the drain, since municipal sewage treatment plants are not well-equipped to remove them.

Management of wastes

Throughout history, four basic methods for managing wastes have been used: dumping; incineration (burning); recycling; and waste prevention. How these four methods are utilized depends on the kind of wastes being managed. Municipal solid waste is much different than industrial, agricultural, or mining waste. And hazardous waste poses such serious problems that it needs to be handled by specialized techniques, even when it is generated with other types of wastes.

Landfills. Early humans did not worry much about waste management. They simply left their garbage where it dropped. But as permanent communities developed, people began to place their waste in designated dumping areas. The use of such open dumps for garbage is still common in some parts of the world.

But open dumps have major disadvantages, especially in heavily populated areas. Toxic chemicals can filter down through a dump and contaminate groundwater. (The liquid that filters through a dump or landfill—just as water percolates or filters through coffee grounds to make coffee—is called leachate.) Dumps also may generate methane, an explosive gas produced when organic wastes decompose under certain conditions.

In many parts of the world today, open dumps have been replaced by landfills, also known as sanitary landfills. The sanitary landfill was apparently invented in England in the 1920s. At a landfill, garbage is covered at the end of every day with several inches of soil. Landfilling became common in the United States in the 1940s. By the late 1950s, it was the dominant solid waste disposal method in the nation.

Early landfills had significant leachate and methane problems. But those have largely been resolved at landfills built in the past 20 years.

Today's landfills are lined with several feet of clay and with thick plastic sheets. Leachate is collected at the bottom, drained through pipes, and processed. Methane gas also is safely piped out of the landfill.

The dumping of waste does not take place on land only. Ocean dumping makes use of barges that carry garbage out to sea. This technique was once used as a disposal method by some U.S. coastal cities and is still practiced by some nations. Sewage sludge, or processed sewage, was dumped at sea in huge quantities by New York City until 1992, when it was finally prohibited. Also called biosolids, sewage sludge is not generally considered solid waste but is sometimes composted with organic municipal solid waste.

Incineration. Incineration has a long history in municipal solid waste management. Some American cities began to burn their garbage in the late nineteenth century in devices called cremators. These devices were not very efficient, however, and cities eventually went back to dumping or other methods. In the 1930s and 1940s, many cities built new types of garbage burners known as incinerators. Many incinerators have now been shut down, primarily because of the air pollution they create.

Waste burning enjoyed yet another revival in the 1970s and 1980s. The new incinerators, many of which are still in operation, are called resource recovery or waste-to-energy plants. In addition to burning garbage,

Fresh Kills landfill in New York was closed in 2001. *(Reproduced by permission of Greenpeace Photos.)*

they produce heat or electricity that is used in nearby buildings or residences or sold to a utility. Many local governments became interested in waste-to-energy plants following the U.S. energy crisis in 1973. But, by the mid-1980s, it had become difficult to find locations to build these facilities, once again mainly because of air quality issues.

Another problem with incineration is that it generates ash, which must be landfilled. Incinerators usually reduce the volume of garbage by 70 to 90 percent. The rest comes out as ash that often contains high concentrations of toxic substances.

Recycling and waste prevention. Municipal solid waste will probably always be landfilled or burned to some extent. Since the mid-1970s, however, nondisposal methods such as waste prevention and recycling have become more popular. Because of public concerns and the high costs of landfilling and incineration, local governments want to reduce the amount of waste that needs to be disposed.

Even the earliest civilizations recycled some items before they became garbage. Broken pottery was often ground up and used to make new pottery, for example. Recycling has taken many forms. One unusual type of recycling, called reduction, was common in large U.S. cities from about 1900 to 1930. In reduction plants, wet garbage, dead horses, and other dead animals were cooked in large vats to produce grease and fertilizer. A more familiar, and certainly more appealing, type of recycling took place during World War II (1939–45), when scrap metal was collected to help the war effort. Modern-day recycling has had two recent booms, from about 1969 to 1974 and another that began in the late 1980s. At the beginning of the twenty-first century, the recycling rate in the United States had risen to 28 percent, an increase of more than 10 percent from a decade before.

Reuse and repair are the earliest forms of waste prevention, which also is known as waste reduction. When tools, clothes, and other necessities were scarce, people naturally repaired them again and again. When they were beyond repair, people found other uses for them.

One form of waste prevention, called source reduction, is a reduction in the quantity or the toxicity of the material used for a product or packaging.

Industrial waste management

Industrial wastes that are not hazardous have traditionally been sent to landfills or incinerators. The rising cost of disposal has prompted many companies to seek alternative methods for handling these wastes. Often, a manufacturing plant can reclaim certain waste materials by feeding them back into the production process.

An estimated 60 percent of all hazardous industrial waste in the United States is disposed of with a method called deep well injection. With this technique, liquid wastes are injected into a well located in a type of rock formation that keeps the waste isolated from groundwater and surface water. Other underground burial methods are also used for hazardous industrial waste and other types of dangerous waste.

Hazardous wastes are disposed of at specially designed landfills and incinerators. A controversial issue in international relations is the export of hazardous waste, usually from industrial countries to developing nations. This export often takes place with the stated intent of recycling, but some of the wastes end up being dumped.

[*See also* **Composting; Pollution; Recycling**]

Water

Water is an odorless, tasteless, transparent liquid that appears colorless but is actually very pale blue. The color is obvious in large quantities of water such as lakes and oceans. Water is the most abundant liquid on Earth. In its liquid and solid (ice) form, it covers more than 70 percent of Earth's surface—an area called the hydrosphere.

Earth's supply of water is constantly being replaced through a natural cycle called the hydrologic cycle. Water is continually evaporating from the surface of the planet, condensing in the atmosphere, and falling back to the surface as precipitation.

It is impossible to overstate the importance of water to almost every process on Earth, from the life processes of the lowest bacteria to the shaping of continents. Water is the most familiar of all chemical compounds known to humans. In fact, the human body is composed mainly of water.

Chemical properties of water

Water is a single chemical compound whose molecules consist of two hydrogen atoms attached to one oxygen atom. The chemical formula of this compound is H_2O. Considering that a hydrogen atom weighs only about one-sixteenth as much as an oxygen atom, most of the weight in water is due to oxygen: 88.8 percent of the weight is oxygen and 11.2 percent is hydrogen. This percentage remains the same from a single water molecule to a lake full of water molecules.

Words to Know

Aquifer: Underground layer of sand, gravel, or spongy rock that collects water.

Estuary: Lower end of a river where ocean tides meet the river's current.

Hydrologic cycle: Continual movement of water from the atmosphere to Earth's surface through precipitation and back to the atmosphere through evaporation and transpiration.

Ion: A molecule or atom that has lost one or more electrons and is, therefore, electrically charged.

Water can be made (synthesized) from hydrogen and oxygen, both of which are gases. When these two gases are mixed, however, they do not react unless the reaction is started with a flame or spark. Then they react with explosive violence. The tremendous energy that is released is a signal that water is an extremely stable compound. It is hard to break a water molecule apart into its components.

The normal boiling point of water is 212°F (100°C) and its freezing point is 32°F (0°C). As water is cooled to make ice, it becomes slightly denser, like all liquids. But at 39.2°F (4°C), it reaches its maximum density. When cooled below that temperature, it becomes less dense. At 32°F (0°C), water freezes and expands. Since ice is less dense than water, ice floats on it.

In pure water, 1 out of every 555 million molecules is broken down into a hydrogen ion and a hydroxide ion (an ion is an electrically charged atom or group of atoms). These ions are enough to make water a slight conductor of electricity. That is why water is dangerous when there is electricity around.

Because water dissolves so many substances (it is called the universal solvent), all of the water on Earth is in the form of solutions.

Saltwater

The oceans contain more than 97 percent of all the water on Earth. However, seawater is unsuitable for drinking because of the large amount of dissolved salts in it. The six most abundant elements making up these salts in seawater are chlorine, sodium, sulfur, magnesium, calcium, and

▼ Hard Water

Hard water is water that contains large amounts of ions (electrically charged particles) of calcium, magnesium, or iron. Hard water often has an unpleasant taste, interferes with the ability of soaps to dissolve, and can cause scaling (the building up of insoluble material) in pipes and hot water systems.

Water hardness is most commonly the result of acidic water containing carbon dioxide passing through limestone or dolomite and dissolving the minerals these rocks contain. The dissolved minerals lead to an increase in the amounts of calcium and magnesium ions in the water.

Hard water can be treated by boiling the water, but this method is effective only for small quantities. A more efficient method is to use ion-exchangers, in which the unwanted calcium and magnesium ions are exchanged or traded for sodium ions that do not cause scaling. Most water softeners work by the ion-exchange method. The soft water that is produced is not free of ions, only of undesirable ions.

potassium. Chlorine and sodium, the most abundant of these elements, combine to form sodium chloride, more commonly known as table salt.

These elements are deposited in seawater through various means. Volcanic activity (on land and on the seafloor) releases chlorine and sulfur. Other elements reach the oceans through runoffs from land. Rain and other precipitation weathers and erodes rocks and soil on land, dissolving the minerals (salts) they contain. This material is then transported to the oceans by rivers.

Salinity is the measure of the amount of dissolved salts in seawater. This measurement is usually the mass of material dissolved in 1,000 grams (35 ounces) of water. The average salinity of seawater is about 35 grams (1.2 ounces) of salts in 1,000 grams (35 ounces) of seawater, or 3.5 percent of the total.

Desalination. Desalination is the process of removing salt from seawater to provide essential water for drinking, irrigation, and industry, especially in desert regions or areas where freshwater is scarce. In the almost 4,000 desalination plants worldwide, most desalination takes place through two methods: distillation and reverse osmosis.

At its simplest, distillation consists of boiling seawater to separate it from dissolved salt. Once the seawater boils, water vapor rises, leaving the salt on the bottom of the tank. The water vapor is then transferred to a separate, cooler tank where it condenses as pure liquid water. Heat for distillation usually comes from burning fossil fuels (oil and coal). Distillation is widely used in the Middle East, where fossil fuel is plentiful but freshwater is scarce.

Reverse osmosis uses high pressure to force pure water out of saltwater. Pressures up to 60 atmospheres (800 to 1,200 pounds per square inch) are applied to saltwater, forcing it through a special membrane that allows only pure water to flow through, trapping the salt on the other side. Reverse osmosis is widely used to desalinate brackish water, which is less salty than seawater and therefore requires pressures only about one-half as great.

Brackish water

Brackish water has a salinity between that of freshwater and seawater. Brackish waters develop through the mixing of saltwater and freshwater. This occurs mostly near the coasts of the oceans in coastal estuaries (the lower course of a river where it flows into an ocean) or salt marshes that are frequently flooded with ocean currents due to the rising and falling of tides.

A freshwater mountain stream in Rocky Mountain National Park. *(Reproduced by permission of JLM Visuals.)*

Most species can tolerate either saltwater or freshwater, but not both. Organisms that live in brackish habitats must be tolerant of a wide range of salt concentrations. The small fish known as killifish are common residents of estuaries, where within any day the salt concentration in tidal pools and creeks can vary from that of freshwater to that of the open ocean. During their spawning migrations, salmon and eels experience a range of salt concentration as they move through all three water environments: seawater, brackish water, and freshwater.

Freshwater

Freshwater is chemically defined as water that contains less than 0.2 percent dissolved salts. Of all the water on Earth, less than 3 percent is freshwater. About two-thirds of all freshwater is locked up in ice, mainly in Greenland and the Antarctic.

The remaining freshwater—less than 1 percent of all the water on Earth—supports most plants and animals that live on land. This freshwater occurs on the surface in lakes, ponds, rivers, and streams and underground in the pores in soil and in subterranean aquifers in deep geological formations. Freshwater also is found in the atmosphere as clouds and precipitation.

Worldwide, agricultural irrigation uses about 80 percent of all freshwater. The remaining 20 percent is used for domestic consumption, as cooling water for electrical power plants, and for other industrial purposes. This figure varies widely from place to place. For example, China uses 87 percent of its available water for agriculture. The United States uses 40 percent for agriculture, 40 percent for electrical cooling, 10 percent for domestic consumption, and 10 percent for industrial purposes.

[*See also* **Hydrologic cycle; Lake; Ocean; River**]

Wave motion

Wave motion is a disturbance that moves from place to place in some medium, carrying energy with it. Probably the most familiar example of wave motion is the action of water waves. A boat at rest on the ocean moves up and down as water waves pass beneath it. The waves appear to be moving toward the shore. But the water particles that make up the wave are actually moving in a vertical direction. The boat itself does not move toward the shore or, if it does, it's at a much slower rate than that of the water waves themselves.

Words to Know

Amplitude: The maximum displacement (difference between an original position and a later position) of the material that is vibrating. Amplitude can be thought of visually as the highest and lowest points of a wave.

Condensation: A region of space with a higher-than-normal density.

Crest: The highest point reached by a wave.

Frequency: The number of wave crests (or wave troughs) that pass a given point per unit of time (usually per second).

Longitudinal wave: A wave that causes the particles of the surrounding medium to vibrate in the same direction as that in which the wave is moving.

Rarefaction: A region of space with a lower-than-normal density.

Transverse wave: A wave that causes the particles of the surrounding medium to vibrate in a direction at right angles to the direction of the wave motion.

Trough: The lowest point reached by a wave.

Wavelength: The distance between any two adjacent wave crests (wave crests that are next to each other) or any two adjacent wave troughs in a wave.

The energy carried by a water wave is obvious to anyone who has watched a wave hit the shore. Even small waves have enough energy to move bits of sand. Much larger waves can, of course, tear apart the shore and wash away homes.

Types of wave motion

Two types of waves exist: transverse and longitudinal. A transverse wave is one that causes the particles of the surrounding medium to vibrate in a direction at right angles to the direction of the wave. A water wave is an example of a transverse wave. As water particles move up and down, the water wave itself appears to move to the right or left.

A longitudinal wave is one that causes the particles of the surrounding medium to vibrate in the same direction as that in which the wave is moving. A sound wave is an example of a longitudinal wave. A sound wave is produced when the pressure in a medium is suddenly increased or decreased. That pressure change causes pulses of rarefactions and condensations to spread out away from the source of the sound. A rarefaction is a region of space with a lower-than-normal density; a condensation is a region with a higher-than-normal density. The sound wave travels from one place to another as particles vibrate back and forth in the medium in the same direction as the sound wave.

Characteristics of a wave

Any wave can be fully characterized by describing three properties: wavelength, frequency, and amplitude. Like any wave, a water wave appears to move up and down in a regular pattern. The highest point reached by the wave is known as the wave crest; the lowest point reached is the wave trough (pronounced trawf).

The distance between any two adjacent (next to each other) wave crests or any two adjacent wave troughs is known as the wavelength of the wave. The wavelength is generally abbreviated with the Greek letter lambda, λ. The number of wave crests (or wave troughs) that pass a given point per unit of time (usually per second) is known as the frequency of the wave. Frequency is generally represented by the letter f. The highest point reached by a wave above its average height is known as the amplitude of the wave. The speed at which a wave moves is the product of its wavelength and its frequency, or, $v = \lambda f$.

Two kinds of waves most commonly encountered in science are sound waves and electromagnetic waves. Electromagnetic radiation includes a wide variety of kinds of energy, including visible light, ultraviolet light, infrared radiation, X rays, gamma rays, radar, microwaves, and radio waves. As different as these forms of energy appear to be, they are all alike in the way in which they are transmitted. They travel as transverse waves with the same velocity, about 3×10^{10} centimeters (1.2×10^{10} inches) per second, but with different wavelengths and frequencies.

Properties of waves

Waves have many interesting properties. They can reflect from surfaces and refract, or change their direction, when they pass from one medium into another. An example of reflection is the light we observe that bounces off an object, allowing us to see that object. An example of refraction is the apparent dislocation of objects when they are placed underwater.

Waves also can interfere, or combine, with each other. For example, two waves can reach a particular point at just the right time for both to disturb the medium in the same way. This effect is known as constructive interference. Similarly, destructive interference occurs when the disturbances of different waves cancel each other out. Interference can also lead to standing waves—waves that appear to be stationary. The medium is still disturbed, but the disturbances are oscillating in place. Standing waves can occur only within confined regions, such as in water in a bathtub or on a guitar string that is fixed at both ends.

[*See also* **Acoustics; Fluid dynamics; Interference; Light**]

Weather

Weather is the state of the atmosphere at any given time and place, determined by such factors as temperature, precipitation, cloud cover, humidity, air pressure, and wind. The study of weather is known as meteorology. No exact date can be given for the beginnings of this science since humans have studied weather conditions for thousands of years. Weather conditions can be regarded as a result of the interaction of four basic physical elements: the Sun, Earth's atmosphere, Earth itself, and natural landforms on Earth.

Snowstorm in Portland, Maine. *(Reproduced courtesy of the National Oceanic and Atmospheric Administration.)*

Words to Know

Humidity: The amount of water vapor contained in the air.

Meteorology: The study of Earth's atmosphere and the changes that take place within it.

Solar energy: Any form of electromagnetic radiation that is emitted by the Sun.

Topography: The detailed surface features of an area.

Solar energy and Earth's atmosphere

The driving force behind all meteorological changes taking place on Earth is solar energy. Only about 25 percent of the energy emitted from the Sun reaches Earth's surface directly. Another 25 percent reaches the surface only after being scattered by gases in the atmosphere. The remaining solar energy is either absorbed or reflected back into space by atmospheric gases and clouds.

Solar energy at Earth's surface is then reradiated to the atmosphere. This reradiated energy is likely to be absorbed by other gases in the atmosphere such as carbon dioxide and nitrous oxide. This absorption process—the greenhouse effect—is responsible for maintaining the planet's annual average temperature.

Humidity, clouds, and precipitation. The absorption of solar energy by Earth's surface and atmosphere is directly responsible for most of the major factors making up weather patterns. When water on the surface (in oceans, lakes, rivers, streams, and other bodies of water) is warmed, it tends to evaporate and move upward into the atmosphere. The amount of moisture found in the air at any one time and place is called the humidity.

When this moisture reaches cold levels of the atmosphere, it condenses into tiny water droplets or tiny ice crystals, which group together to form clouds. Since clouds tend to reflect sunlight back into space, an accumulation of cloud cover may cause heat to be lost from the atmosphere.

Clouds also are the breeding grounds for various types of precipitation. Water droplets or ice crystals in clouds combine with each other, eventually becoming large enough to overcome upward drafts in the air and falling to Earth as precipitation. The form of precipitation (rain, snow, sleet, hail, etc.) depends on the atmospheric conditions (temperature, winds) through which the water or ice falls.

Atmospheric pressure and winds. Solar energy also is directly responsible for the development of wind. When sunlight strikes Earth's surface, it heats varying locations (equatorial and polar regions) and varying topography (land and water) differently. Thus, some locations are heated more strongly than others. Warm places tend to heat the air above them, causing that air to rise upward into the upper atmosphere. The air above cooler regions tends to move downward from the upper atmosphere.

In regions where warm air moves upward, the atmospheric pressure tends to be low. Downward air movements bring about higher atmospheric pressures. Areas with different atmospheric pressures account for the movement of air or wind. Wind is simply the movement of air from a region of high pressure to one of lower pressure.

Earth, land surface, and the weather

Earth's surface ranges from oceans to deserts to mountains to prairies to urbanized areas. The way solar energy is absorbed and reflected from each of these regions is different, accounting for variations in local weather patterns.

However, the tilt of Earth on its axis and it's varying distance from the Sun account for more significant weather variations. The fact that Earth's axis is tilted at an angle of 23.5 degrees to the plane of its orbit means that the planet is heated unevenly by the Sun. During the summer, sunlight strikes the Northern Hemisphere more directly than it does the Southern Hemisphere. In the winter, the situation is reversed.

At certain times of the year, Earth is closer to the Sun than at others. This variation means that the amount of solar energy reaching the outer atmosphere will vary from month to month depending on Earth's location in its path around the Sun.

Even Earth's rotation on its own axis influences weather patterns. If Earth did not rotate, air movements on the planet would probably be relatively simple. Air would move in a single overall equator-to-poles cycle. Earth's rotation, however, causes the deflection of these simple air movements, creating smaller regions of air movement that exist at different latitudes.

Weather and climate

The terms weather and climate often are used in place of each other, but they refer to quite different phenomena. Weather refers to the day-to-day changes in atmospheric conditions. Climate refers to the average weather pattern for a region (or for the whole planet) over a much longer period of time (at least three decades according to some authorities).

[*See also* **Air masses and fronts; Atmosphere, composition and structure; Atmospheric circulation; Atmospheric pressure; Clouds; Cyclone and anticyclone; Drought; El Niño; Global climate; Monsoon; Thunderstorm; Weather forecasting; Wind**]

Weather forecasting

Weather forecasting is the attempt by meteorologists to predict weather conditions that may be expected at some future time. Weather forecasting is the single most important practical reason for the existence of meteorology, the study of weather, as a science. Accurate weather forecasts help save money and lives.

Humans have been looking for ways to forecast the weather for centuries. Modern weather forecasting owes its existence to the invention of many weather recording instruments, such as the hygrometer, barometer, weather balloon, and radar. Three major technological developments have led weather forecasting to its current status: the development of instant communications with distant areas beginning in the late 1800s, remote sensing devices starting in the early 1900s, and computers in the late 1900s.

Weather recording instruments

In the fifteenth century, Italian artist and scientists Leonardo da Vinci (1452–1519) invented the hygrometer (pronounced hi-GROM-e-ter), an instrument that measures atmospheric humidity (moisture in the air). Around 1643, Italian physicist Evangelista Torricelli (1608–1647) created the barometer to measure air pressure differences. These instruments have been improved upon and refined many times since.

Weather information has long been displayed in map form. In 1686, English astronomer Edmond Halley (1656–1742) drafted a map to explain regular winds, tradewinds, and monsoons. Nearly 200 years later, in 1863, French astronomer Edme Hippolyte Marie-Davy published the first isobar maps, which have lines (isobars) connecting places having the same barometric pressure.

Weather data allowed scientists to try to forecast what the weather would be at some later time. In 1870, the U.S. Weather Service was established under the supervision of meteorologist Cleveland Abbe (1838–1916), often called America's first weatherman. Networks of telegraphs made it possible to collect and share weather reports and predictions. By the twentieth century, the telephone and radar further increased meteorologists' ability to collect and exchange information.

Remote sensing (the ability to collect information from unmanned sources) originated with the invention of the weather balloon by French meteorologist Léon Teisserenc de Bort (1855–1913) near the beginning of the twentieth century. Designed to make simple preflight tests of wind patterns, these balloons were eventually used as complete floating weather stations with the addition of a radio transmitter to the balloon's instruments.

Scientific advances

Many scientists added to the pool of meteorological knowledge. During World War I (1914–18), the father-son team of Vilhelm and Jacob

A weather map showing high and low centers of air pressure. The isobar with solid triangles crossing the southern states denotes a cold front, and the isobar at the top left with triangles and half-circles on opposite sides is a stationary front. *(Reproduced by permission of JLM Visuals.)*

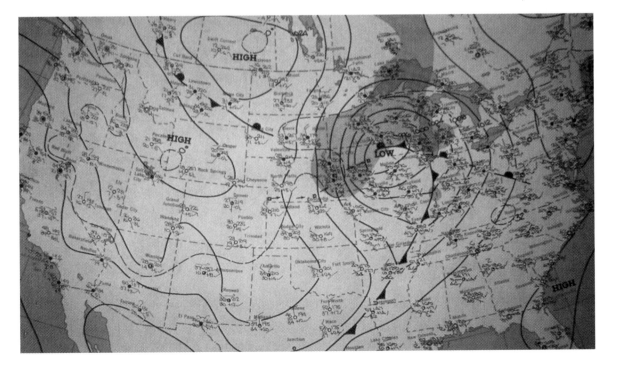

Daily Weather Map

The weather map that appears in daily newspapers can be used to predict with some degree of accuracy weather conditions in the next few days. The major features of the daily weather map include isobars and high and low pressure areas.

An isobar is a line connecting locations with the same barometric pressure. Isobars often enclose regions of high or low pressure, indicated on the map as H or L. The outer edge of an isobar marks a front. The nature of the front is indicated by means of solid triangles, solid half-circles, or a combination of the two. An isobar with solid triangles attached represents a cold front; one with solid half-circles, a warm front; one with triangles and half-circles on opposite sides, a stationary front.

The daily weather map also may include simplified symbols that indicate weather conditions. A T enclosed in a circle may stand for thunderstorms, an F for fog, and a Z for freezing rain. Precipitation (rain, showers, snow, flurries, ice) is often represented by different designs, such as small circles, stars, and slash marks. Differences in sunshine and cloudiness are often represented by differently shaded areas.

Bjerknes organized a nationwide weather-observing system in their native Norway. With the data available, they formulated the theory of polar fronts: the atmosphere is made up of cold air masses near the poles and warm air masses near the tropics, and fronts exist where these air masses meet.

During World War II (1939–45), American military pilots flying above the Pacific Ocean discovered a strong stream of air rapidly flowing from west to east, which became known as the jet stream.

The development of radar, rockets, and satellites greatly improved data collection. Weather radar first came into use in the United States in 1949 with the efforts of Horace Byers (1906–1998) and Roscoe R. Braham. Conventional weather radar shows the location and intensity of precipitation. In the 1990s, the more advanced Doppler radar, which can continuously measure wind speed and precipitation, came into wide use.

Calculators and computers make it possible for meteorologists to process large amounts of data and make complex calculations quickly.

Weather satellites, first launched in 1960, can now produce photographs showing cloud and frontal movements, water-vapor concentrations, and temperature changes.

Long-range forecasting

Because of the complexity of atmosphere conditions, long-range weather forecasting remains an elusive target. Usual forecasts do not extend beyond a week to ten days. This reality does not prevent meteorologists from attempting to make long-term forecasts. These forecasts might predict the weather a few weeks, a few months, or even a year in advance. One of the best known (although not necessarily the most accurate) of long-term forecasts is found in the annual edition of the *Farmer's Almanac*.

[*See also* **Air masses and fronts; Atmosphere, composition and structure; Atmospheric circulation; Atmospheric pressure; Global climate; Weather**]

Winds shown on Doppler weather radar. Wind speed and direction is a major factor in determining weather conditions. *(Reproduced by permission of National Center for Atmospheric Research.)*

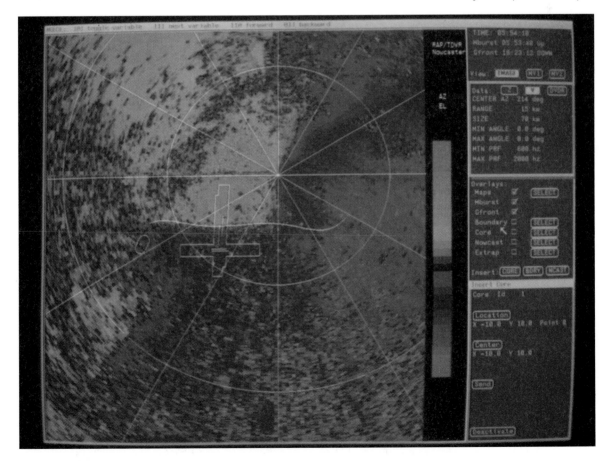

Wetlands

Wetlands are low-lying ecosystems that are saturated with water at or close to the surface. (An ecosystem consists of all the animals, plants, and microorganisms that make up a particular community living in a certain environment.) The most common types of wetlands are swamps, marshes, and bogs. Wetlands provide habitats for an incredibly wide variety of plants and animals. They also are important because they absorb heavy rainfalls and prevent flooding. In addition, wetlands protect the ground water humans depend on for drinking by capturing and neutralizing surface pollutants.

However, wetlands are rapidly disappearing because they are being drained and filled for farming and urban growth. Wetlands also are being destroyed by pollution, especially the runoff of agricultural fertilizers and sewage dumping.

Swamps

Swamps are shallow bodies of water in a low-lying, poorly drained area. These wetlands support a wide range of plant life, especially trees and high shrubs. In southeastern North America, swamp forests are typically dominated by such tree species as bald cypress, water tupelo, swamp

Sunset on a wetland near Lake Erie in Crane Creek State Park. During low water periods, mud flats are exposed, providing nesting platforms for waterfowl like this Canadian goose. *(Reproduced by permission of Field Mark Publications.)*

> ### Words to Know
>
> **Biodiversity:** Existence of a variety of plant and animal species in an ecosystem.
>
> **Ecosystem:** The collection of plants, animals, and microorganisms in an area considered together with their environment.
>
> **Peat:** Soil composed chiefly of decaying plant matter.
>
> **Primary succession:** Natural replacement over time of one plant community with another more complex one.

tupelo, and eastern white cedar. More northern temperate swamps are usually dominated by red maple, silver maple, American elm, and green or swamp ash.

Swamps provide a habitat for numerous species of animals. For example, swamps of bald cypress provide dwelling for the pileated woodpecker, red-shouldered hawk, Carolina wren, and many other small birds. These swamps also provide a nesting habitat for colonies of wading birds such as herons and egrets. Mammals supported by cypress swamps include swamp rabbits, white-tailed deer, and panthers. Many species of amphibians and reptiles—including the American alligator—live in cypress swamps.

Marshes

Marshes are large wetlands dominated by rushes, sedges, and low-lying grasses. Typical plants of North American marshes include cattails, reeds, bulrushes, and saw-grass. Marshes can support relatively large populations of birds and certain mammals such as muskrats. Relatively small, fringing marshes around lakes and ponds are common in the prairies of North America. The borders of these marshy areas, called potholes, have historically provided major breeding habitats for surface-feeding ducks such as mallards, pintails, and blue-winged teals.

Bogs

Bogs are areas of wet spongy ground composed chiefly of peat (soil composed chiefly of decaying plant matter). The water underneath the surface-floating peat contains very little oxygen and other nutrients. It is also very acidic. As a result, bogs are dominated by acid-loving vegetation such as sphagnums (an order of mosses), sedges, and heaths.

Wetland ecology

Wetlands are dynamic ecosystems that are in transition between land and water habitats. Over time, most wetlands gradually fill in, a natural process known as primary succession. All wetlands were originally lakes or other bodies of water. Tons of plants, animals, and insects grow and die each year. The decaying material from these organisms gradually accumulates in small lakes. After a while, the lake becomes a wetland. The process continues with the wetland filling in more and more. Eventually, the wetland becomes a meadow, which in turn becomes a forest.

Wetlands also are delicate ecosystems. The biodiversity (the existence of a variety of plant and animal species in an ecosystem) of a particular wetland is maintained by the conditions that exist in that wetland. The plants and animals that thrive in a specific wetland have done so by adapting to the soil, water, nutrient supply, and other conditions found there. In general, wetlands that are well supplied with phosphorus (in the form of phosphate) and to a lesser degree nitrogen (as nitrate or ammonium) sustain relatively large populations of plants and animals. This is commonly the case for marshes, which are among the most productive natural ecosystems on Earth. In contrast, wetlands with low supplies of nutrients, such as bogs, sustain only small populations of plants and animals.

Wetland destruction

All wetlands have great value as natural ecosystems, and they all support species of plants and animals that occur nowhere else. Their usefulness in providing essential habitat for fish, birds, and other wildlife cannot be overstated. Similarly, humans gain from wetlands, which control floods and erosion, cleanse the water that flows through them, and extend supplies of water for drinking or irrigation. In addition, wetlands have an aesthetic (beauty) value that is priceless.

Unfortunately, most of the world's wetlands are being lost rapidly. Land developers drain and fill them in. Since the beginning of European settlement in America, more than 65 million acres have been lost. Often, wetlands are used for the disposal of municipal solid wastes and sewage. Run-offs of chemical pollutants from farmland further pollute wetlands, disturbing their delicate soil-water balance and endangering their many plant and animal species.

[*See also* **Biodiversity; Water**]

White dwarf

Words to Know

Black dwarf: Cooling remnants of a white dwarf that has ceased to glow.

Nebula: Cloud of interstellar gas and dust.

Nuclear fusion: Reaction involving the merging of two hydrogen nuclei into one helium nucleus, releasing a tremendous amount of energy in the process.

Red giant: Stage in which an average-sized star spends the final 10 percent of its lifetime; its surface temperature drops and its diameter expands to 10 to 1,000 times that of the Sun.

White dwarf

A white dwarf is the fate awaiting the Sun and other average-sized stars. It is the core of a dead star left to cool for eternity.

An image of the binary star system R Aquarii, consisting of a red giant star and a white dwarf (the two black areas at center left). The halo in this image was formed by gas that was pulled away from the red giant star by the gravity of the white dwarf. *(Reproduced by permission of Photo Researchers, Inc.)*

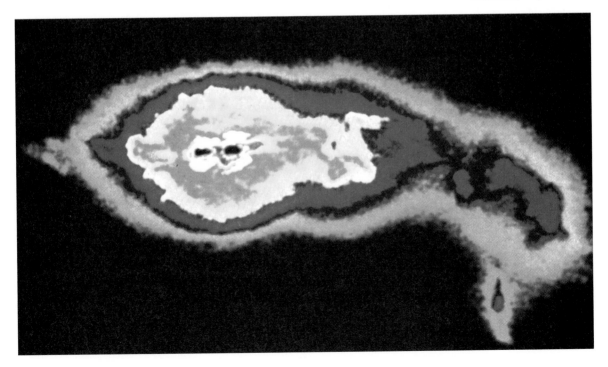

Nuclear fusion is the merging of two hydrogen nuclei into one helium nucleus, with the release of a tremendous amount of energy in the process. This occurs in the early stages of every star's life. It fuels the star and provides an outward pressure that acts as a balance to the star's tremendous gravity. In the absence of fusion, gravity takes over and causes a star to collapse upon itself. The larger the original star, the smaller a white dwarf it becomes. The reason for this pattern is that larger stars have stronger gravitational fields, which produce a more complete collapse.

An average-sized star like the Sun will spend the final 10 percent of its life as a red giant. In this phase of a star's evolution, the star's surface temperature drops to between 3,140 and 6,741°F (1,727 and 3,727°C) and its diameter expands to 10 to 1,000 times that of the Sun. The star takes on a reddish color, which is what gives it its name.

Buried deep inside the star is a hot, dense core, about the size of Earth. The core makes up about 1 percent of the star's diameter. The helium left burning at the core eventually ejects the star's atmosphere, which explodes off into space as a planetary nebula (gas and dust cloud). All that remains of the star is a glowing core, a white dwarf.

The term white dwarf is a bit misleading. The core starts out white, but as it cools it displays a range of colors—from yellow to red. When all heat within the core has escaped, the body ceases to glow and becomes a black dwarf. Billions of white dwarfs exist within our galaxy, many of them now in the form of black dwarfs. These cold, dark globes, however, are next to impossible to detect.

[*See also* **Red giant; Star**]

Wind

Wind refers to any flow of air above Earth's surface in a roughly horizontal direction. A wind is always named according to the direction from which it blows. For example, a wind blowing from west to east is a west wind.

The ultimate cause of Earth's winds is solar energy. When sunlight strikes Earth's surface, it heats that surface differently. Newly turned soil, for example, absorbs more heat than does snow. Uneven heating of Earth's surface, in turn, causes differences in air pressure at various locations. Heated air rises, creating an area of low pressure beneath. Cooler air descends, creating an area of high pressure. Since the atmosphere constantly seeks to restore balance, air from areas of high pressure always flow into

Words to Know

Coriolis effect: A force exemplified by a moving object appearing to travel in a curved path over the surface of a spinning body.

Local winds: Small-scale winds that result from differences in temperature and pressure in localized areas.

Pressure gradient force: Difference in air pressure between two adjacent air masses over a horizontal distance.

adjacent areas of low pressure. This flow of air is wind. The difference in air pressure between two adjacent air masses over a horizontal distance is called the pressure gradient force. The greater the difference in pressure, the greater the force and the stronger the wind.

The Coriolis effect and wind direction

An important factor affecting the direction in which winds actually blow is the Coriolis effect, named for French mathematician Gaspard-Gustave de Coriolis (1792–1843). In 1835, Coriolis discovered that a force appears to be operating on any moving object situated on a rotating body, such as a stream of air traveling on the surface of a rotating planet. Because of the spinning of Earth, any moving object above the planet's surface tends to drift sideways from its course of motion. Thus winds are deflected from their straightforward direction. In the Northern Hemisphere, the Coriolis effect tends to drive winds to the right. In the Southern Hemisphere, it tends to drive winds to the left.

Friction and wind movement

The Coriolis effect and pressure gradient forces are the only factors affecting the movement of winds in the upper atmosphere. Such is not the case near ground level, however. An additional factor affecting air movements near Earth's surface is friction. As winds pass over the surface, they encounter surface irregularities (hills, mountains, etc.) and slow down. The decrease in wind speed means that the Coriolis effect acting on the winds also decreases. Since the pressure gradient force remains constant, the wind direction is driven more strongly toward the lower air pressure, often resulting in gusts.

Local winds

Local winds are small-scale winds that result from differences in temperature and pressure in localized areas. Sea and land breezes are typical of such winds. Along coastal areas, winds tend to blow onshore during the day and offshore during the evening. This is because dry land heats up and cools down quicker than water. During the day, air over land heats up and rises. Cooler air over the water then moves onshore (sea breeze). At night, air over the water remains warm and rises. The now-cooler air over land is then pushed out to sea (land breeze).

The presence of mountains and valleys also produces specialized types of local winds. For example, Southern Californians are familiar with the warm, dry Santa Ana winds that regularly sweep down out of the San Gabriel and San Bernadino Mountains, through the San Fernando Valley, and into the Los Angeles Basin. As the air blows over the mountains and sinks down into the valleys, it creates high pressure. The high pressure, in turn, compresses the air and heats it. These warm winds often contribute to widespread and devastating wildfires.

Wind chill

Wind chill is the temperature felt by humans as a result of air blowing over exposed skin. The temperature that humans actually feel can be

Winds from a 1945 hurricane in Florida. *(Reproduced courtesy of the Library of Congress.)*

quite different from the temperature measured in the same location with a thermometer. In still air, skin is normally covered with a thin layer of warm molecules that insulates the body, keeping it slightly warmer than the air around it. When the wind begins to blow, that layer of molecules is swept away, and body heat is lost to the surrounding atmosphere. An individual begins to feel colder than would be expected from the actual thermometer reading at the same location. The faster the wind blows, the more rapidly heat is lost and the colder the temperature appears to be.

The National Weather Service has published a wind chill chart that shows the relationship among actual temperature, wind speed, and wind chill factor. Wind chill factor is the temperature felt by a person at the given wind speed. According to this chart, individuals do not sense any change in temperature with wind speeds of 4 miles (6 kilometers) per hour or less. The colder the temperature, the more strongly the wind chill factor is felt. When the wind chill factor is below −58°F (−50°C), flesh will freeze in about one minute.

Wind shear

Wind shear occurs between two air currents in the atmosphere that are traveling at different speeds or in different directions. The friction that occurs at the boundary of these two currents is an indication of wind shear.

Wind shear is a crucial factor in the development of other atmospheric phenomena. For example, as the difference between adjacent wind currents increases, the wind shear also increases. At some point, the boundary between currents may break apart and form eddies (circular currents) that can develop into clear air turbulence or, in more drastic circumstances, tornadoes and other violent storms.

Under certain storm conditions, a wind shear will travel in a vertical direction. The phenomenon is known as a microburst, a strong downdraft or air which, when it reaches the ground, continues to spread out horizontally. An airplane that attempts to fly through a microburst feels, in rapid succession, an additional lift from headwinds and then a sudden loss of lift from tailwinds. In such a case, a pilot may not be able to maintain control of the aircraft in time to prevent a crash.

[*See also* **Atmospheric circulation; Atmospheric pressure; Tornado**]

X ray

X rays are a form of electromagnetic radiation with wavelengths that range from about 10^{-7} to about 10^{-15} meter. No sharp boundary exists between X rays and ultraviolet radiation on the longer wavelength side of this range. Similarly, on the shorter wavelength side, X rays blend into that portion of the electromagnetic spectrum called gamma rays, which have even shorter wavelengths.

X rays have wavelengths much shorter than visible light. (Wavelengths of visible light range from about 3.5×10^{-9} meter to 7.5×10^{-9} meter.) They also behave quite differently. They are invisible, are able to penetrate substantial thicknesses of matter, and can ionize matter (meaning that electrons that normally occur in an atom are stripped away from that atom). Since their discovery in 1895, X rays have become an extremely important tool in the physical and biological sciences and the fields of medicine and engineering.

History

X rays were discovered in 1895 by German physicist William Roentgen (1845–1923) quite by accident. Roentgen was studying the conduction of electricity through gases at low pressure when he observed that a fluorescent screen a few meters from his experiment suddenly started to glow. Roentgen concluded that the glow was caused by certain unknown rays that were given off in his experiment. Because of its unknown character, he called this radiation X rays.

Roentgen discovered that these rays were quite penetrating. They passed easily through paper, wood, and human flesh. He was actually able

Words to Know

Anode: Also known as target electrode; the positively charged electrode in an X-ray tube.

Cathode: The negatively charged electrode in an X-ray tube.

Computerized axial tomography (CAT scan): An X-ray technique in which a three-dimensional image of a body part is put together by computer using a series of X-ray pictures taken from different angles along a straight line.

Electrode: A material that will conduct an electrical current, usually a metal, used to carry electrons into or out of an electrochemical cell.

Hard X rays: X rays with high penetrating power.

Nondestructive testing: A method of analysis that does not require the destruction of the material being tested.

Soft X rays: X rays with low penetrating power.

Synchrotron radiation: Electromagnetic radiation from certain kinds of particle accelerators that can range from the visible region to the X-ray region.

X-ray tube: A tube from which air has been removed that is used for the production of X rays.

to insert his hand between the source and the screen and see on the screen the faint shadow of the bones in his hand. He concluded that more dense materials such as bone absorbed more X rays than less dense material such as human flesh. He soon found that photographic plates were sensitive to X rays and was able to make the first crude X-ray photographs.

Production of X rays

The method by which X rays were produced in Roentgen's first experiments is basically the one still used today. As shown in the accompanying X-ray tube drawing, an X-ray tube consists of a glass tube from which air has been removed. The tube contains two electrodes, a negatively charged electrode called the cathode and a positively charged target called the anode. The two electrodes are attached to a source of direct (DC) current. When the current is turned on, electrons are ejected from the cathode. They travel through the glass tube and strike a target. The energy released when the electrons hit the target is emitted in the form of X rays. The wavelength of the X rays produced is determined by the metal used for the target and the energy of the electrons released from the cathode. X rays with higher frequencies and, therefore, higher penetrating power are known as hard X rays. Those with lower frequencies and lower penetrating power are known as soft X rays.

Applications of X rays

Medical.   The earliest uses of X rays were based on the discoveries made by Roentgen, namely their ability to distinguish bone and teeth

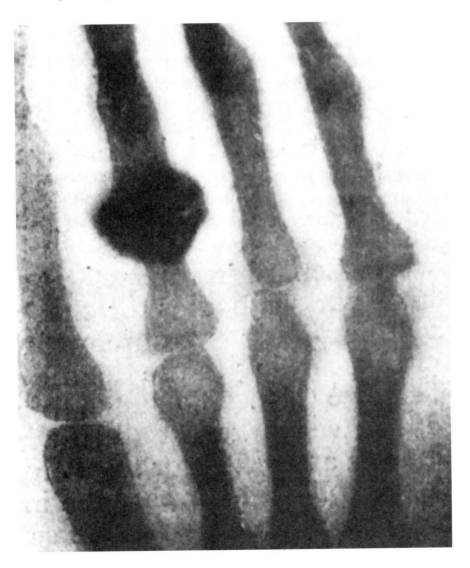

The first X ray, of Bertha Roentgen's hand. *(Reproduced by permission of Royal Institute of Technology.)*

from flesh in X-ray photographs. When an X-ray beam is focused on a person's hand or jaw, for example, the beam passes through flesh rather easily but is absorbed by bones or teeth. The picture produced in this case consists of light areas that represent bone and teeth and dark areas that represent flesh. Some applications of this principle in medicine are the diagnosis of broken bones and torn ligaments, the detection of breast cancer in women, or the discovery of cavities and impacted wisdom teeth.

X rays can be produced with energies sufficient to ionize the atoms that make up human tissue. Thus, X rays can be used to kill cells. This is just what is done in some types of cancer therapy. X-radiation is directed against cancer cells in the hope of destroying them while doing minimal damage to nearby normal cells. Unfortunately, too much exposure of normal cells to X rays can *cause* the development of cancer. For this reason, great care is taken by physicians and dentists when taking X rays of any type to be sure that the exposure to the rest of the patient's body is kept at an absolute minimum.

A relatively new technique for using X rays in the field of medicine is called computerized axial tomography, producing what are called CAT scans. A CAT scan produces a cross-sectional picture of a part of the body that is much sharper than a normal X ray. Normal X rays are taken through the body, producing a picture that may show organs and body parts super-

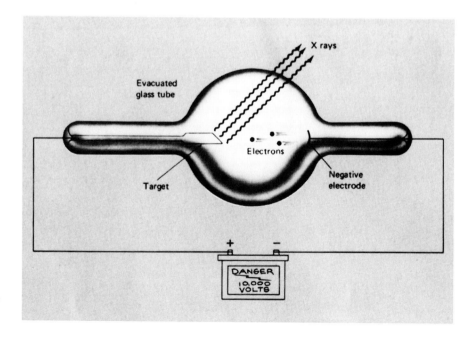

Figure 1. An X-ray tube. (Reproduced by permission of Robert L. Wolke.)

imposed on one another. In contrast, in making a CAT scan, a narrow beam of X rays is sent through the region of interest from many different angles. A computer is then used to reconstruct the cross-sectional picture of that region.

Nondestructive testing. The term nondestructive testing refers to methods that can be used to study the structure of a material without destroying the material itself. For example, one could find out what elements are present in a piece of metal alloy by dissolving the alloy in acid and conducting chemical tests. But this process of testing obviously destroys the alloy being tested.

X rays can be used to study the structure of a material without actually destroying it. One approach is based on the usual method of producing X rays. A sample of unknown material is used as the target in an X-ray machine and bombarded with high energy electrons. The X-ray pattern produced by the sample can be compared with the X-ray patterns for all known elements. Based on this comparison, the elements present in the unknown sample can be identified. A typical application of this technique is the analysis of hair or blood samples or some other material being used as evidence in a criminal investigation.

X rays are used for nondestructive testing in business and industry in many other ways. For example, X-ray pictures of whole engines or engine parts can be taken to look for defects without having to take an engine apart. Similarly, sections of oil and natural gas pipelines can be examined for cracks or defective welds. Airlines also use X-ray detectors to check the baggage of passengers for guns or other illegal objects.

Synchrotron radiation. In recent years an interesting new source of X rays has been developed called synchrotron radiation. Synchrotron radiation is often produced by particle accelerators (atom-smashers). A particle accelerator is a machine used to accelerate charged particles, such as electrons and protons, to very high speeds. As these particles travel in a circle around a particle accelerator, they may give off energy in the form of X rays. These X rays are what make up synchrotron radiation.

One of the more important commercial applications of synchrotron radiation is in the field of X-ray lithography. X-ray lithography is a technique used in the electronics industry for the manufacture of high density integrated circuits. (A circuit is a complete path of electric current, including the source of electric energy.) The size of the circuit elements is limited by the wavelength of the light used in them. The shorter the wavelength the smaller the circuit elements. If X rays are used instead of light, the circuits can be made much smaller, thereby permitting the manufacture of smaller electronic devices such as computers.

[*See also* **Electromagnetic spectrum; Particle accelerators**]

X-ray astronomy

Stars and other celestial objects radiate energy in many wavelengths other than visible light, which is only one small part of the electromagnetic spectrum. At the low end (with wavelengths longer than visible light) are low-energy infrared radiation and radio waves. At the high end of the spectrum (wavelengths shorter than visible light) are high-energy ultraviolet radiation, X rays, and gamma rays.

X-ray astronomy is a relatively new scientific field focusing on celestial objects that emit X rays. Such objects include stars, galaxies, quasars, pulsars, and black holes.

Earth's atmosphere filters out most X rays. This is fortunate for humans and other life on Earth since a large dose of X rays would be deadly. On the other hand, this fact makes it difficult for scientists to observe the X-ray sky. Radiation from the shortest-wavelength end of the X-ray range, called hard X rays, can be detected at high altitudes. The only way to view longer X rays, called soft X rays, is through special telescopes placed on artificial satellites orbiting outside Earth's atmosphere.

First interstellar X rays detected

In 1962, an X-ray telescope was launched into space by the National Aeronautics and Space Administration (NASA) aboard an Aerobee rocket. The rocket contained an X-ray telescope devised by physicist Ricardo Giacconi (1931–) and his colleagues from a company called American Science and Engineering, Inc. (ASEI). During its six-minute flight, the telescope detected the first X rays from interstellar space, coming particularly from the constellation Scorpius.

Later flights detected X rays from the Crab Nebula (where a pulsar was later discovered) and from the constellation Cygnus. X rays in this latter site are believed to be coming from a black hole. By the late 1960s, astronomers had become convinced that while some galaxies are sources of strong X rays, all galaxies (including our own Milky Way) emit weak X rays.

Words to Know

Black holes: Remains of a massive star that has burned out its nuclear fuel and collapsed under tremendous gravitational force into a single point of infinite mass and gravity.

Electromagnetic radiation: Radiation that transmits energy through the interaction of electricity and magnetism.

Electromagnetic spectrum: The complete array of electromagnetic radiation, including radio waves (at the longest-wavelength end), microwaves, infrared radiation, visible light, ultraviolet radiation, X rays, and gamma rays (at the shortest-wavelength end).

Gamma rays: Short-wavelength, high-energy radiation formed either by the decay of radioactive elements or by nuclear reactions.

Infrared radiation: Electromagnetic radiation of a wavelength shorter than radio waves but longer than visible light that takes the form of heat.

Pulsars: Rapidly spinning, blinking neutron stars.

Quasars: Extremely bright, starlike sources of radio waves that are the oldest known objects in the universe.

Radiation: Energy transmitted in the form of subatomic particles or waves.

Radio waves: Longest form of electromagnetic radiation, measuring up to 6 miles (9.7 kilometers) from peak to peak.

Ultraviolet radiation: Electromagnetic radiation of a wavelength just shorter than the violet (shortest wavelength) end of the visible light spectrum.

Wavelength: The distance between two troughs or two peaks in any wave.

X rays: Electromagnetic radiation of a wavelength just shorter than ultraviolet radiation but longer than gamma rays that can penetrate solids and produce an electrical charge in gases.

In 1970, NASA launched *Uhuru,* the first satellite designed specifically for X-ray research. It produced an extensive map of the X-ray sky. In 1977, the first of three High Energy Astrophysical Observatories (HEAO) was launched. During its year and a half of operation, it provided constant monitoring of X-ray sources, such as individual stars, entire galaxies, and pulsars. The second HEAO, known as the Einstein Observatory, operated from November 1978 to April 1981. It contained a high resolution X-ray telescope that discovered that X rays are coming from nearly every star.

In July 1999, NASA launched the Chandra X-ray Observatory (CXO), named after the Nobel Prize-winning, Indian-born American astrophysicist Subrahmanyan Chandrasekhar (1910–1995). About one billion times more powerful than the first X-ray telescope, the CXO has a resolving power equal to the ability to read the letters of a stop sign at a distance of 12 miles (19 kilometers). This will allow it to detect sources more than twenty times fainter than any previous X-ray telescope. The CXO orbits at an altitude 200 times higher than the Hubble Space Telescope. During each orbit around Earth, it travels one-third of the way to the Moon.

The purpose of the CXO is to obtain X-images and spectra of violent, high-temperature celestial events and objects to help astronomers better understand the structure and evolution of the universe. It will observe galaxies, black holes, quasars, and supernovae (among other objects) billions of light-years in the distance, giving astronomers a glimpse of regions of the universe as they existed eons ago. In early 2001, the

An all-sky X-ray map compiled by a High Energy Astrophysical Observatory (HEAO). *(Reproduced courtesy of the U.S. Naval Research Laboratory.)*

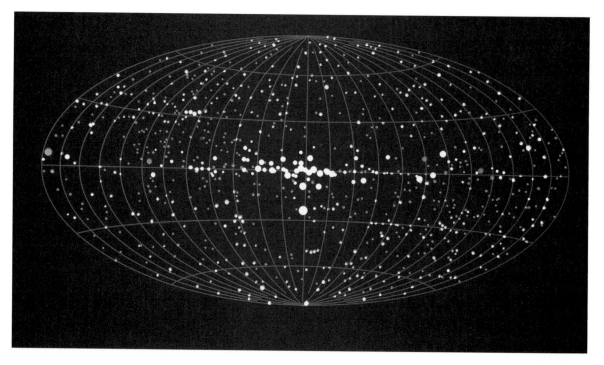

CXO found the most distant X-ray cluster of galaxies astronomers have ever observed, located about 10 billion light-years away from Earth. Less than a month later, it detected an X-ray quasar 12 billion light-years away. These are both important discoveries that may help astronomers understand how the universe evolved.

[*See also* **Telescope; X rays**]

Yeast

Yeast are microscopic, single-celled organisms that are classified in the family Fungi. Individual yeast cells multiply rapidly by the process of budding, in which a new cell begins as a small bulge along the cell wall of a parent cell. In the presence of an abundant food source, huge populations of yeast cells gather. The cells often appear as long chains with newly formed cells still attached to their parent cells, due to the short budding time of two hours.

Yeast are among the few living organisms that do not need oxygen in order to produce energy. This oxygen-independent state is called anaerobic (pronounced a-na-ROE-bik; "without oxygen"). During such anaerobic conditions, yeast convert carbohydrates—starches and sugars—to alcohol and carbon dioxide gas. This process is known as fermentation.

The fermentation process of yeast is caused by enzymes, catalysts in chemical reactions similar to the digestive enzymes in the human body. In fact, the word enzyme means "in yeast." Certain enzymes in yeast act on starch to break down the long chainlike molecules into smaller units of sugar. Then other yeast enzymes convert one kind of sugar molecule to another. Still other enzyme reactions break apart the sugar molecule (composed of carbon, hydrogen, and oxygen atoms) into ethyl alcohol and carbon dioxide. The series of reactions provides the yeast cells with the energy necessary for their growth and division (form of reproduction).

In nature, yeast enzymes break down the complex carbon compounds of plant cell walls and animal tissues, feeding on the sugar produced in the process. In this way, yeast function as natural decomposers in the environment.

Words to Know

Anaerobic: Living or growing in an atmosphere lacking oxygen.

Budding: Process by which a small outgrowth on a simple organism grows into a complete new organism of the same species.

Enzyme: An organic compound that speeds up the rate of chemical reactions in living organisms.

Fermentation: Chemical reaction in which enzymes break down complex organic compounds into simpler ones.

The importance of yeast for humans

The by-products of fermentation—carbon dioxide and alcohol—have been used by humans for centuries in the production of breads and alcoholic beverages. Before the mid-nineteenth century, however, bakers and brewers knew very little about the nature of the organisms that helped

Yeast, or *Anthrocobia muelleri*. (Reproduced by permission of Phototake.)

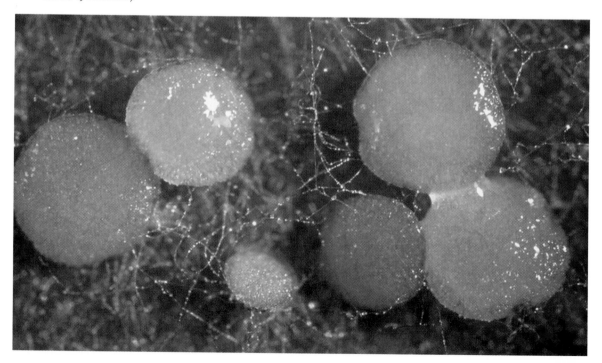

make their products. The experiments of French microbiologist Louis Pasteur (1822–1895) showed that fermentation could only take place in the presence of living yeast cells. He also deduced that anaerobic conditions were necessary for proper fermentation of wine and beer (in the presence of oxygen, yeast convert alcohol to acetic acid [vinegar]).

Brewer's yeast is added to liquids derived from grains and fruits to brew beer and wine. The natural starches and sugars in the liquids provide food for the yeast. Deprived of oxygen during the fermentation process, yeast produce alcohol as a by-product of incomplete sugar breakdown. Yeast that occur naturally on the skins of grapes also play a vital role in fermentation, converting the sugars of grapes into alcohol for wine production.

Baker's yeast, another variety of yeast, are added to a dough made from the starchy portion of ground grains (such as wheat or rye flour). The yeast break down some of the starch and sugar present in the mixture, producing carbon dioxide. The carbon dioxide bubbles through the dough, forming many air holes and causing the bread to rise. Since oxygen is present, no alcohol is produced when the bread is rising. When the bread is baked, the air holes give the bread a lighter texture.

In recent times, yeast have been used to aid in the production of alternative energy sources that do not produce toxic chemicals as by-products. Yeast are placed in huge vats of corn or other organic material. When fermentation takes place, the yeast convert the organic material into ethanol fuel. Present-day geneticists are working on developing yeast strains that will convert even larger organic biomasses (living material) into ethanol more efficiently.

[*See also* **Brewing; Fermentation; Fungi**]

Z

Zero

The most common meaning of the term zero is the absence of any magnitude or quantity. For example, a person might say that he or she has zero children, meaning that he or she has no children. In this respect, zero is a number, like 2, +9, −45, or 0.392. It can be used in mathematical operations in nearly all of the same ways that nonzero numbers can be used. For example, 4 + 0 = 4 is a legitimate mathematical operation. One mathematical operation from which zero is omitted is division. One can divide 0 by any number (in which case the answer is always zero), but one cannot divide any number by zero. That is, the mathematical operation 4 ÷ 0 has no meaning.

Zeroes also have other functions. For example, a zero may indicate the beginning of some counting system. A temperature of zero degrees kelvin (0 K), for example, is the starting point for the absolute temperature scale.

Zero also is used as a placeholder in the Hindu-Arabic numeration system. The zero in the number 405 means that the number contains no tens. An expanded definition of the number is that 405 = 4 hundreds (4 × 100) plus 0 tens (0 × 10) plus 5 ones (5 × 1).

History

The history of the zero in numeration systems is a fascinating one. The symbol for zero (0) was not used by early Greek, Roman, Chinese, Egyptian, and other civilizations because they did not need it. In the Roman numeration system, for example, the number 405 is represented by CDIV.

The symbol for zero is believed to have first been used in the fourth century B.C. by an unknown Indian mathematician. When he wanted to record a more permanent answer on his beaded counting board, he used a simple dot. This dot was called a *sunya* and indicated columns in which there were no beads. While the *sunya* was not a true zero symbol, its use in place value notation was very important.

The actual 0 symbol for zero first appeared in about A.D. 800 when it was adopted as part of the Hindu-Arabic numeration system. The symbol was originally a dot, or *sifr,* as it was called in Arabic. Over time, the dot gradually evolved to a small circle and then to the familiar oval we recognize today.

The zero symbol reached Europe around the twelfth century. However, Europeans did not adopt the symbol eagerly. In fact, many were reluctant to abandon their familiar Roman numerals, and hostile battles took place between supporters of the two systems. Such battles sometimes took the form of bloody physical encounters. It was not until three centuries later, therefore, that the Hindu-Arabic numeration system—including the zero—was widely accepted and adopted throughout Europe.

[*See also* **Numeration systems**]

Where to Learn More

Books

Earth Sciences

Cox, Reg, and Neil Morris. *The Natural World*. Philadelphia, PA: Chelsea House, 2000.

Dasch, E. Julius, editor. *Earth Sciences for Students*. Four volumes. New York: Macmillan Reference, 1999.

Denecke, Edward J., Jr. *Let's Review: Earth Science*. Second edition. Hauppauge, NY: Barron's, 2001.

Engelbert, Phillis. *Dangerous Planet: The Science of Natural Disasters*. Three volumes. Farmington Hills, MI: UXL, 2001.

Gardner, Robert. *Human Evolution*. New York: Franklin Watts, 1999.

Hall, Stephen. *Exploring the Oceans*. Milwaukee, WI: Gareth Stevens, 2000.

Knapp, Brian. *Earth Science: Discovering the Secrets of the Earth*. Eight volumes. Danbury, CT: Grolier Educational, 2000.

Llewellyn, Claire. *Our Planet Earth*. New York: Scholastic Reference, 1997.

Moloney, Norah. *The Young Oxford Book of Archaeology*. New York: Oxford University Press, 1997.

Nardo, Don. *Origin of Species: Darwin's Theory of Evolution*. San Diego, CA: Lucent Books, 2001.

Silverstein, Alvin, Virginia Silverstein, and Laura Silverstein Nunn. *Weather and Climate*. Brookfield, CN: Twenty-First Century Books, 1998.

Williams, Bob, Bob Ashley, Larry Underwood, and Jack Herschbach. *Geography*. Parsippany, NJ: Dale Seymour Publications, 1997.

Life Sciences

Barrett, Paul M. *National Geographic Dinosaurs*. Washington, D.C.: National Geographic Society, 2001.

Fullick, Ann. *The Living World*. Des Plaines, IL: Heinemann Library, 1999.

Gamlin, Linda. *Eyewitness: Evolution*. New York: Dorling Kindersley, 2000.

Greenaway, Theresa. *The Plant Kingdom: A Guide to Plant Classification and Biodiversity*. Austin, TX: Raintree Steck-Vaughn, 2000.

Kidd, J. S., and Renee A Kidd. *Life Lines: The Story of the New Genetics*. New York: Facts on File, 1999.

Kinney, Karin, editor. *Our Environment*. Alexandria, VA: Time-Life Books, 2000.

Nagel, Rob. *Body by Design: From the Digestive System to the Skeleton.* Two volumes. Farmington Hills, MI: UXL., 2000.

Parker, Steve. *The Beginner's Guide to Animal Autopsy: A "Hands-in" Approach to Zoology, the World of Creatures and What's Inside Them.* Brookfield, CN: Copper Beech Books, 1997.

Pringle, Laurence. *Global Warming: The Threat of Earth's Changing Climate.* New York: SeaStar Books, 2001.

Riley, Peter. *Plant Life.* New York: Franklin Watts, 1999.

Stanley, Debbie. *Genetic Engineering: The Cloning Debate.* New York: Rosen Publishing Group, 2000.

Whyman, Kate. *The Animal Kingdom: A Guide to Vertebrate Classification and Biodiversity.* Austin, TX: Raintree Steck-Vaughn, 1999.

Physical Sciences

Allen, Jerry, and Georgiana Allen. *The Horse and the Iron Ball: A Journey Through Time, Space, and Technology.* Minneapolis, MN: Lerner Publications, 2000.

Berger, Samantha, *Light.* New York: Scholastic, 1999.

Bonnet, Bob L., and Dan Keen. *Physics.* New York: Sterling Publishing, 1999.

Clark, Stuart. *Discovering the Universe.* Milwaukee, WI: Gareth Stevens, 2000.

Fleisher, Paul, and Tim Seeley. *Matter and Energy: Basic Principles of Matter and Thermodynamics.* Minneapolis, MN: Lerner Publishing, 2001.

Gribbin, John. *Eyewitness: Time and Space.* New York: Dorling Kindersley, 2000.

Holland, Simon. *Space.* New York: Dorling Kindersley, 2001.

Kidd, J. S., and Renee A. Kidd. *Quarks and Sparks: The Story of Nuclear Power.* New York: Facts on File, 1999.

Levine, Shar, and Leslie Johnstone. *The Science of Sound and Music.* New York: Sterling Publishing, 2000

Naeye, Robert. *Signals from Space: The Chandra X-ray Observatory.* Austin, TX: Raintree Steck-Vaughn, 2001.

Newmark, Ann. *Chemistry.* New York: Dorling Kindersley, 1999.

Oxlade, Chris. *Acids and Bases.* Chicago, IL: Heinemann Library, 2001.

Vogt, Gregory L. *Deep Space Astronomy.* Brookfield, CT: Twenty-First Century Books, 1999.

Technology and Engineering Sciences

Baker, Christopher W. *Scientific Visualization: The New Eyes of Science.* Brookfield, CT: Millbrook Press, 2000.

Cobb, Allan B. *Scientifically Engineered Foods: The Debate over What's on Your Plate.* New York: Rosen Publishing Group, 2000.

Cole, Michael D. *Space Launch Disaster: When Liftoff Goes Wrong.* Springfield, NJ: Enslow, 2000.

Deedrick, Tami. *The Internet.* Austin, TX: Raintree Steck-Vaughn, 2001.

DuTemple, Leslie A. *Oil Spills.* San Diego, CA: Lucent Books, 1999.

Gaines, Ann Graham. *Satellite Communication.* Mankata, MN: Smart Apple Media, 2000.

Gardner, Robert, and Dennis Shortelle. *From Talking Drums to the Internet: An Encyclopedia of Communications Technology.* Santa Barbara, CA: ABC-Clio, 1997.

Graham, Ian S. *Radio and Television.* Austin, TX: Raintree Steck-Vaughn, 2000.

Parker, Steve. *Lasers: Now and into the Future.* Englewood Cliffs, NJ: Silver Burdett Press, 1998.

Sachs, Jessica Snyder. *The Encyclopedia of Inventions*. New York: Franklin Watts, 2001.

Wilkinson, Philip. *Building*. New York: Dorling Kindersley, 2000.

Wilson, Anthony. *Communications: How the Future Began*. New York: Larousse Kingfisher Chambers, 1999.

Periodicals

Archaeology. Published by Archaeological Institute of America, 656 Beacon Street, 4th Floor, Boston, Massachusetts 02215. Also online at www.archaeology.org.

Astronomy. Published by Kalmbach Publishing Company, 21027 Crossroads Circle, Brookfield, WI 53186. Also online at www.astronomy.com.

Discover. Published by Walt Disney Magazine, Publishing Group, 500 S. Buena Vista, Burbank, CA 91521. Also online at www.discover.com.

National Geographic. Published by National Geographic Society, 17th & M Streets, NW, Washington, DC 20036. Also online at www.nationalgeographic.com.

New Scientist. Published by New Scientist, 151 Wardour St., London, England W1F 8WE. Also online at www.newscientist.com (includes links to more than 1,600 science sites).

Popular Science. Published by Times Mirror Magazines, Inc., 2 Park Ave., New York, NY 10024. Also online at www.popsci.com.

Science. Published by American Association for the Advancement of Science, 1333 H Street, NW, Washington, DC 20005. Also online at www.sciencemag.org.

Science News. Published by Science Service, Inc., 1719 N Street, NW, Washington, DC 20036. Also online at www.sciencenews.org.

Scientific American. Published by Scientific American, Inc., 415 Madison Ave, New York, NY 10017. Also online at www.sciam.com.

Smithsonian. Published by Smithsonian Institution, Arts & Industries Bldg., 900 Jefferson Dr., Washington, DC 20560. Also online at www.smithsonianmag.com.

Weatherwise. Published by Heldref Publications, 1319 Eighteenth St., NW, Washington, DC 20036. Also online at www.weatherwise.org.

Web Sites

Cyber Anatomy (provides detailed information on eleven body systems and the special senses) *http://library.thinkquest.org/11965/*

The DNA Learning Center (provides in-depth information about genes for students and educators) *http://vector.cshl.org/*

Educational Hotlists at the Franklin Institute (provides extensive links and other resources on science subjects ranging from animals to wind energy) *http://sln.fi.edu/tfi/hotlists/hotlists.html*

ENC Web Links: Science (provides an extensive list of links to sites covering subject areas under earth and space science, physical science, life science, process skills, and the history of science) *http://www.enc.org/weblinks/science/*

ENC Web Links: Math topics (provides an extensive list of links to sites covering subject areas under topics such as advanced mathematics, algebra, geometry, data analysis and probability, applied mathematics, numbers and operations, measurement, and problem solving) *http://www.enc.org/weblinks/math/*

Encyclopaedia Britannica Discovering Dinosaurs Activity Guide *http://dinosaurs.eb.com/dinosaurs/study/*

The Exploratorium: The Museum of Science, Art, and Human Perception *http://www.exploratorium.edu/*

ExploreMath.com (provides highly interactive math activities for students and educators) *http://www.exploremath.com/*

ExploreScience.com (provides highly interactive science activities for students and educators) *http://www.explorescience.com/*

Imagine the Universe! (provides information about the universe for students aged 14 and up) *http://imagine.gsfc.nasa.gov/*

Mad Sci Network (highly searchable site provides extensive science information in addition to a search engine and a library to find science resources on the Internet; also allows students to submit questions to scientists) *http://www.madsci.org/*

The Math Forum (provides math-related information and resources for elementary through graduate-level students) *http://forum.swarthmore.edu/*

NASA Human Spaceflight: International Space Station (NASA homepage for the space station) *http://www.spaceflight.nasa.gov/station/*

NASA's Origins Program (provides up-to-the-minute information on the scientific quest to understand life and its place in the universe) *http://origins.jpl.nasa.gov/*

National Human Genome Research Institute (provides extensive information about the Human Genome Project) *http://www.nhgri.nih.gov:80/index.html*

New Scientist Online Magazine *http://www.newscientist.com/*

The Nine Planets (provides a multimedia tour of the history, mythology, and current scientific knowledge of each of the planets and moons in our solar system) *http://seds.lpl.arizona.edu/nineplanets/nineplanets/nineplanets.html*

The Particle Adventure (provides an interactive tour of quarks, neutrinos, antimatter, extra dimensions, dark matter, accelerators, and particle detectors) *http://particleadventure.org/*

PhysLink: Physics and astronomy online education and reference *http://physlink.com/*

Savage Earth Online (online version of the PBS series exploring earthquakes, volcanoes, tsunamis, and other seismic activity) *http://www.pbs.org/wnet/savageearth/*

Science at NASA (provides breaking information on astronomy, space science, earth science, and biological and physical sciences) *http://science.msfc.nasa.gov/*

Science Learning Network (provides Internet-guided science applications as well as many middle school science links) *http://www.sln.org/*

SciTech Daily Review (provides breaking science news and links to dozens of science and technology publications; also provides links to numerous "interesting" science sites) *http://www.scitechdaily.com/*

Space.com (space news, games, entertainment, and science fiction) *http://www.space.com/index.html*

SpaceDaily.com (provides latest news about space and space travel) *http://www.spacedaily.com/*

SpaceWeather.com (science news and information about the Sun-Earth environment) *http://www.spaceweather.com/*

The Why Files (exploration of the science behind the news; funded by the National Science Foundation) *http://whyfiles.org/*

Index

Italic type indicates volume numbers; **boldface** type indicates entries and their page numbers; (ill.) indicates illustrations.

A

G

H

O

P